LANGSTON HUGHES

COLUMBIA INTRODUCTIONS TO
TWENTIETH-CENTURY
AMERICAN POETRY
JOHN UNTERECKER, GENERAL EDITOR

Langston Hughes

AN INTRODUCTION
TO THE POETRY

ONWUCHEKWA JEMIE

COLUMBIA UNIVERSITY PRESS

NEW YORK

1976

811.09
J

Library of Congress Cataloging in Publication Data

Jemie, Onwuchekwa, 1940–
    Langston Hughes: an introduction to the
poetry.

    (Columbia introductions to twentieth-century
American poetry)
    Bibliography: p.
    Includes index.
    1. Hughes, Langston, 1902–1967—Criticism and
interpretation.
PS3515.U274Z664   811'.5'2   76-18219
ISBN 0-231-03780-5

Columbia University Press
New York—Guildford, Surrey

COLUMBIA INTRODUCTIONS TO
TWENTIETH-CENTURY
AMERICAN POETRY

*Theodore Roethke: An Introduction to
the Poetry*　　　　　　　　　　　Karl Malkoff

*Hart Crane: An Introduction to the
Poetry*　　　　　　　　　　　Herbert Leibowitz

*Marianne Moore: An Introduction to
the Poetry*　　　　　　　　　　George W. Nitchie

*Ezra Pound: An Introduction to the
Poetry*　　　　　　　　　Sister Bernetta Quinn

*Langston Hughes: An Introduction
to the Poetry*　　　　　　　　Onwuchekwa Jemie

Contents

JOHN UNTERECKER

Foreword

As Onwuchekwa Jemie puts it, Langston Hughes was a writer who faced opposition both from the white audience that largely supported his work and from many members of the black audience for whom a great deal of it was written. During his lifetime, he suffered not so much from a lack of "success" as from casual critical neglect. Over the course of more than forty years his books of poems, fiction, essays, and autobiography were produced in an almost uninterrupted flow. Yet precisely because Hughes did exactly what he set out to do, and did it well, critics—accustomed to his voice—relegated him to the territory of "popular" writer and by-passed serious consideration of his work. This neglect was as widespread, on the whole, in black critical circles as in their white counterparts. In a time when it was fashionable to be difficult, Hughes—even in the name of one of his characters—risked being simple.

What almost all critics—black and white—failed to recognize—and what Jemie conspicuously demonstrates—is that Hughes's great achievement was to build popular literature into a significant art form. Writing not for the ultraconservative university-based "new critics," who from the twenties into the early sixties acted as judge and jury of literary excellence, but rather for a much wider audience, one that responded less to "literature" than to its roots, Hughes linked his art to the most vital black artists of his time—the blues-singing, jazz-playing men and women whose voices could be heard on street corners, in slum bars, in a few night clubs, and, if you had good ears, in kitchens and bedrooms. Here, Hughes felt, was authentic poetic material that many black writers had ignored either in favor of white models or more sophisticated black ones.

Like its sources in an essentially oral tradition, Hughes's poetry relies more on tone and inflection than it does on any traditional Western literary metrical structure. Its link is with music rather than with "poetics," and though Hughes could and often did turn out perfectly conventional verse, his inclination was to respond to far more subtle cadences of language. Behind the spoken words of a great deal of his poetry, the half-heard melodies of blues, the syncopation of jazz, and the abrupt intrusion of prose statement clue the careful reader into a proper performance. For this is poetry to be performed rather than to be read. The man who studies Langston Hughes's work in a public library under the SILENCE PLEASE placards is in deep trouble. Unless he's trained himself to hear the melodies of language—melodies that have only the most oblique relationship to iambs and anapests—he confuses delicate and carefully contrived effects with "mistakes."

In examining the sources of Hughes's poetry, Jemie teaches us how to read that poetry. And in countering the formalist criticism that so conspicuously underrated not only Hughes's poetry but poetry as different as that of Robert Frost, William Carlos Williams, Gary Snyder, and dozens of other black and white counter-reactionary poets, Jemie does a major service in restoring to his proper eminence a determined, intelligent, and richly gifted artist all of us need to know. A pioneering and important book, this one shows how very much Hughes was not only a product of significant but undervalued forces of his time, but as well a poet who anticipates the rich variety of both the black and the white antiestablishment poetry of our own day. Onwuchekwa Jemie, a fine poet in his own right, offers a poet's insight into a neglected major American poet.

Preface

This book is intended as an introduction to Langston Hughes's poetry, not as an exhaustive study. It is limited to his collected poems (approximately a third of his poems have not been collected), with a brief glance at his prose fiction. My approach is broadly judicial: I have attempted to delineate Hughes's major themes and techniques, especially as they relate to Afro-American oral tradition, rather than to offer a close reading of many individual poems. Chapter 1 is an examination of Hughes's artistic objectives as enunciated early in his career in "The Negro Artist and the Racial Mountain" and as modified over the years. Chapter 2 considers his blues poems in relation to the popular blues of his day. Chapter 3 deals with the jazz poems, including *Montage of a Dream Deferred* and *Ask Your Mama*. Chapter 4 discusses poems on black life and protest not modeled on jazz or blues, including the proletarian poetry of the 1930s and *The Panther and the Lash*. Chapter 5 is a brief look at the lyric, apolitical poetry, including *Fields of Wonder*, and at the prose fiction. And chapter 6 is a selective chronological survey of Afro-American poetry from the point of view of Hughes's esthetic.

Hughes was a prolific writer. In the forty-odd years between his first book in 1926 and his death in 1967, he published some sixteen books of poems, two novels, three collections of short stories, four volumes of "editorial" or "documentary" fiction (the Simple stories), some twenty plays, musicals, and operas, three history books, eight books for younger readers, two autobiographies, a dozen radio and television scripts, and dozens of magazine articles. In addition, he edited seven anthologies.

Hughes's work is swept by what may well be the most powerful positive compulsions or radical energies in Afro-American literature, energies manifest in the persistence or even predominance of elements that derive from the folk culture and oral tradition, and that are intimately concerned with the black struggle. These energies flow naturally from the history of blacks in America: since oppression has kept blacks a lower-class people for the most part, black culture has remained essentially a lower-class or folk culture. Understandably, therefore, black written literature is much closer to oral folk traditions than is the literature of the "mainstream." And since black life has been so deeply involved in struggle, black literature is also deeply involved in struggle. The literature mirrors the life, is a part of the life. Afro-American literature is preeminently one in which we watch in process the transmutation of oral into written forms, and is preeminently a literature of struggle. This is probably what Saunders Redding meant when he called it a "literature of necessity." [1]

Hughes's work is very much a "literature of necessity." Much of its living substance is made of folk material, folk forms, folk characters and folk speech, and most of it is related in an organic, inseparable way to the black struggle. I have therefore attempted to examine his poetry from the dual perspective of the oral tradition and the tradition of struggle and protest. This dual perspective, articulated in its classic form in his essay "The Negro Artist and the Racial Mountain" (1926), embodies the principles of what today has come to be discussed as a "Black Esthetic." In that essay, and in subsequent essays and speeches, Hughes rebuked those writers who thought they had to run away from themselves in order to be "universal," those who said they wanted to be "a writer, not a Negro [or black or African] writer"; those writers who saw no beauty in black life and who therefore avoided black themes and styles or deprecated the black heritage or apologized for it in their writings. Such avoidance, deprecation or apology I have designated a "negative compulsion," the reverse of the "positive compulsion" whose direction in art is towards affirmation of the black heritage and embracement of the black struggle. That the deadening power of the "negative compulsion" has been felt in every era of Afro-American literature is demonstrated in the brief survey of Afro-American poetry in chapter 6. In his call to black writers to look to black life for themes and to black folk culture for techniques—a call that was to be echoed and amplified in later eras by Richard Wright, Hoyt Fuller, Ron Karenga, Amiri Baraka (LeRoi Jones) and others [2]—Hughes prefigures the cultural nationalism of the writers of the 1960s and 70s.

In Hughes's poetry, the oral tradition is perhaps strongest in those poems modeled on black music—the jazz and blues poems. Hughes came to maturity in the 1920s, the classic age of jazz and blues; and feeling as he did about the beauty of black life, it is not surprising that he should see black music as a paradigm of the human experience ("The rhythm of life/Is a jazz rhythm,/Honey") and a suitable mold for his poetry. His blues poems parallel the popular blues and capture, more fully than the work of any other writer, that "ironic laughter mixed with tears" which is the spirit and essence of the genre. The blues spirit in fact pervades Hughes's work in all genres. Similarly, the jazz poems move with the essential gaiety and swiftness of the music, developing from the controlled counterpoint of "Closing Time" and "The Cat and the Saxophone" to the sustained complexity of *Montage of a Dream Deferred* and *Ask Your Mama.*

Regardless of form, however, the subject of an overwhelming portion of Hughes's poetry is the black struggle for political power and economic well-being within the American framework of the Declaration of Independence and the Constitution. Hughes has coded this struggle into his concept of the *dream deferred.* The black dream of well-being is an aspect of the "American Dream"—that segment of it whose fulfillment has constantly been obstructed by racism. Hughes depicts black life, including and in particular the efforts to fulfill the dream, not only in his blues and jazz poems but also in his free verse proletarian poetry of the 1930s, in his Freedom and Democracy poems of the World War II years, and in his final bitter, threatening, Third-World-conscious poetry of the mid-60s collected in *The Panther and the Lash.*

Hughes was primarily a social poet, and recognized himself as such; but he was also a lyricist of the first order. His lyric, apolitical poems, for the most part built on the techniques of Imagism and the poetic conceit, are rich and original. His love poems, for instance, compare with the best in the language for their freshness, tenderness, musicality, and evocative power.

Hughes's poetry is both surface-simple and deep, both lucid and profound. It glitters with laughter—the understated, ironic humor of the blues. In his blues and jazz poems, and in the black sensibility which, against the opposition of his "respectable" readers, he succeeded in infusing into contemporary free verse in general, Hughes is a technician and innovator of the first rank and a seminal figure in American literature.

I would like to express my gratitude to Quentin Anderson, Robert Bone, Wilfred Cartey, Chinweizu, Hollis Lynch, Stanley Macebuh, Ihechukwu Madubuike, Walter Ofonagoro, Ellease Southerland, and John Unterecker. They read the manuscript at various stages of its development and offered me valuable criticisms and suggestions. Needless to say, my reading of Hughes and of Afro-American literature did not always agree with theirs, and the judgments and errors in this book are solely my responsibility. To my wife Patricia, who lived with this work so patiently for so long, I owe more than words can express.

ONWUCHEKWA JEMIE

Minneapolis, Minn.
November 1975

Acknowledgments

Grateful acknowledgment is made to the following for permission to quote copyrighted material:

To Alfred A. Knopf, Inc. for selections from the following works by Langston Hughes: *The Panther and the Lash,* copyright © 1967 by Arna Bontemps and George Houston Bass, Executors of Langston Hughes; *Ask Your Mama: 12 Moods for Jazz,* copyright © 1959, 1961 by Langston Hughes; *The Weary Blues,* copyright © 1926 by Alfred A. Knopf, Inc. and renewed 1954 by Langston Hughes; *Shakespeare in Harlem,* copyright 1942 by Alfred A. Knopf, Inc. and renewed 1970 by Arna Bontemps and George Houston Bass; *Fields of Wonder,* copyright 1947 by Langston Hughes; *One-Way Ticket,* copyright 1936, 1940, 1942, 1943, 1945, 1947, 1948 by Alfred A. Knopf, Inc; *Selected Poems,* copyright © 1959 by Langston Hughes.

To Harold Ober Associates, Inc. for selections from the following works by Langston Hughes: *Fine Clothes to the Jew,* Alfred A. Knopf, 1927; *Dear Lovely Death,* Troutbeck Press, 1931; *The Negro Mother,* Golden Stair Press, 1931; *Scottsboro Limited,* Golden Stair Press, 1932; *A New Song,* International Workers

Order, 1938; *Jim Crow's Last Stand,* Negro Publication Society, 1943; *Montage of a Dream Deferred,* Henry Holt, 1951; *The Big Sea,* Alfred A. Knopf, 1940; *Good Morning Revolution,* Lawrence Hill, 1973.

To Dodd, Mead and Company, Inc. for selections from the following: *Rendezvous with America* by Melvin B. Tolson, copyright 1944 by Dodd, Mead and Company, Inc.; *The Complete Poems of Paul Laurence Dunbar,* copyright 1913 by Dodd, Mead and Company, Inc.

To Broadside Press for selections from the following: *Don't Cry, Scream* by Don L. Lee, copyright © 1969 by Don L. Lee; *We Walk the Way of the New World* by Don L. Lee, copyright © 1970 by Don L. Lee; *We a BaddDDD People* by Sonia Sanchez, copyright © 1970 by Sonia Sanchez Knight; *Riot* by Gwendolyn Brooks, copyright © 1969 by Gwendolyn Brooks; *Family Pictures* by Gwendolyn Brooks, copyright © 1970 by Gwendolyn Brooks.

To City Light Books for selections from *Howl* by Allen Ginsberg, copyright © 1956, 1959 by Allen Ginsberg.

To Dover Publications, Inc. for selections from *Early Negro American Writers* by Benjamin Brawley.

To Music Sales Corporation for selections from *The Poetry of the Blues* by Samuel Charters, copyright © 1963 by Oak Publications, A Division of Embassy Music Corporation. All rights reserved.

To Macmillan Publishing Co., Inc. for selections from *The Collected Poems of Vachel Lindsay,* copyright 1914 by the Macmillan Publishing Co., Inc., renewed 1942 by Elizabeth C. Lindsay.

To William Morrow and Co., Inc. and The Sterling Lord Agency, Inc. for selections from *Home: Social Essays* by LeRoi Jones, copyright © 1965, 1966 by LeRoi Jones.

To Corinth Books, Inc. and The Sterling Lord Agency, Inc. for selections from *Preface to a Twenty Volume Suicide Note* by LeRoi Jones, copyright © 1961 by LeRoi Jones.

To The Bobbs-Merrill Co., Inc. and The Sterling Lord Agency, Inc. for selections from *Black Magic Poetry 1961–1967* by LeRoi Jones, copyright © 1969 by LeRoi Jones.

To Grove Press, Inc. for selections from *The Dead Lecturer* by LeRoi Jones, copyright © 1964 by LeRoi Jones.

To The Sterling Lord Agency, Inc. for selections from *It's Nation Time* by Imamu Amiri Baraka (LeRoi Jones), copyright © 1970 by Imamu Amiri Baraka (LeRoi Jones).

To Harper and Row, Publishers, Inc. for selections from the following: *The World of Gwendolyn Brooks* by Gwendolyn Brooks, copyright © 1971 by Gwendolyn Brooks; *Color, Copper Sun, The Black Christ* by Countee Cullen.

To G. P. Putnam's Sons for selections from *Selected Poems* by William Stanley Braithwaite, copyright 1948 by William Stanley Braithwaite.

To Liveright Publishing Corporation for selections from *Angle of Ascent: New and Selected Poems* by Robert Hayden, copyright © 1975, 1972, 1970, 1966 by Robert Hayden.

To Twayne Publishers, Inc. for selections from the following: *Harlem Gallery* by Melvin B. Tolson, copyright 1965 by Twayne Publishers, a Division of G. K. Hall & Co., Boston; *Selected Poems of Claude McKay*, copyright 1953 by Twayne Publishers, a Division of G. K. Hall & Co., Boston.

To Horizon Press and Cassell & Co., Ltd. for selections from *Blues Fell This Morning: The Meaning of the Blues* by Paul Oliver, copyright 1960 by Paul Oliver.

Langston Hughes: A Chronology and Sketch

Information on the last twenty-seven years of Hughes's life (1940–67) is scanty; and until a fuller biography is written, readers will have to continue to depend on his two autobiographies, *The Big Sea* (1940) and *I Wonder as I Wander* (1956), which carry his life up to 1939, and on Milton Meltzer's biography, *Langston Hughes* (1968), which is based almost entirely on the autobiographies. This chronology and sketch is drawn from these three works and, to a lesser degree, from the chronologies in James Emanuel's *Langston Hughes* (1967) and Donald Dickinson's *A Bio-Bibliography of Langston Hughes* (1967).

Hughes was a genius at making light of life's tragedies, his own included. He wrote the most when he was most unhappy, he tells us; and if we take him at his word (and is there any reason not to?), he must, considering his vast output, have had enormous doses of unhappiness. He was born James Mercer Langston Hughes, on February 1, 1902, in Joplin, Missouri, to James Nathaniel Hughes and Carrie Mercer Langston Hughes. His parents separated shortly after he was born. His father left the U.S., moved first to Cuba, then to Mexico where he settled and lived the rest of his life as a lawyer and businessman.

Hughes's childhood was, by his own account, a lonesome, "passed-around" childhood, not unlike that of young Sandy in his novel *Not Without Laughter*, or, later, of Jesse B. Semple (nick-

named Simple). Except for a short-lived period of marital accord
during which he lived with both parents in Mexico (1907–8), and a
summer (1919) and then a year (1920–21) which he spent with his
father in Mexico, Hughes lived his entire childhood and early
youth with his mother, maternal grandmother, and family friends.
His father lived apart and prosperous in Mexico; but Langston
grew up in dire poverty (despite his fame as a writer, he never
made much money, and lived in poverty or near-poverty much of
his life).

His mother had had a year of college, and at one time belonged
to a literary society at which she delivered papers, read her own
poems, and recited dramatic monologues in costume. But she was
unable to find any but menial jobs (cook, waiter, etc.). She moved
constantly from city to city (Topeka, Kansas City, Colorado
Springs, etc.) looking for work, sometimes taking Langston with
her. Most of the time Langston lived with his grandmother in
Lawrence, Kansas, and after her death in 1914, he lived briefly
with her friends, the Reeds. It was in the Reed household, he
reports, that for the first time he had enough to eat.

Hughes describes his father as a man who was "only interested
in making money" and who despised anyone who either was not
interested or not successful in making money. In particular, he
despised blacks, Mexicans, and Indians, all of whom he considered
ignorant, backward, lazy, and dishonest:

> My father hated Negroes. I think he hated himself, too, for being a
> Negro. He disliked all of his family because they were Negroes and
> remained in the United States, where none of them had a chance to
> be much of anything but servants. . . . My father had a great con-
> tempt for all poor people. He thought it was their own fault that they
> were poor.

(Big Sea, pp. 39–41, 49)

Hughes found his relationship with his father so unmanageable
that he came within a trigger-breadth of suicide that summer of

1919 in Mexico. His visit the following year stretched into a year-long war of nerves, at the end of which his father relented and agreed to send him to college in New York, which Langston insisted upon, rather than to Europe. Father and son were antipodes apart in personality, temperament, and interests; and when Langston dropped out of Columbia University in 1922 after only a year, the breach between them was to become final and complete. From then on they exchanged occasional letters but never saw each other again. And when the father died twelve years later in 1934 he left his entire estate to three Spanish Catholic spinsters who had looked after him in his closing years. Langston was not even mentioned in his will.

Hughes reserves some of his harshest words for his father; but although he spares his mother from explicit censure, an unflattering mosaic of her nevertheless emerges from the autobiographies. Her second marriage was marked by innumerable separations and reunions, each separation-reunion propelling her to yet another city in search of yet another job, or in search of her older son (she had a son by her second marriage): New York, Pittsburgh, Washington, D.C., Atlantic City, Chicago, Cleveland. The strain of her continuous financial dependence on her son's meager earnings is explicitly related over and over in the autobiographies; and the sensitive reader will feel just as readily the emotional strain.

It is hard to say who was the more restless and rootless, Langston Hughes or his mother. The mother's pattern of constant movement is replayed by the son. Hughes sums up this telling feature of his life when he says to Richard Wright: "Six months in one place is long enough to make one's life complicated" (Meltzer, p. 228).

1914   Went to live with the Reeds after grandmother's death.

1915   Went to Lincoln, Illinois, to live with mother, her new husband, Homer Clark, and his half-brother, Kit. Started writing poetry after he was elected class poet by his graduating grammar school class.

1916   Family moved to Cleveland, Ohio. Attended Central High School, Cleveland, and published poems in school magazine, the *Belfry Owl*. Read Dunbar, Longfellow, Sandburg, Lindsay, Amy Lowell, and Edgar Lee Masters. Wrote dialect poems in Dunbar style, free verse poems in Sandburg style. Many of the students were children of recent European immigrants, therefore less racially discriminatory. They introduced him to leftist literature and ideas.

1918   Spent summer vacation in Chicago where mother was employed as a cook. Back in Cleveland, lived alone in a rooming house while completing high school. Read Schopenhauer, Nietzsche, de Maupassant, Edna Ferber, and Dreiser. Was one of school's leading athletes.

1919   Spent summer in Mexico with father. Wrote "When Sue Wears Red."

1920   Graduated from high school. Wrote "The Negro Speaks of Rivers" on the train to Mexico.

1920–21   Spent a year in Mexico teaching English. *June 1921:* "The Negro Speaks of Rivers" published in *The Crisis*. Poetry and prose published in *The Brownie's Book*, a junior version of *The Crisis*.

1921–22   Freshman at Columbia University. Met editorial staff of *The Crisis*. Dropped out of Columbia, June 1922.

1922–23   Lived in Harlem. Worked at odd jobs—office boy, clerk, waiter, bus boy, farm hand on Staten Island, flower boy, deck hand on dock-bound ship. Wrote "The Weary Blues." Gave his first public reading.

1923   *June–November:* six-month voyage to West Africa as cabin boy on merchant freighter *S.S. Malone*. Before sailing, threw all his books into the sea in symbolic repudiation. On his return, visited mother, step-father, and half-brother at McKeesport, near Pittsburgh, Pa. *December:* took a job on a ship sailing to Holland.

1924   *January–February:* second voyage to Holland on same ship. In Rotterdam, resigned and boarded train for Paris, arriving with

$7 in his pocket. Shared a room in Montmartre with Sonya, a penniless Russian girl whose ballet troupe had disbanded for lack of funds. Sonya found a low-paying job at a nightclub; over a month later, Hughes found a job as nightclub doorman for 5F (less than 25c) a night plus dinner. Later, a job as dishwasher at the Grand Duc nightclub for 15F a night plus breakfast. Had a chance to hear leading black musicians then in Paris. *Spring:* met and fell in love with Mary, mulatto daughter of Nigerian businessman. Her father disapproved, had her taken back to London. Alain Locke visited Hughes in Paris to ask for poems for special Harlem issue of *Survey Graphic*, an issue which became the nucleus of *The New Negro* (1925). *July:* the Grand Duc, having lost its star performer, closed for the summer. Hughes accompanied two coworkers to their villages in Italy. Toured Venice with Alain Locke. Arranged to visit Claude McKay in Toulon on the French Riviera. Was robbed of his passport and money on the train to Toulon. Got off train at Genoa, fearing he couldn't enter France without a passport. Lived in a flophouse and hustled with a band of beachcombers. Finally found a job on a ship, working without pay in exchange for passage home. *November:* arrived New York, went to Washington, D.C. to join mother who was again separated from her husband and living with some well-to-do relatives.

1925   Worked in a laundry for $12 a week. Moved into unheated two-room apartment with mother and brother. Worked briefly for black historian Carter G. Woodson. Won poetry prizes from *The Crisis* and *Opportunity.* Began writing poems in idiom of blues and spirituals. *December:* while working as busboy at Wardman Park Hotel, placed three poems at poet Vachel Lindsay's dining table. That night, Lindsay announced he had discovered a "Negro busboy poet" and read Hughes's poems to his audience. Next day, nationwide publicity for Hughes.

1926   *February:* entered Lincoln University with a scholarship from Amy Spingarn and a semester's credit for previous work at Columbia. *The Weary Blues* published.

1927   *Spring and summer:* poetry reading tour of the South, his first visit South. Took boat to Cuba, then back to New Orleans for the rest of the summer. Ran into Zora Neale Hurston, who was collecting folklore, and they rode back North together in her car, occasionally stopping to collect folklore. *Fine Clothes to the Jew* published.

1928   Introduced to Mrs. Rufus Osgood Mason, elderly widow of a physician. She lived on wealthy Park Avenue and was patron ("godmother," as she preferred to be called) to Zora Neale Hurston and Louise Thompson. She became Hughes's patron also, provided him a steady income and a suburban cottage while he worked on his novel, *Not Without Laughter*, in summer of 1928 and 1929 and after.

1929   *June:* graduated from Lincoln.

1930   *July: Not Without Laughter* published. Collaborated with Zora Neale Hurston on *Ham Bone*, a black folk comedy. Wrote "Advertisement for the Waldorf-Astoria." Mrs. Mason objected to this poem, preferred to think of Hughes as a "primitive," not as a radical political poet. Tension built up between them, and Hughes ended the relationship that winter. Moved to Cleveland, where mother was now living, reunited with her husband.

1931   Received the Hammond Gold Award for Literature ($400) for *Not Without Laughter. Dear Lovely Death* privately printed by Amy Spingarn at her hand press. Met Zell Ingram, a student at the Cleveland School of Art. *March:* Hughes and Ingram, with $300 apiece, set out in Ingram's mother's car on a tour of the South. Visited Bethune-Cookman College in Daytona Beach, Florida. Mary McLeod Bethune encouraged Hughes to make a living with his poetry, to tour the South reading his poems and inspiring black youth. Hughes and Ingram sailed to Cuba, spent the summer in Haiti, mostly in the revolutionary fortress town of Cap Haitien. *August:* both returned to New York via Daytona, taking Mary McLeod Bethune in the car with them. *October:* with $1000 grant from the Rosenwald Fund, Hughes set out on a poetry reading tour of the South and West, accompanied by former Lincoln classmate Radcliffe Brown who served as chauffeur and manager and shared half the earnings. Carried with him, to be sold at readings, a special dollar edition of *Weary Blues* and a new booklet, *The Negro Mother and other Dramatic Recitations*. Read at Hampton Institute, University of North Carolina at Chapel Hill, Tuskegee Institute, and to the Scottsboro Boys at Kilby Prison. Ended up in San Francisco early the following year as guest of Noel Sullivan, to whom he brought a letter of introduction from mutual friends.

1932   *May:* received a telegram inviting him to join twenty-one other blacks on a movie-making trip to the Soviet Union. *June:* movie group sailed. In Moscow, Hughes found movie script bad, and most of his group lacking in acting experience and talent. *August:* movie project cancelled. Group dispersed. For six months Hughes toured Soviet Asia alone. On return to Moscow, wrote articles for Moscow papers. Inspired by reading D. H. Lawrence's short stories, wrote some short stories which he sent to New York for publication. *The Dream Keeper* and *Scottsboro Limited* published.

1933   Traveled the Trans-Siberian Express from Moscow to Vladivostok. Toured Korea and Japan, then Shanghai on mainland China. On return to Tokyo, Hughes was detained and questioned as a suspected communist spy; was asked to leave Japan and never come back. Sailed back to San Francisco. Trip to Russia and Asia lasted fifteen months.

1933–34   Lived rent-free for a year in Noel Sullivan's cottage *Ennesfree* in Carmel, California. Worked 10 to 12 hours a day and completed at least one article or story a week. Sold stories to various magazines, with much of the earnings going to his sick mother, once again separated from her husband. *The Ways of White Folks,* a collection of his stories, published in 1934. Joined radical protest movements on the West Coast; participated in fund-raising campaigns for defense of Scottsboro Boys and relief of migrant farm workers. Was visited by a steady stream of intellectuals, artists, and entertainers.

1934   *Late summer:* telegram announcing his father's death. Borrowed money to travel to Mexico for the reading of the will. Father left all his estate to three elderly ladies who had looked after him in his closing years when he was partially crippled from a stroke. Langston was not even mentioned in his will. The three women offered to share the estate with him, but he refused, eventually accepting only a portion of his father's cash savings.

1934–35   Remained in Mexico for the winter, earning his return fare by tutoring and translating. Read *Don Quixote* in Spanish, and credits it with influencing his conception, some years later, of the character Jesse B. Semple.

1935   *June:* returned to California to collaborate with Arna Bontemps on a book of children's stories. Visited his sick mother in Oberlin, Ohio, and lived and wrote there for a while. Mother's illness used up most of his income, including a Guggenheim Fellowship. Was refused employment by the WPA because his income was "too high." *Fall:* traveled to New York to attempt to sell his stories, and was surprised to find his play, *Mulatto*, in rehearsal. Much changed from the original, the play ran successfully on Broadway for a year (a record for black plays), then went on the road for two seasons.

1936   Lived most of the year in Cleveland with his ailing mother. His play *Angelo Herndon Jones* won first prize in *New Theatre* magazine competition. Six of his plays were produced in Cleveland in 1936–37 by the Gilpin Players at Karamu House, the community center.

1937   *June–December:* spent six months in Spain covering the civil war for the *Baltimore Afro-American*. Teamed with Cuban poet Nicolas Guillen, also a war correspondent. Wrote poems praising and exhorting the Spanish peasants and workers and the soldiers of the International Brigade fighting against Franco.

1938   *January:* returned to New York via Paris. Founded the Harlem Suitcase Theatre, an experimental theatre-in-the-round. His play *Don't You Want to Be Free?*, which they staged in April, ran for 135 weekend performances. His radical poetry celebrating the international workers' movements published in *A New Song*. *July:* Hughes and novelist Theodore Dreiser represented the U.S. at the International Congress of Writers for the Defense of Culture, held in Paris. Mother died of breast cancer.

1939   Founded the New Negro Theatre in Los Angeles. Wrote script for Hollywood film, *Way Down South*. *May–September:* lived in Chicago while completing his first autobiography.

1940   *The Big Sea* published. Received a Rosenwald Fellowship to write historical plays. Lived and wrote in Noel Sullivan's Hollow Hills Farm near Monterey, California.

1941   Founded the Skyloft Players in Chicago, who produced his musical, *The Sun Do Move*.

1942   Returned to Harlem and shared a three-room apartment with Emerson and Toy Harper, two old family friends who were like adopted uncle and aunt. Wrote verses and slogans to help sell U.S. Defense Bonds. *Shakespeare in Harlem* published.

1943   Began Tales of Simple in his weekly column in the *Chicago Defender*. Received honorary Doctor of Letters from Lincoln University.

1947   *Fields of Wonder* published. Moved into his own home on West 127th Street in Harlem. This was to remain his home for the rest of his life. Was Visiting Professor of Creative Writing for a semester at Atlanta University.

1949   *One-Way Ticket* published. *Troubled Island*, a musical, staged in New York.

1949–50   Poet-in-Residence for two years at the Laboratory School, University of Chicago. *Simple Speaks His Mind* published, 1950. *The Barrier*, a musical version of *Mulatto*, staged in New York.

1951   *Montage of a Dream Deferred* published.

1952   *The First Book of Negroes* and *Laughing to Keep From Crying* published.

1953   Received *Saturday Review*'s Anisfield-Wolf Award for best book of the year on race relations for *The First Book of Negroes*. *Simple Takes a Wife* published. *March 26:* was interrogated by Senator Joseph McCarthy's anticommunist Congressional committee (Senate Permanent Subcommittee on Investigations of the Committee on Government Operations).

1954   *Famous American Negroes* and *First Book of Rhythms* published.

1955   *First Book of Jazz* and *Famous Negro Music Makers* published. Also *Sweet Flypaper of Life*, with text by Hughes and photographs by Roy de Carava.

1956   Second autobiography, *I Wonder as I Wander*, published. Also *First Book of the West Indies* and (with Milton Meltzer) *A Pictorial History of the Negro in America*.

1957   *Simple Stakes a Claim* published. *Simply Heavenly*, a play based on *Simple Takes a Wife*, staged on Broadway.

1958   *The Langston Hughes Reader, Tambourines to Glory* (novel), and *Famous Negro Heroes of America* published.

1959   *Selected Poems* published.

1960   *The First Book of Africa* and *An African Treasury* (anthology of African writing) published. Awarded NAACP's Spingarn Medal.

1961   *The Best of Simple* and *Ask Your Mama* published. *Black Nativity* staged in New York.

1962   *Fight for Freedom: The Story of the NAACP* published. Attended literary conferences in Africa. Began Simple column in the *New York Post*.

1963   *Something in Common* and *Five Plays* (ed. Webster Smalley) published. *Tambourines to Glory* (play) staged on Broadway. Received honorary Doctor of Letters from Howard University. *Jericho-Jim Crow* staged in New York.

1964   Received honorary Doctor of Letters from Western Reserve University.

1965   *Simple's Uncle Sam* published. *The Prodigal Son* staged in New York. Lectured in Europe under auspices of the U.S. Information Agency.

1967   *The Panther and the Lash* published. Also, *Black Magic: a Pictorial History of the Negro in American Entertainment*, with Milton Meltzer. *May 22:* Hughes died in New York's Polyclinic Hospital from complications following surgery.

LANGSTON HUGHES

CHAPTER 1

Hughes's Black Esthetic

Perhaps the most remarkable fact about Langston Hughes's career is his singlemindedness. It would appear that relatively early in life he discovered what he wanted to do and how he wanted to do it, and he spent most of his life doing it. What he wanted to do was to record and interpret the lives of the common black folk, their thoughts and habits and dreams, their struggle for political freedom and economic well-being. He wanted to do this using their own forms of expression: their language, humor, music, and folk verse. And consistently, through a career of four decades and in the face of opposition not only from much of the white world which constituted the majority of his audience, but from an important portion of his black audience who objected to his matter and manner, Hughes did what he set out to do, and did it well. Unlike Countee Cullen, for instance, who wore his color like a shroud,[1] Hughes wore his "Like a banner for the proud / . . . . Like a song soaring high."[2]

To say that Hughes matured early, or that he was singleminded, is not to say that he did not grow and change. In his first book he demonstrated mastery of his craft and spoke in his own authentic voice, but still his technique improved over the years, and his

angle of attack shifted with the times. What is unique, however, is
that for a career that lasted so long, Hughes's subject matter and
his commitment to black folk expression remained stubbornly
undiluted. And literary history has vindicated him, for the
"temples for tomorrow" which he and his fellow believers in a distinctive black art insisted on building, regardless of the pleasure or
displeasure of their contemporaries, are the temples in which pan-
African artists of the *negritude* school worshipped in the 1930s and
40s, and in which Afro-American artists of the 1960s and 70s still
worship.[3]

Hughes's argument in favor of a distinctive black art was ham-
mered out in the heat of controversy. Even before the abolition of
slavery, what might be called the Great Black Controversy had already made its appearance, for instance, in the heated debates
over "colonization": should blacks be integrated into the body poli-
tic (could they?), or should they (could they?) be repatriated en
masse to West Africa? First of all, are they Americans, or are they
Africans? Or are they some separate new mutation, neither one
nor the other? Or are they (could they be) all three? The question
of Afro-American identity is at the heart of the Great Black Controversy. The terms of the dispute have shifted from generation to
generation, but its core is perennial, its essence unchanging. As
W. E. B. DuBois so accurately stated it, the black man in
America is burdened with a double identity, a "double-consciousness. . . . two souls, two thoughts, two unreconciled strivings;
two warring ideals in one dark body."[4] The controversy involves
an effort to bring this double consciousness to an end; an effort to
achieve a harmonious, healthy self by excising one or other of
the two selves, or by welding them together into a single and
undivided whole.

The terms of the dispute involve the means by which a healthy
self is to be achieved. Through the years, a portion of the Afro-
American people have urged and attempted total effacement of the

African self and total assimilation into white American culture and identity. But the very conditions (racism) which created that option also made it impossible to fulfill. So that in the final analysis, the most enduring voices in Afro-American life and history have been those who have insisted that the African identity is fundamental and definitive, that it is a positive structure onto which additions borrowed from white American culture and elsewhere are to be built, not a structure to be razed and replaced.

Without reducing the pan-African dimensions of his vision, Marcus Garvey could be said to have been the purveyor, during the 1920s, of this latter, "nationalist" position, a position of which Langston Hughes was to become the most eloquent articulator in the field of arts and letters. Although rarely acknowledged by the black writers of his day, and frequently maligned by his fellow-Jamaican Claude McKay, Garvey's magnetic presence, and the sweeping power of his philosophy, nevertheless left a firm imprint on the art and thought of the period, including Claude McKay's. Indeed, it was Garvey's rhetoric, his pride of ancestry, his dreams of a rebuilt and once again powerful African homeland, that provided the infrastructure of the nationalist revival that was the Harlem Renaissance.

As in other eras, black nationalism did not flourish unchallenged in the 1920s, whether in politics and public life, or in the arts. In 1925 Garvey was thrown into the penitentiary, a political prisoner on trumped-up charges, and his Universal Negro Improvement Association fell into disarray. Garvey had a program and was therefore "politically dangerous"; the artists and intellectuals had none and could carry on their debates "harmlessly."

In June 1926, in the pages of a prestigious journal, two young black writers, Langston Hughes and George S. Schuyler, joined issue on the esthetic aspects of the Great Black Controversy. Schuyler's lofty contempt for the idea of a distinctive black art and esthetic, so highly touted especially in the pages of Alain Locke's anthology, *The New Negro* (1925), is unmistakable even from the title of his essay, "The Negro-Art Hokum." [5] Black art, he declares, exists in Africa, but to suggest that it also exists in America is "self-evident foolishness." Spirituals, blues, ragtime, jazz and the Charleston, usually regarded as examples of a distinct black art, are, he argues, not so much the products of an ethnic group as of a peasant class or caste, and as such have less in common with the soul and sense of Afro-Americans as a people than with peasant music and dance the world over. "Any group under similar circumstances would have produced something similar," and it is sheer coincidence that this peasant group happens to be black. Furthermore, he argues, this peasant music is not universal to blacks: it is "foreign" to blacks in the North, in the West Indies and in Africa, and therefore could no more be regarded as "expressive or characteristic of the Negro race than the music and dancing of the Appalachian highlanders or the Dalmatian peasantry are expressive or characteristic of the Caucasian race."

As with folk art, so with the self-conscious productions of the middle classes: these are, he argues, "identical in kind with the literature, painting, and sculpture of white Americans: that is, [they show] more or less evidence of European influence." Black artists are trained in the same schools as white artists, and their work could not therefore be said to be "expressive of the Negro soul."

Schuyler founds his argument on the faulty premises that "education and environment [have been] about the same for blacks and whites," and that the Afro-American is "merely a lampblacked Anglo-Saxon," a white man in everything but skin color. He assumes that blacks have already been assimilated into white culture; that America is a melting pot and blacks have not only melted but have melted as totally and irretrievably as the various waves of European immigrants were presumed to have melted. And if the latter could not (or did not choose to) claim for themselves an ethnic culture and art distinct from the "mainstream," how could (or why should) blacks?

Schuyler paints a picture of harmonious assimilation so replete with half-truths and inaccuracies that it deserves to be quoted at length:

> Again, the Aframerican is subject to the same economic and social forces that mold the actions and thoughts of the white Americans. He is not living in a different world as some whites and a few Negroes would have us believe. When the jangling of his Connecticut alarm clock gets him out of his Grand Rapids bed to a breakfast similar to that eaten by his white brother across the street; when he toils at the same or similar work in mills, mines, factories, and commerce alongside the descendants of Spartacus, Robin Hood, and Erik the Red; when he wears similar clothing and speaks the same language with the same degree of perfection; when he reads the same Bible and belongs to the Baptist, Methodist, Episcopal, or Catholic church; when his fraternal affiliations also include the Elks, Masons, and Knights of Pythias; when he gets the same or similar schooling, lives in the same kind of houses, owns the same makes of cars (or rides in them), and nightly sees the same Hollywood version of life on the screen; when he smokes the same brands of tobacco and avidly peruses the same puerile periodicals; in short, when he responds to the same political, social, moral, and economic stimuli in precisely the same manner as his white neighbor, it is sheer nonsense to talk about "racial differences" as between the American black man and the American white man.[6]

Schuyler ignores profound differences, qualitative and quantitative, in favor of superficial resemblances. And when he carries his argument to Europe, he is equally obtuse: overlooking the very crucial differences between the black experience in Europe and in America, he argues that if European blacks such as Pushkin, Latino, and the elder and younger Dumas could produce work that "shows the impress of nationality rather than race," why not blacks in America? "Why should Negro artists of America vary from the national artistic norm when Negro artists of other countries have not done so?"

Schuyler's perspective, compounded from inaccurate observation and wishful thinking, was not uncommon in that era, nor, for that matter, in earlier and later eras. Nor was his perspective unique to blacks. Many white liberals were just as anxious to forget the shameful history of slavery and inequality, and to usher in a new era largely by proclaiming that such an era was already there. Or they subscribed, sometimes unconsciously, to some variant of the myths of the "white man's burden," "manifest destiny" and "civilizing mission"—except that they were convinced that the mission had already been accomplished, and that blacks had been (or should be or were about to be) duly inducted to full membership in white civilization. In the face of such high purpose and good will it seemed almost impertinent to insist on racial differences. Such a high-minded believer, for instance, was Melville Herskovits, a white liberal scholar whose reputation today rests superbly on his contention, supported with a mass of data painstakingly gathered from all over the pan-African world, that blacks in the Americas did not lose nearly as much of their African culture and life style as was popularly supposed, but in fact retained so much of it as to distinguish them radically from the white "mainstream." [7] But that was in 1941. Back in 1925, young Herskovits was blithely asserting, as Schuyler does, that the black community of Harlem was "just like any other American community. The same pattern, only a different shade":

> What there is today in Harlem distinct from the white culture which surrounds it, is, as far as I am able to see, merely a remnant from the peasant days in the South. Of the African culture, not a trace. . . . Black America represents a case of complete acculturation. [8]

Seconding Schuyler but with none of his vitriol were such leading black writers of the period as Countee Cullen and William Stanley Braithwaite. Cullen was notorious for his repeated insistence that he saw himself and wished that others would see him as "a poet, not a Negro poet." [9] In so saying he was of course, as he explained, defending himself against the condescension and double standard of some white critics. But at the same time there is the implication, much as Schuyler would have it, that there were or should be no discernible differences between black artists and white artists, or between black art and white art. And if, as Schuyler claims, education and environment have been about the same for black artists and white artists, and if, as would have to be the case, their education and environment were controlled by the mainstream, then it follows that the art they produce would be faithful replicas of the mainstream sensibility and tradition. In other words, their art would be white. Thus, there would be no discernible differences in the artistic productions of blacks and whites only when the mainstream sensibility and tradition are exclusive or dominant in those productions; when, in other words, the black artist has erased from his work all traces of his African heritage. Only then (if then) would he be, in the given time and place that is racist America, just another artist instead of a Negro or black artist. For over and beyond the fact of color, it is his concern with the black situation and, above all, the black sensibility which suffuses his work, that defines the black artist.

Countee Cullen swam against the current of his natural inclinations only to find, to his dismay, that the racial theme would not leave him alone, and that his strongest poems tended to be those rooted in his experience as a black man, those that defined him as a distinctly black poet.

> A number of times I have said I wanted to be a poet and known as such and not as a Negro poet. . . . In spite of myself, however, I find that I am activated by a strong sense of race consciousness. This grows upon me, I find, as I grow older, and although I struggle against it, it colors my writing. . . . Somehow or other I find my poetry treating of the Negro, of his joys and sorrows, mostly of the latter and of the heights and depths of emotion which I feel as a Negro. [10]

But no writer of the period went further out of his way to avoid identifiably racial themes and styles than William Stanley Braithwaite. His poetry, almost uniformly colorless and lifeless, is a study in assiduous racial self-effacement. In addition, Braithwaite was an editor and critic with a national reputation, but few of his readers were aware that he was black. And it seems he was anxious to keep it that way; and if Claude McKay is to be believed, he even advised younger black writers to do the same:

> He [Braithwaite] said that my poems were good, but that, barring two, any reader could tell that the author was a Negro. And because of the almost insurmountable prejudice against all things Negro, he said, he would advise me to write and send to magazines only such poems as did not betray my racial identity.[11]

The wilful McKay rejected this advice, arguing that his [McKay's] poetic expression was "too subjective, personal, and tell-tale"—not unlike those of the poets he admired most—to be thus suppressed and whitewashed:

> I felt more confident in my own way because, of all the poets I admire, major and minor, Byron, Shelley, Keats, Blake, Burns, Whitman, Heine, Baudelaire, Verlaine and Rimbaud and the rest—it seemed to me that when I read them—in their poetry I could feel their race, their class, their roots in the soil, growing into plants, spreading and forming the backgrounds against which they were silhouetted. I could not feel their reality without that. So likewise I could not realize myself writing without conviction.[12]

Langston Hughes, too, was of a quite different persuasion from Schuyler, Cullen, and Braithwaite. He would have agreed with McKay that the writers usually held up as examples of raceless universality were indeed as time-and-place-bound as anyone, as expressive of their particular *race, moment, milieu,* to borrow Taine's classic formulation,[13] as the most consciously racial artist could ever be. If their works carry universal appeal, it is not because they avoid the local and particular, but, if anything, at least partly because they so intimately and profoundly embrace the local and particular as particles of general human experience. But more on universality later.

In his seminal essay "The Negro Artist and the Racial Mountain," written as a rebuttal to Schuyler and appearing in *The Nation* the following week,[14] Hughes contends that far from being totally assimilated into American life, blacks had in fact retained their ethnic distinctness. Hughes does not go into the historical reasons for this, but he welcomes it, regards it as an asset for black people and a boon to the black artist. For he sees it as one of the writer's challenges to translate into literature this ethnic distinctness, with its "heritage of rhythm and warmth, [and] incongruous humor that so often, as in the Blues, becomes ironic laughter mixed with tears." Whatever his medium, the work of the black artist who uses material from his own rich culture cannot but be identifiably racial. Therefore for him to wish to be regarded as an artist but not as a black artist—as though the two things were mutually exclusive—is, in Hughes's view, in effect to turn his back on his identity, to cast aspersions on his heritage, to wish to be other, to wish he were white. It is to accept the white world's definition of his people as ugly and inferior, unworthy of serious exploration in art.

Longstanding white prejudice against things black (Braithwaite's argument) is, in Hughes's view, no excuse for such abandonment of self. Prejudice has bred self-hate—"this urge within the race toward whiteness," this reaching for "Nordic manners, Nordic faces, Nordic art . . . and an Episcopal heaven" so common among the Negro middle and upper classes. But the artist's mission is to counter self-hate, not to pander to it.

> To my mind, it is the duty of the younger Negro artist, if he accepts any duties at all from outsiders, to change through the force of his art that old whispering "I want to be white," hidden in the aspirations of his people, to "Why should I want to be white? I am a Negro—and beautiful!"

The writer who accepts this mission will find a sturdy ally and positive example in the black masses, the "low-down folks," with their confident humanity, their indifference to white opinion, their *joie de vivre* amidst depressing circumstances. Unlike the middle and upper classes, the common folk "accept what beauty is their own without question." They are the uncontaminated reservoir of the strength of the race, the body and vehicle of its traditions. In their lives, and in black-white relations "with their innumerable overtones and undertones," the writer will find "a great field of unused material ready for his art. . . . an inexhaustible supply of themes." The writer will also find two temptations, two monsters conspiring to swallow him: he must steer a straight course between the scylla of stereotyped portraits of blacks so beloved by much of the white public who comprise the majority of his audience, and the charybdis of idealized and compensatory portraits sometimes demanded by vigorous defenders of the race. The transforming energy of his art would have to radiate from accurate representations of black people in all their human splendor—and human deformity. "We know we are beautiful. And ugly too." Like other races of mankind, the black race is neither uniformly admirable nor uniformly despicable. There is therefore no need either to apologize for it or to exaggerate its virtues. The artist's currency is reality and truth, and he should offer these "without fear or shame." He should create with an inner freedom, refusing to give in to pressure from any camp.

> If white people are pleased we are glad. If they are not, it doesn't matter. . . . If colored people are pleased we are glad. If they are not, their displeasure doesn't matter either.

Succumbing to pressure from the racist majority is unthinkable. But it is equally important to avoid, on the one hand, artistic propaganda of the "best foot forward" type, and, on the other, the romanticism of the "primitivists" and bohemians for whom all things black or non-Western are beautiful and pure. Hughes calls instead for *critical realism*—a balanced presentation as free from chauvinism as from apology, a view in which blacks are neither monsters nor saints but richly and complexly human.

Hughes's essay amounts to a manifesto, an apologia not only for his work but for the black art of his generation and the generations before and after him. It is an admonition to his fellow writers to "cast down your bucket where you are" (if I might quote Booker T. Washington in such an alien context). The creators of great black music and dance, including the blues and jazz artists of the day, invariably rooted themselves in black tradition. Naturally and without urging, they have utilized the vast cultural wealth into which they were born. This is what gives their music its depth and power. Their music is black folk music elaborated and extended. Of the black masses, Hughes says: "Jazz is their child." What black musicians have done with black folk music, he argues, black writers, sculptors, painters, and dramatists can and should do with black folklore and folk life. Moreover, writers like Dunbar and Chesnutt, and in Hughes's own day, Jean Toomer, had already shown that it could be done in literature.

> Now I await the rise of the Negro theater. . . . And within the next decade I expect to see the work of a growing school of colored artists who paint and model the beauty of dark faces and create with new technique the expressions of their own soul-world.

In his own work, Hughes attempted to follow the example of Dunbar and Chesnutt and the musicians: "Most of my own poems are racial in theme and treatment, derived from the life I know. In many of them I try to grasp and hold some of the meanings and rhythms of jazz." His "theme" (matter) is black people and their concerns; and for his "treatment" (manner, style, technique, point of view) he adopts the technical resources of the culture: black idiom and dialect; black folk humor, including the tragicomic irony of the blues; the form and spirit of jazz. The "meaning" of black life in America, Hughes implies, is to be found in black music: in the *blues,* a philosophy of endurance of the apparently unendurable ("pain swallowed in a smile"); in *jazz,* subversion of the status quo ("revolt against weariness in a white world, a world of subway trains, and work, work, work"). *Black music, in short, is a paradigm of the black experience in America.* It is not only black America's most profound cultural expression and "product," but, in its most complex, representative contemporary forms of blues and jazz, it encompasses the polar extremes of that experience, namely: *resignation,* or the impulse towards assimilation; and *revolt,* or the impulse towards nationalism.

Implicit in Hughes's essay is a call for the reeducation not only of the black artist but of the black middle class public as well; a call for the emergence of a black audience that would take the initiative in recognizing and patronizing black talent, instead of waiting for white public approval first. To do this, of course, implies a proper valuation of black culture, the communal recognition, in other words, of a black esthetic. A critically alert black audience, Hughes seems to imply, might have been able to prevent the works of important artists, such as Dunbar and Chesnutt, from going out of print, or Jean Toomer's *Cane* from suffering so total a commercial failure. But of course what is involved here, among other things, is the ancillary issue of black control of black publishing, an issue which Hughes does not explore.

Hughes's insistence on a distinct black art utilizing black themes and styles is an affirmation of black existence, a recognition of the fact that Afro-Americans are a distinct people within the American nation, and an insistence on their continued ethnic distinctness. Hughes, in other words, could accurately be described as a nationalist although he did not articulate his position in those terms. The revolutionary potential which he perceives in black art will be redefined and given ideological direction in the following decade.

The 1930s was a Marxist decade for Hughes as it was for some other American writers. Communism promised an alternative to the capitalist order which feeds on racism and the exploitation of the working classes. It emphasized the identity of interests of all oppressed peoples, regardless of race or nationality, and called upon them to unite and overthrow their oppressors. Unlike Richard Wright, Hughes never specifically joined the Communist Party; but he found in its ideology a fresh perspective, an effective tool of social analysis, a broader conception of the black struggle as part of a world-wide struggle against oppression.

Hughes dates his involvement with communism as commencing with the Scottsboro case in 1931 and ending with the Nazi-Soviet Pact of 1939.[15] Under Marxist influence he reworked his esthetic somewhat, giving it a consciously political and ideological thrust. The central document of this period is his essay "To Negro Writers," [16] a militant blueprint for an expository and hortatory literature serving the cause of the proletarian revolution. It should be pointed out right away that except for its vocabulary and tone of urgency, this essay says little that was not already said in "Racial Mountain." Hughes calls on black writers to address their work to the masses, both black and white, and seek to unify them, and to use their work to lay bare the true nature of America: the hypocrisy of philanthropy and of organized religion; the betrayal of workers by white labor leaders, and of the black masses by false Negro leaders who were controlled by the ruling class; the manipulation of patriotic sentiment in support of wars which destroy the citizenry and profit the ruling class. The black writer should use his art to expose "all the economic roots of race hatred and race fear."

In short, Hughes calls for a functional literature, or what Jean-Paul Sartre was to call a *littérature engagée*, a literature committed to revolution. As he sees it, the black writer has a clear and unequivocal role in the struggle for revolution, for that struggle is being waged for him and his. Writers who place themselves aloof from the struggle at best condemn themselves to social irrelevance; at worst, they are aiders and abetters of the status quo, partners in oppression, whether they are aware of it or not.[17] In the literature of struggle there is no place for the romanticisms of the Harlem Renaissance which celebrated the gaiety and rhythm of black life; and the tragicomic laughter of the blues is to be transformed into laughter that "chokes the proletarian throat and makes the blood run to fists that must be increasingly, militantly clenched to fight the brazen terror" of capitalism. Black laughter has to become menacing, as in Burck's cartoons, foreshadowing "the marching power of the proletarian future," a future which the oppressor cannot laugh off so easily.[18]

Such a literature cannot have at its center celebrations of nature, of moonlight and roses:

> Or would you rather write about the moon?
> Sure, the moon still shines over Harlem. Shines over Scottsboro. Shines over Birmingham, too, I reckon. Shines over Cordie Cheek's grave, down South.
> Write about the moon if you want to. Go ahead. This is a free country.[19]

Hughes's radical concerns during the 1930s are reflected in *Scottsboro Limited* (1932) and *A New Song* (1938), and in numerous uncollected magazine pieces written to Marxist specifications. Years later, he was to describe these works as "outdated," unrepresentative of his ideals:

> I was strongly attracted by some of the promises of Communism, but always with the reservations, among others, of a creative writer wishing to preserve my own freedom of action and expression—and as an American Negro desiring full integration into our body politic.[20]

The fact that this plea was entered on the occasion of a Congressional witchhunt against communists and "fellow travelers" should automatically render it suspect. Hughes's immersion in communist dogma may not have been total, but neither the shock of the Nazi-Soviet Pact of 1939 nor the punitive terror of Senator McCarthy's committee in the early 1950s was enough to annul his communist sympathies. On the contrary, he held on to his Marxist vision and terms of rhetoric—with this concession, that, no doubt for reasons of expediency, he routed them underground, as it were: he continued to publish Marxist proletarian poetry and prose in various periodicals, but, with the significant exception of "Good Morning Stalingrad," which was included in *Jim Crow's Last Stand* (1943), he excluded them from his collected works.[21]

Hughes abandoned Marxist terms of rhetoric in his collected works, but not the principle of literature as an instrument of social change. On the contrary, as we have seen, he had enunciated this principle as early as "The Negro Artist and the Racial Mountain," and only elaborated and extended it in his more specifically Marxist declarations. Indeed it would be fair to say that "The Negro Artist and the Racial Mountain" is the basic document of his esthetic, and future pronouncements are restatements and elaborations, footnotes and glosses. In subsequent statements he downplays the hortatory functions of literature and expands on the expository. He continues to stress the social responsibility of the black artist, and no doubt saw his own career as fulfilling that socially responsible role. In "My Adventures As a Social Poet," [22] his most important restatement of the 1940s, Hughes defines himself as a primarily social as distinct from a primarily lyric poet, thus giving formal recognition to a bias which became visible quite early in his career. "The major aims of my work have been to interpret and comment upon Negro life, and its relations to the problems of Democracy." [23] Taking the American Dream as his cue, Hughes had developed his poetic metaphor of the dream, a concept which was to become a strategic theme, a major artery running through the body of his work. The dream is transmitted along two channels: first, as an assortment of romantic fantasies and desires, including the desire for a life rich in love and adventure; secondly, as the dream of political freedom and economic well-being. The latter is an extension of the former, and it is this latter that is the "dream deferred" of the black man and black race. Although he did not coin the phrase itself until *Montage of a Dream Deferred* (1951), which came in mid-career, his dual vision of the dream is introduced in his first book, *The Weary Blues.*

As might be expected, the theme of the "dream deferred" finds its fullest expression in his social poetry, whereas his lyric poetry is the particular vehicle of the dream as romantic fantasy ("love, roses and moonlight"). [24] *The Weary Blues* (1926) was evenly divided between social and lyric poetry; but his second volume, *Fine Clothes to the Jew* (1927), showed an unmistakable swing toward social themes, so much so that one contemporary critic heralded it as a "final frank turning to the folk life of the Negro." [25] Hughes preferred his second book for precisely the reason that it was less conventionally lyrical, "more impersonal, more about other people than myself . . . about work and the problems of finding work, that are always so pressing with the Negro people." [26]

Hughes did not then cease writing lyric poetry, but the balance had tipped heavily in the direction of social poetry. In "My Adventures as a Social Poet" he explains why: much as he had stated in his Marxist essay, beauty and lyricism, or poems about love, moonlight, and roses, are "really related to another world, to ivory towers, to your head in the clouds, feet floating off the earth," rather than to the everyday world of poverty and Jim Crow in which he was born and bred and still lived. In his world, the sentiment of romantic love, for example, is all too often twisted and blasted by the economic imperative, as the ghetto wasteland of *Montage of a Dream Deferred* was to demonstrate. Roses are fine, but "almost all the prettiest roses I have seen have been in rich white people's yards—not in mine." And as for moonlight,

> sometimes in the moonlight my brothers see a fiery cross and a circle of Klansmen's hoods. Sometimes in the moonlight a dark body swings from a lynching tree.[27]

Roses and moonlight, yes, but their thorny dark sides. To Hughes's thinking, the social realities of black life in America are so overwhelming that the concerned black artist could not but make these realities the central matter of his art. Hughes is not attempting to legislate subject matter for the black artist; but he is insisting, stubbornly, that given the Afro-American situation, beauty and lyricism, love and moonlight and roses, are insufficient matter. Whether they are sufficient for the rich, middle class, comfortable and white, is something else.

Because he deals with sensitive public issues, the social poet invariably runs into censorship and confrontations with authority, with the upholders of the status quo. Hughes was no exception, and "My Adventures as a Social Poet" is, among other things, a humorous inventory of the unpleasantnesses he had been subjected to because of his poetry.

It was during this same period (1940s) that to the the question, "Is Hollywood Fair to Negroes?" Hughes answered an unequivocal "No." [28] Hollywood, he argues, presents a one-sided picture of blacks: the same age-old stereotypes dating back to minstrelsy. The motion picture industry had in effect replaced the minstrel stage, and had become perhaps the most powerful propaganda and educational medium yet invented. "Millions of people take what they see on the screen to be an approximate representation of contemporary life in America," and accordingly find in the fantasies, caricatures, distortions, and lopsided portrayals of blacks a confirmation of their inherited prejudices and further reason to continue supporting (or ignoring) the oppression of blacks.

Hollywood propaganda is even more effective in that black actors lend their talents to this racial betrayal. The economic argument, says Hughes, "explains, but can never excuse" black complicity. The artist's social responsibility overrides all others; and he calls on black actors to cease and desist: "it is time now, actors, for you-all to stop."

If Hollywood were fair to blacks, he argues, it would present a rounded, realistic picture of black life in which "educated, well-groomed, self-respecting" blacks appear at least as regularly as loose women and comic servants.

The need for realistic portraiture of black life is a theme that Hughes returns to again and again. From his earliest days his own work had been repeatedly denounced by "respectable" Negroes for focussing on lower-class life and for daring to portray prostitutes, pimps, and other disreputable characters. But Hughes had always resisted the "best foot forward" argument. His theory and practice was to portray the ugliness as readily as the beauty of black life, the unsavory as readily as the admirable. Critical realism demanded both. However, toward the end of his career we find what on the surface might appear like a shift toward the position of his critics. Dismayed by the alienation and despair, foul language, and explicit sexuality with which so much of the literature of the early 1960s by and about blacks was replete, Hughes urged black artists

> not necessarily to put our *best* foot forward, but to try at least to put a balanced foot forward, so that we do not all appear to be living in a *Cool World* in *Another Country* in the *Crazy House of the Negro* in which the majority of *The Blacks* seem prone to little except the graffiti of *The Toilet* or the deathly behavior of a *Slow Dance on the Killing Ground.* [29]

If there is a shift, it is more semantic than substantive, for the demand for "a balanced foot" is a demand for proportion, for an exacting fidelity to fact which would preclude biassed and exaggerated concern with either the unsavory aspects of black life, or the admirable. The politics of the civil rights era would, in his view, make such balance even more urgent:

> The Negro image deserves objective, well-rounded (rather than one-sided) treatment, particularly in the decade of a tremendous freedom movement in which all of us can take pride. [30]

I said before that Hughes recognized music as the quintessential Afro-American art. Into music more than any other art form, black people from earliest times have poured their daily concerns. Music accompanied the African, newly arrived in the Americas, at work in the slavemaster's house and in his fields, and at work or play in the slave quarters. From slavery to freedom, music has provided a salve for the cut and hurt soul and body. It has served as an ec-stasy-inducer, an escape, a manifestation and affirmation of the transcendent beauty of life.

Hughes's experience with black music began in early youth:

> It was fifty years ago the first time I heard the Blues on Independence Avenue in Kansas City. Then State Street in Chicago. Then Harlem in the twenties with J. P. and J. C. Johnson and Fats and Willie the Lion and Nappy playing piano—with the Blues running all up and down the keyboard through the ragtime and the jazz. House rent party cards. I wrote *The Weary Blues*. . . . [31]

He came to maturity in the 1920s, a decade of overwhelming im-portance for the development and diffusion of black music, and the classic age of both jazz and blues. From their homes in the lower Mississippi River region (for jazz, New Orleans in particular), jazz and blues had traveled north with the Great Migration and es-tablished themselves in various regional centers, especially Kansas City, Chicago, and New York. And through the 1920s each of these regions developed its own styles and orientations (Kansas City jazz, for instance, was noted for its strong blues orientation), but not in isolation: all the while a process of cross-fertilization, of fusion and diffusion, was taking place. This cross-fertilization, and the spread of black music on the national and international scene, was greatly facilitated by the introduction of commercial phonograph recordings of black music in 1923. In fact the so-called jazz age may be said to have properly begun in 1923 when black music first became readily available on phonograph records.

It was during that same decade that Fletcher Henderson, based in New York, developed precision in jazz instrumentation, introduced orchestral arrangements, and organized the jazz orchestra into what was to become the Big Band. Many of the best known names in jazz, including Coleman Hawkins, J. C. Higginbotham, Russell Procope, Benny Carter, Ben Webster, Don Redman, Cootie Williams, Dicky Wells, and Eddie Barefield played in Henderson's band at one time or another. Even Louis Armstrong, the first great jazz virtuoso, played briefly with Henderson before returning to Chicago to found his famous Hot Five and Hot Seven groups. And it was in the 20s that Armstrong established what came to be regarded as the standard jazz structure, including solo and improvisation, and introduced the trumpet as the prime solo instrument (a preeminence which the trumpet was to enjoy until the 1940s when Charlie Parker supplanted it with the saxophone). And while these developments were taking place, Duke Ellington, a young man, was learning his craft and was to emerge in the following decade as one of the great jazz leaders.

It was also in the 1920s that the classic blues structure was established: three lines of lyric, the second line a repetition in whole or part of the first line, the third line rhyming with the first two. The era was dominated by women singers, worthy successors to Ma Rainey, with Bessie Smith as "Empress" and Ida Cox, Victoria Spivey, and the other Smiths—Mamie, Laura, Clara and Trixie—

in attendance. These singers were frequently accompanied by jazz orchestras. Toward the end of the 20s, however, commercial interest in classic blues declined, and by 1929 the blues women had been forced out of the spotlight and out of the recording studios. The recording industry had discovered fresh sources: male blues singers who had recently migrated north to Chicago. And the depression ushered in the era of Blind Lemon Jefferson, Bill Broonzy, Tampa Red, and Georgia Tom (Thomas A. Dorsey, "Father of Gospel Music") and their Chicago city blues.[32]

In 1921 Hughes persuaded his father to send him to college in New York rather than in Europe, out of "an overwhelming desire to see Harlem. . . . the greatest Negro city in the world." [33] And he more than saw Harlem: he attended shows, followed the progress of black musicians, singers, and actors, and sat up in the gallery night after night watching Noble Sissle and Eubie Blake's "Shuffle Along"—the black musical which became the prototype of the Broadway musical comedy.[34]

Hughes, in short, was from his early youth a sensitive and involved witness to the growth and maturation of what in the mid-1920s emerged as classic black music; and even in that early era black music was universally acknowledged as the greatest indigenous American music (as against the musics inherited from Europe), and was enjoyed and imitated the world over. In tune as he was with the currents of life around him, it is not surprising that he came to regard this music as a paradigm of the black experience and a metaphor for human life in general. "The rhythm of life / Is a jazz rhythm," he declared in 1926.[35] Conversely, a poem in jazz rhythm has the rhythm of life; to capture the rhythm of jazz is to capture (an aspect of, a slice of) life. And the rhythm of life: long, incantative, endless like the jazz, with its riffs and breaks and repetitions, with love and joy and pain interchanging, alternating in "Overtones, / Undertones, / To the rumble of street cars, / To the swish of rain" [36]—the hard fierce beat of street cars and rain an appropriate urban metaphor for the movements and vibrations and cycles of which human life is composed.

Jazz is everyone's life, everyone's heartbeat: "Jazz is a heartbeat—its heartbeat is yours" [37]—whoever you may happen to be and even if you cannot comprehend or define it. Recalling Louis Armstrong's rebuke—"Lady, if you have to ask what it is, you'll never know"—Hughes says: "Well, I wouldn't be so positive. The lady just might know—without being able to let loose the cry—to follow through—to light up before the fuse blows out." [38] The lady may feel and know in her marrows "the meanings and rhythms of jazz" even if she is unable to articulate them.

Again, jazz is "a montage of a dream deferred. A great big dream—yet to come—and always *yet*—to become ultimately and finally true." [39] And that same or other lady, "dressed so fine," who has not bop but Bach on her mind, if she was to listen she would surely hear, "way up in the treble" of the Bach, that same music of a dream deferred, that same "tingle of a tear," of mixed sorrow and hope that is jazz. [40] Jazz is process-music, a dynamic force whose thrust is forwards towards the future. It is anti-static, developing, moving. Its impulse is recalcitrant, rebellious, revolutionary. With its free and easy, open-ended improvisational construction, its invitation to joy and the uninhibited movements of the body, jazz constitutes rebellion in a puritan society. It goes against the grain of the accepted and expected in music (Western music) and in life (Puritan Christian life). It challenges the established: Western industrial society and its weary materialism, its demand of "work, work, work," its destruction of human beings with inhuman machineries. Jazz carries within it the vision of an alternative mode of life; and just as continued black existence in circumstances of deprivation is a reproach to American democracy, so is jazz (and by extension, all black music and culture) a rival and subverter of the mainstream culture.

It should of course be pointed out that this view of jazz as a music of revolt is not entirely original with Hughes. It is adapted from J. A. Rogers's essay of the year before.[41] Also, the bohemian rebellion in the America of the 1920s, of which the Harlem Renaissance was a manifestation, generally viewed black music and culture in this light. And this view is in keeping with the history of European thought of the last half millenium which, surveying the world through the elaborate manichean binoculars of Judeo-Christianity, saw in the non-Western world, its manners and morals, an exotic "other" antithetical to the West, a magnetic pole whose powerful attraction is fatal to "civilization" and "reason," whose embrace would mean drastic change or revolution. What Hughes did was to convert this idea into an operative principle of black art.

When Hughes speaks of jazz in these terms he is to be understood to mean black music in general. Jazz in this broad sense stands for the Afro-American Spirit out of which the total musical culture flows. Jazz, he says, is a big sea "that washes up all kinds of fish and shells and spume and waves with a steady old beat, or off-beat." [42] That Spirit, that sea, is the source of blues, gospel, and rock and roll, as it was of spirituals, work songs, field hollers, shouts, and ragtime. These varied emanations of the Spirit come and go: "A few more years and Rock and Roll will no doubt be washed back half forgotten into the sea of jazz." [43] And other forms will emerge and take its place.

Life, too, is such a sea: "Life is a big sea / full of many fish. / I let down my nets / and pull." [44] And literature: "Literature is a big sea full of many fish. I let down my nets and pulled. I'm still pulling." [45] Jazz and literature are the same sea of life out of which all things of human significance and meaning emerge, and to which they return. Jazz, literature, and life share the same heartbeat and constitute a unity. Each is a metaphor for the others; in their structures and significances they parallel and illuminate and reinforce one another.

Hughes therefore proposes to pour life as he knows it into the molds so magnificently provided by black music. He proposes to do in literature what others were doing in music, to create, in effect, a literary equivalent of black music. He wants to create literature that is as *rooted* in the life of the folk and as *deep* and *accessible* to them as black music is. Literature in which the masses of black people would find their life experiences reflected and illuminated; in which the community would find itself expressed. Accordingly, he devoted the opening section of his first book to "poems mostly about jazz in which I tried to capture the rhythms of jazz and the blues," [46] and named the volume *The Weary Blues.* His subsequent works are similarly suffused with the spirit of black music. *Fine Clothes to the Jew* opens and closes with a section of blues poems, with a section of gospel shouts, moans, and prayers in the center, and a multitude of ballads, blues, and jazz poems in between. Of the eight sections of *Shakespeare in Harlem* (1942), three are entirely in the blues mode, the rest mixtures of jazz, blues, ballads, and free verse. *One-Way Ticket* (1949) and *The Panther and the Lash* (1967) include poems in the blues and jazz modes. But it is in *Montage of a Dream Deferred* (1951) and *Ask Your Mama* (1961) that Hughes attains the highest peaks of complexity in his life-long effort to integrate his poetry with music. *Montage* is written in the powerful be-bop mode of the mid-40s and the 50s, and *Ask Your Mama* is a straight jazz-poem sequence set to the accompaniment of jazz and blues. Hughes's major poetry lives and breathes, to use his own phrase, in the "shadow of the blues." [47]

The characteristic quality of Hughes's poetry is simplicity, and one of its strategic ingredients is humor. His poems are stark, unadorned, crystal-clear surfaces through which may be glimpsed tremendous depths and significant human drama. In "The Negro

Artist and the Racial Mountain" he spoke of his efforts to capture
and express the ironic humor of the blues. (In his Marxist pronouncement he seemed to consider humor out of place—unless it
was the laughter of a triumphant proletariat—and the two Marxist-
influenced works are uncharacteristically humorless.) Hughes
never seemed to take himself too seriously, was rarely in too
deadly earnest to be able to laugh. However tragic or serious his
subject matter, he usually manages to see the humorous and ironic
side—which is precisely what the blues artist does. Commenting
on black life and its relations to the problems of democracy is a
serious matter; but still, Jim Crow is so "desperately and gro-
tesquely funny" [48] that the comedy often outweighs the tragedy.
He criticizes the "serious colored magazines" like *The Crisis* and
Phylon which "evidently think the race problem is too deep for
comic relief." But most black people do not think so; it is the ability of the black masses to see the funny side that has helped them
survive oppression.

> Colored people are always laughing at some wry Jim Crow incident
> or absurd nuance of the color line. If Negroes took all the white
> world's daily boorishness to heart and wept over it as profoundly as
> our serious writers do, we would have been dead long ago.[49]

But of course Jim Crow is not always funny. "The race problem in
America is serious business, I admit. But must it *always* be written
about seriously?" [50] To Hughes, lack of humor is unnatural, something akin to lack of humanity. And he speculates that there might
be a connection between humorlessness and rabid racism and brutality.

> Personally, I know that not all white Americans practice Jim Crow at
> home and preach democracy abroad. But what puzzles me about
> those who do is their utter lack of humor concerning their own absur-
> dities.
>   I have read that Hitler had no sense of humor either. Certainly,
> among Hitler's hunting trophies today are thousands of human heads,

scattered across the world in the bloody mud of battle. I suppose the greatest killers cannot afford to laugh. Those most determined to Jim Crow me are grimly killing America. [51]

Afro-American humor represents a profound criticism of America, a sane antidote to an insane circumstance. And if Jim Crow humor is sometimes macabre, it is a quality inherent in the situation, certainly not the fault of the victims. Following the example of the black masses and of the blues, Hughes seeks to capture, in all its density and complexity, that humor that is "too deep for fun." [52]

Hughes's people are the lower classes, the urban folk: porters, bell boys, elevator boys, shoe shine boys, cooks, waiters, nurse maids, rounders, gamblers, drunks, piano players, cabaret singers, chorus girls, prostitutes, pimps, and ordinary, decent, hard-working men and women. These are the "low-down folks, the so-called common element," [53] the ones who crowd the street corners, stoops, bars, beauty shops and barber shops and churches, hot rented rooms and stuffy apartments all over the black sections of cities. They are the dwellers on Beale Street, State Street and Seventh Street, Central Avenue and Lenox Avenue. They are the ones who made Chicago's South Side and New York's Harlem both famous and infamous. Hughes has himself listed them in "Laughers." [54] His treatment of them is stark and unsentimental, capturing at once the wretchedness and beauty of their lives. As Charles S. Johnson has pointed out, there is in Hughes's depiction of them "no pleading for sympathy, or moralizing; there is a moment's blinding perception of a life being lived fiercely beneath the drunken blare of trombones, or in blank weariness of the Georgia roads." [55]

Hughes's particular world is the inner city and, specifically, Harlem. The "colored middle class" or "black bourgeoisie" rarely appear, and when they do they are " 'buked and scorned." The disrespect was mutual: the "black bourgeoisie" and their spokesmen denounced his work vehemently. Critic Allison Davis called

Hughes's poems "vulgar," "sordid" and "sensational." [56] Benjamin Brawley, whom Hughes has described as "our most respectable critic," wrote of *Fine Clothes to the Jew* that "it would have been just as well, perhaps better, if the book had never been published. No other ever issued reflects more fully the abandon and vulgarity of its age." [57] To them and the many who thought like them, Hughes's answer is a shrug of the shoulders: "I have never pretended to be keeping a literary grazing pasture with food to suit all breeds of cattle." [58] The "respectable" people hated his preference for blues and jazz and the cabaret and its habitués over the middle class (white) arts and places and people. Hughes's supreme creation, Jesse B. Semple, and his exemplary urban domain, for instance, were to the "black bourgeoisie" no more than reminders of a heritage they were struggling to leave behind in their "progress forward and upward." To Hughes, however, it is the Simples that are the soul of the race and that most deserve to be expressed in black art. It is the *simple* folk, their life styles, their dreams, their stupidities, and their deep wisdom that Hughes immortalizes in his work.

Hughes's speech on accepting the Spingarn Medal in 1960 [59] is an homage to these simple folk, an expression of profound gratitude for the things they gave him. They are, he says, the source and substance of his poems and stories, plays and songs. It was their singing in the little churches of his childhood that opened his ears to "the lyric beauty of living poetry not of books." It was a blind guitar player on a Kansas City street corner singing, "Going down to the railroad, lay my head on the track—but if I see the train a-coming, I'll jerk it back," that opened his eyes to the laughter and sadness of the blues which was to become a part of his own poetry. It was the old folks recounting their memories of slavery that made possible his great heritage poems such as "The Negro Speaks of Rivers," "Aunt Sue's Stories," "Mother to Son," and "The Negro Mother." And it was the endless stories, tall tales, jokes, comments, and complaints, which he assiduously listened to in black communities across the nation, that enabled him to create the irrepressible, lifelike figure of Jesse B. Semple and the cycle of Simple tales. Hughes's relentless mining of this literary black gold is in keeping with his prescription in "Racial Mountain" and a lesson for all black writers.

Hughes entertained no doubts as to the sufficiency and greatness of the molds provided by black music, nor of black life as subject matter. On the question of whether such black matter and manner could attain "universality," Hughes in his Spingarn Speech issued a definitive answer:

> There is so much richness in Negro humor, so much beauty in black dreams, so much dignity in our struggle, and so much universality in our problems, in us—in each living human being of color—that I do not understand the tendency today that some American Negro artists have of seeking to run away from themselves, of running away from us, of being afraid to sing our own songs, paint our own pictures, write about ourselves—when it is our music that has given America its greatest music, our humor that has enriched its entertainment media, our rhythm that has guided its dancing feet from plantation days to the Charleston, the Lindy Hop, and currently the Madison. . . .
>
> Could you possibly be afraid that the rest of the world will not accept it? Our spirituals are sung and loved in the great concert halls of the whole world. Our blues are played from Topeka to Tokyo. Harlem's jive talk delights Hong Kong. Those of our writers who have concerned themselves with our very special problems are translated and read around the world. The local, the regional can—and does—become universal. Sean O'Casey's Irishmen are an example. So I would say to young Negro writers, do not be afraid of yourselves. You are the world.[60]

Hughes's confidence in blackness is a major part of his legacy, for the questions he had to answer have had to be answered over again by subsequent generations of black artists. Black culture is still embattled; and Hughes provides a model for answering the questions and making the choices. Whether they say so or not, those who, like Cullen and Braithwaite, plead the need to be "universal" as an excuse for avoiding racial material, or for treating such material from perspectives rooted in alien sensibilities, invariably equate "white" or "Western" with "universal," and "black" or "non-Western" with its opposite, forgetting that the truly universal—that is, the foundation elements of human experience, the circumstances attending birth, growth, decline, and death, the emotions of joy and grief, love and hate, fear and guilt, anger and pain—are common to all humanity. The multiplicity of nations and cultures in the world makes it inevitable that the details and particulars of human experience will vary according to time, place, and circumstance, and it follows that the majority of writers will dramatize and interpret human life according to the usages of their particular nation and epoch. Indeed, the question whether a writer's work is universal or not rarely arises when that writer is European or white American. It arises so frequently in discussions of black writers for no other reason than that the long-standing myth of white superiority and black inferiority has led so many to believe that in literature, and in other areas of life as well, the black particular of universal human experience is less appropriate than the white particular.

The question of universality, in the terms in which it has invariably been raised, usually by hostile critics of black literature, is a false issue. The real issue is whether the drama is lively, whether the portrait is vivid and memorable, whether the interpretation is perceptive and accurate; in short, whether the work is well done. But of course, to be able to judge whether the work is well done, one must have standards of judgement derived from the nation, epoch, and milieu from which the work itself derives. One cannot judge a European sonnet and a Japanese haiku by exactly the same criteria; nor a German lieder and an Afro blues; nor a Beethoven symphony and a Coltrane set; nor Wordsworth's "Intimations of

Immortality" and Hughes's "Mother to Son." The cultures are that distinct, each autonomous, governed by its own laws. Which brings us to the central issue involved in the idea of a black esthetic, namely, the extrapolation of standards for judging black art from within the culture-sensibility.

Whatever the technical excellences of a work of imaginative literature by a black writer, if it is rooted in an alien sensibility it cannot be central or important to blacks. On the other hand, mere fidelity to the culture-sensibility is not enough: what is required is a happy marriage of technical excellence and sensibility. Langston Hughes is a great poet because, among other things, he combines *to an unusual degree* such poetic virtues as economy, lucidity, evocativeness of imagery, and mellifluousness of movement, with a deep-rooted fidelity to the Afro-American sensibility. He is therefore a proper source for extracting some of the governing principles of black art, some of the standards by which black literature, and in particular black poetry, is to be judged. These principles are implicit in his work, as follows:

(1) His central concern is the central concern of the Afro-American people, namely, their struggle for freedom. His is, from first to last, a socially committed literature, ulilizing, for a brief period of time at least, a Marxist ideological frame. Whether he says it in these terms or not, one of the aims and ultimate effects of his work is the raising of our consciousness, the strengthening of black people in their struggle in America and elsewhere. Starting with black America, he expands into the pan-African world in his later years, especially in *Ask Your Mama* and *The Panther and the Lash*.

(2) Hughes has anchored his work in Afro-American oral tradition, thereby serving the vital function of cultural transmission. His utilization of black musical forms—jazz, blues, spirituals, gospel, sermons—is the most comprehensive and profound in the history of Afro-American literature. Blues appears in various guises:

in the strict, classic, three-line verse form; in a variety of modified verse forms paralleling the infinite variety of folk blues which do not conform to the classic verse pattern; and in the blues spirit and world view incorporated into non-blues poems and into his prose fiction and drama. His jazz poems are appropriately cast in free verse and often in black idiom, and they approximate the bouncy rhythms and light-hearted exuberance of the music. Much of his poetry is in Afro-American idiom, usually Northern urban, sometimes unalloyed, sometimes modified with standard English usage. In addition, he employs the forms and techniques of contemporary "street poetry"—rapping, signifying, toasting, and playing the dozens (ranking, screaming, sounding, louding, woofing). The effect of his choice of forms, and his ease and smoothness in handling them, is to situate his works brilliantly and unequivocally in the black world.

(3) Finally, Hughes's black characters are authentic and memorable, the greatest of them being Jesse B. Semple, Madam Alberta K. Johnson of "Madam to You," and the Black Madonnas of "Mother to Son" and "The Negro Mother." Hughes is essentially *a dramatic poet*. He speaks in a multiplicity of voices, through a multitude of personas, each of them the purveyor of authentic black attitudes—attitudes, views, and life-styles that are as heterogeneous as the Afro-American population.

The matter of greatness in art extends beyond the narrow limits of formal esthetics into the realm of politics. However well written, it is unlikely that a pro-Nazi novel would be well received at this time in Western Europe or America, or in Israel. If blacks had greater power in America, it would have been impossible, for instance, for William Styron to receive a national award for his novel, *The Confessions of Nat Turner* (1968), which turns history upside down, slanders the Afro-American people and their heroes, and mocks black suffering. In short, the question of an autonomous black esthetic is centrally involved with politics, as all questions of esthetics, which is itself a branch of ethics, ultimately are. When therefore I speak of the qualities that make for greatness in Hughes's work, I speak with awareness of the political existence of black people in America as a suppressed nation within a nation. If it were not for oppression, the matter of commitment to liberation and raising of consciousness might not arise. But it is from the standpoint of the distinctive character and needs of a long oppressed people that the conservation and transmission of the folk heritage, of which Hughes is so smooth a vehicle, becomes not merely and indifferently "desirable," but *essential* to cultural coherence and group survival.

Charles S. Johnson, a perceptive contemporary observer and interpreter of the arts of the Harlem Renaissance, wrote of the new racial poetry of which Hughes's was a leading example:

> The new racial poetry of the Negro is the expression of something more than experimentation in a new technique. It marks the birth of a new racial consciousness and self conception. It is a first frank acceptance of race, and the recognition of difference without the usual implications of disparity. It lacks apology, the wearying appeals to pity, and the conscious philosophy of defense. In being itself it reveals its greatest charm. In accepting this life it invests it with a new meaning. . . . Who would know something of the core and limitations of this life should go to the Blues. In them is the curious story of disillusionment without a saving philosophy and yet without defeat.[61]

Hughes had forecast that perhaps the common people, the folk whose lives formed the axis on which the new poetry revolved, "will give to the world its truly great Negro artist, the one who is not afraid to be himself." Hughes is himself the fulfillment of that dream. His work stands as a Great Pyramid against which all other monuments in the Valley of Afro-American Poetry will have to be measured.

CHAPTER 2

Shadow of the Blues

When blues traveled north and settled in the cities, its character, like that of the migrants, gradually changed from southern to northern, rural to urban. The industrial urban environment became the main source of blues themes and imagery; the lone minstrel became a nightclub singer and his guitar one instrument in an orchestra. City blues grew distinct from the country blues of the South. Jazz and blues became commercial arts, and the cabaret or nightclub became their home. During the 1920s especially, in the hey-day of the Harlem Renaissance, black nightclubs were the haunt of white pleasure-seekers from all over the nation and abroad, soaking in the music and indulging their appetite for the exotic and forbidden, including bootleg liquor and interracial sex. In some of his poems of that period, especially in the opening section of the *The Weary Blues,* Hughes successfully evokes the cabaret atmosphere: its sensuous gaiety, heady music, explosive vitality. The dominant attitude is the conventional "carpe diem": Have fun now; tomorrow . . . who knows? To its habitués, the cabaret is a refuge, an escape from routine and drudgery, a temple of worship.[1]

"Jazzonia" is the gilded gateway onto the dazzling altar of the goddesses of the cabaret. Hughes captures the harmonious concert of sounds and sights, of raucous music and sparkling lights, of the dancing girl with bold eyes seductively lifting high her "dress of silken gold." He conveys the impression of speechless wonder with the exclamatory, ecstatic fragments: "Oh, silver tree! / Oh, shining rivers of the soul!" This becomes a refrain, alternated with two brief stanzas describing the action, and as it is repeated river and tree interchange modifiers: the river becomes "silver," the tree "shining" and "singing." A singing, shining, silver tree; a shining, silver river of the soul. They own the same qualities: each is otherworldly, occult, mythic. The dancing girl is both a jaded Eve recently shorn of her innocence at that tree of knowledge, and an ultra-sophisticated Cleopatra. The traditional significances of silver and gold, tree and garden, river and soul are intended. The cabaret is all gorgeous glitter. The artificial tree, now garlanded with song and dance and light, is metamorphosed from something cheap and commercial into something sacred. The girl in the gaudy costume becomes a pagan love deity. And in this holy place the ritual reaffirmation of life is enacted. Of Harlem nightclubs and dance halls generally, Hughes will write in a later poem that they start out drab and ordinary, until the band begins to play and the dancers begin to dance—then, "Suddenly the earth was there, / And flowers, / Tree, / And air, / And like a wave the floor— / That had no dignity before." [2] It is the power of black musical art that transfigures.

While "Jazzonia" might be described as the powerful first impression of one just walking in, most of the other cabaret poems are delivered from the point of view of a seated observer-participant, a refined listener with a sensitive ear who knows that the drama is not only on the stage but equally in the lives of the people about him; a listener gifted with sight, who knows the people, their stereotypical histories, their secret yearnings that surface and burst into flower all around him. "Jazz Band in a Parisian Cabaret" [3] is a roll call of the audience: lords and ladies, dukes and counts, whores and gigolos, millionaires and tourist school teachers. The spectrum of personae is considerable; and while a Harlem nightclub might be less cosmopolitan than a Parisian one, it would be no less microcosmic.

Audience participation is one of the definitive characteristics of pan-African theatre, and in these poems the poet-observer, standing in for the typical black audience, hollers his applause freely from his secular amen-corner: "Sing your Blues song, / Pretty baby" ("To Midnight Nan"); "Play that thing, / Jazz band!" ("Parisian Cabaret"); "So beat dat drum, boy! / Shout dat song: / Shake 'em up an' shake 'em up / All night long." [4] At the same time he provides a running commentary on the action and on the lives of the performers and of selected members of the audience.

The poems are arranged in thematic pairs, each pair a contrast in mood, style, or point of view. The happy dancing couple of "Negro Dancers" who know two more ways to do the buck, are complemented by the couple in "The Cat and the Saxophone" whose cool love dialogue is underscored by the blues lyric running through the poem. The joyous excitement of "Song for a Banjo Dance" is contrasted to the sadness and loneliness of "Blues Fantasy." Two views of the cabaret girls emerge: as bold, aggressive hussies, all body and no soul, in "Midnight Nan," "Harlem Night Club," and "Young Prostitute," and as innocents, victimized and violated, in "To a Little Lover-Lass, Dead," "Nude Young Dancer," and "To a Black Dancer in The Little Savoy." The first group are action poems written in the black idiom in a fast-paced dance meter, while the second group are reflective poems in the diction, imagery and soft sentiments of the conventional romantic lyric. The girls of the first group are affirmers of the life force. They scatter brilliant sparks of joy, but their own joy is impermanent: beneath all the glitter flows a deep river of sadness—brought to the surface and made visible especially in poems of the second group.

Their lives are filled with tragic possibilities. They are condemned to loneliness, for "no good fellow" would be their man. Their destitution is foreshadowed in the young prostitute whose face withered like a flower on a broken stem; their wretched deaths in the little lover-lass who even in death still walks the streets searching for lovers, giving her kiss "to nothingness," the emptiness and stillness of the street now distanced from the noisy jazz-tuned nights where once she reigned. The cabaret girls are unfulfilled; they are symbols of deferred dreams, of the incompleteness of life.

Less is said about the male performers, but they are there. Their presence is above all in the masculine energy of the music which envelopes the scene. It is they for whom life must be "the shivering of / A great drum / Beaten with swift sticks"; [5] they whose music speaks in seven languages, even if they do come from provincial Georgia. [6] And it is to them that the amen-prayer, "play that thing," is addressed. Their music is larger than themselves, larger than life. Life in its presence appears small, begins to take its cue from the music, becomes a copy of the song. In "The Cat and the Saxophone," "Negro Dancers," "Midnight Nan," and "Banjo Dance," the lovers, performers, and general audience live and move in the shadow of the music, their beings in harmony with it, their emotions paralleled and expressed in the song.

The music celebrates the body, and the soul through the body. Jazz is conventionally thought of as a music of gaiety and simple happiness, a music of escape from life. However, in his cabaret poems Hughes holds jazz as a reproduction and interpretation of the complexities of life, its boredoms, lonelinesses, and death as well as its excitement and joy. It is in the brilliance with which it captures life that the music achieves transcendence. This is what Hughes means when he says that the rhythms of life and of jazz are one.

Amidst the boisterous dances of the cabaret, the poet asks, "Does a jazz-band ever sob? / They say a jazz-band's gay" ("Cabaret"). And years later, recreating "the boogie-woogie rumble / Of a dream deferred," he will repeat the question: "You think / It's a happy beat?" [7] Only fools and foreigners think it's a happy beat. Frederick Douglass pointed out their error a century earlier, and what he said of black slaves then is true of black folks now.

I have often been utterly astonished, since I came to the north, to find persons who could speak of the singing, among slaves, as evidence of their contentment and happiness. It is impossible to conceive of a greater mistake. Slaves sing most when they are most unhappy. The songs of the slave represent the sorrows of his heart; and he is relieved by them, only as an aching heart is relieved by its tears. At least, such is my experience. I have often sung to drown my sorrow, but seldom to express my happiness. Crying for joy, and singing for joy, were alike uncommon to me while in the jaws of slavery. The singing of a man cast away upon a desolate island might be as appropriately considered as evidence of contentment and happiness, as the singing of a slave; the songs of the one and of the other are prompted by the same emotion. [8]

Beneath the glittery surface of the jazz, gin, and jargon of the cabaret flows the silent Deep River of the spirituals, the river of slavery and poverty and frustrated dreams, the circus of wasted lives entangled in the nightmare mesh of American history. And after the clang and whir and syncopation of the night quickly follows the silence wherein the burden of black reality resumes its soul-crushing weight. The celebrants—musicians, dancers and audience—are tightly cornered; their dreams are deferred.

The wild laughter of Harlem's nights, if it is an escape, is but a temporary escape: behind the bright mask of jazz waits the sombre sadness of the blues. It is therefore fitting that Hughes chose to introduce the boisterous opening section of *The Weary Blues* with the sombre title poem. The poem is a masterpiece of the blues mood. The pianist's feelings are reflected in the objects around him: an old gas lamp giving out a pale dull light; an old piano with a rickety stool. The tune he plays is "drowsy," his singing voice is "melancholy," and his lazy sway parallels that weariness of body and soul that is the subject of his song. The turbulence of his emotions is mirrored in the song: first he resolves to put aside his troubles and keep on living, then he seems to succumb and wishes that he were dead. These contradictory emotions are consistent with his mood.

But despair is not the dominant emotion. His reserve of strength is felt in the "thump, thump, thump" of his foot relentlessly hammering out the rhythm on the floor. The things around him may be old, but they have character—like the blues. He "can't be satisfied" not only because the means of satisfaction are not immediately at hand, but also because his soul strains for more than life is capable of giving. His moan starts slow, ends powerfully ("thump, thump, thump"). His music is life-affirming. The blues well up from the center of his being until his system is purged of depression, the tension is released, and he sleeps with the heavy stillness of a rock or a corpse. Is this perhaps what Leopold Senghor meant when he spoke of God creating heaven and earth in six days out of the laughter of a saxophone, and on the seventh day sleeping the great black sleep? [9] Creation: a supreme act of expulsion, a birth, an ecstasy-release deep from the center of the being, exhausting the energies and vaulting the artist-god into death-like slumber. It is through the mediation of the creative imagination that the slumber is not of death but only deathlike. Imagination channels and sublimates the negative emotions into art. Singing the blues (the making of art) is cathartic: it transforms pain into melodic beauty.

As the singer sleeps, the blues echo through his head. He has gained a brief respite from his pain, enough to keep living and struggling. The process will repeat itself.

Hughes describes the blues as "sad funny songs—too sad to be funny and too funny to be sad"—songs "containing all the laughter and pain, hunger and heartache, search and reality of the contemporary scene." [10] Blues originated in the rural South, but you don't have to be a Southerner to feel or appreciate it. Wherever life is hard or disappointing—that's the blues:

> I'm not a Southerner. I never worked on a levee. I hardly ever saw a cotton field except from the highway. But women behave the same on Park Avenue as they do on a levee: When you've got hold of one part of them the other escapes you. That's the Blues!
>
> Life is hard on Broadway as it is in Blues-originating-land. The Brill Building Blues is just as hungry as the Mississippi Levee Blues. [11]

And you don't have to be black to appreciate the blues either, "for the Blues have something that goes beyond race or sectional limits, that appeals to the ear and heart of people everywhere." [12] But the response to hardship or disappointment which takes the specific form of blues is, Hughes recognizes, a uniquely Afro-American one.

> [To these life situations] the Negro Artist can give his racial individuality, his heritage of rhythm and warmth, and his incongruous humor that so often, as in the Blues, becomes ironic laughter mixed with tears. [13]

This incongruous, ironic humor, this quality of "laughing to keep from crying," is at the heart of the blues. Hughes once noted that more often than not the blues mood is gloomy, yet when a blues is sung, people laugh. [14] Blues is the music "that laughs and cries at the same time." [15] Blues humor frequently works by subtlety and understatement. In "Out of Work," [16] for instance, the singer has walked the streets looking for work till his shoes wore off his feet. He finally goes to the WPA, a federal agency of the depression years, but they tell him he must reside in that city for a year and a day before he could qualify for employment.

> A year and a day, Lawd,
> In this great big lonesome town!
> A year and a day in this

Great big lonesome town!
I might starve for a year but
That extra day would get me down.

We might have expected a dramatic denunciation of the WPA; but blues logic works by contrary motion. The singer focusses not outwards but inwards, on himself and his response to adversity. That response is sharp and controlled, handled from an esthetic distance that allows for no self-pity. What should have been anger or despair is mellowed into humor by the comment of his closing line. He does not attempt to divert attention from his problem, nor to seek consolation in fantasy or religion; rather, he recognizes the full seriousness of his problem—the fact that there is no solution or redress. His audience is aware of this too; and it is this awareness that makes his closing line an occasion of general laughter, a victory of the human spirit over pain.

There is no dramatic denunciation of the WPA; but much of the laughter is directed at it, at the absurdity of its requirements, at the extremes to which the system will go to keep a man down, at a system that has to go to such absurd extremes to keep the poor down. The victory in laughter is a limited one, but it is nevertheless a victory, for under the circumstances, sheer survival is a victory; under conditions of struggle, survival to fight on a more favorable day is a victory.

In "Hard Luck" [17] the singer is broke and decides to pawn his clothes. But the pawn-broker gives him only a dollar and a half—nowhere near the value of the clothes, and far too little to serve his needs. Now he is worse off, having lost his clothes, and he compounds his loss by using the money to get drunk to stave off dejection. Using the money to get drunk is absurdly logical, and laughable. He has played the fool; he has gone from fryingpan to fire, and by his own miscalculation. He compares himself to a mule, concludes he is worse off than a mule which at least has a stall. Nothing fails like failure, one might say, and nothing has greater potential for comedy. The people in the audience recognize themselves in the singer, for they too have failed in similar ways recently. The singer is their representative, a mirror of their lives, a priest and chief celebrant in a ritual of confession and cleansing. By admitting their failures, singer and audience admit to the simultaneous absurdity and beauty of life. It is not unlike the effect which Aristotle envisaged for the audience of a dramatic tragedy: a purgation (in this case through laughter) of the emotion of despair, a restoration of balance to the emotions, bringing stability to the being and new strength to contend with the ills of life.

One final example from the popular blues: Lonnie Johnson sings:

> They tell me blues and trouble walk hand in hand.
> They tell me blues and trouble walk hand in hand.
> But you ain't had no trouble 'til your woman falls
> for some no good man. [18]

It is bad enough that your woman should fall for another man; but when she falls for a man you consider inferior to yourself, the shock can be devastating. All logic has been overturned. You must now reevaluate yourself. You are the butt of an absurd joke, deserving to be both pitied and laughed at.

Hughes classified the blues as follows:

> There are many kinds of Blues. There are the family Blues, when a man and woman have quarreled, and the quarrel can't be patched up. There's the loveless Blues, when you haven't even got anybody to quarrel with. And there's the left-lonesome Blues, when the one you care for's gone away. Then there's also the broke-and-hungry Blues, a stranger in a strange town. And the desperate going-to-the-river Blues. . . . [19]

Hughes's classification focusses on what might be termed the "down and out" subgroup of blues. But often, in Hughes's blues and elsewhere, the lines between his five types are too thin to be visible. The categories are fluid: a song might start out with the family blues and progress through the loveless blues to the left-lonesome blues, sometimes ending with the desperate going-to-the-river blues. And in black life the broke-and-hungry blues have always been just around the corner.

Ray Charles has listed the following as the major themes of the blues: (1) love; (2) someone's running his mouth too much (gossiping); (3) having fun; (4) jobs are hard to get.[20] The commonest themes of the blues are indeed love and its betrayal; hard luck (pennilessness); joblessness; weariness from overwork; loneliness; a longing for rest and good times; frustration; despair; restlessness and wanderlust. The list is far from exhaustive; indeed, as Sterling Brown has pointed out, blues subject matter is practically endless:

> It is a popular misconception that the Blues are merely songs that ease a woman's longing for her rambling man. Of course, this pattern has been set, especially by certain priestesses of the Blues cult. Nevertheless, the Blues furnish examples of other concerns. And as the lost-lover line may be dragged into a levee moan, so may an excellent bit of farm advice be found in a song about a long-lost mama. Blues will be found ranging from flood songs to graphic descriptions of pneumonia.[21]

One important category omitted in Ray Charles's and Hughes's lists is the topical or occasional blues commenting on the events of the day, e.g., Joe Louis's fights; [22] cyclones, floods, and other natural disasters bemoaned in the "St. Louis Cyclone Blues," "Mississippi Water Blues," "Backwater Blues" and others; [23] or political matters commented on in Leadbelly's "Hitler Song" and "National Defense Blues" [24] and in the "Drafting Blues":

> When Uncle Sam
> Calls out yo' man . . .
> Don't dress in black,
> 'Cause dat won't bring him back.
> Jus' say I've got dose drafted blues.[25]

Blues subject matter is inexhaustible mainly because in the final analysis the subject of the blues is the singer himself, his experiences, problems, emotions, and moods. His theme is the world as it touches upon his world, life as it affects his life. Nothing is irrelevant that is relevant to him; nothing is out of place. What he has experienced, he briefly recounts; what he strongly feels, he strongly expresses. His thought process is associative; his song is reflective. This is how he is able to give farm advice in one verse, moan about his woman that left him in the next. Such leapfrogging results in a formal thematic inconsistency, in an apparent chaos of concerns. But singer and audience feel no chaos, no inconsistency. The singer's person provides the logical bridges; the varied emotions he expresses in telling his life story are the tissues connecting verse to verse, creating coherence. The singer is his or her blues.

But the life whose story is told may not be the singer's. Indeed, it may not be one life at all but a composite of lives; for, like any gifted artist, the blues singer is able to enter into the lives of others, to draw into his song their experiences, problems, emotions, and moods, and to render these as though they were his own.

As indicated earlier, the blues verse was systematized in the 1920s into what came to be regarded as its classic form: three lines of verse (sung to twelve bars of music), the second line repeating the first, and the third rhyming with the first two. Sometimes the second line is slightly altered, sometimes omitted altogether.

In Hughes, as in the popular blues, the classic form is only one of a multitude of blues forms. Generally speaking, Hughes's blues fall into four formal categories: (1) blues in the classic form; (2) blues in a variety of other verse forms; (3) poems in which the classic and other forms are mixed; (4) fragments of blues themes, images, and vocabulary worked into prose or verse.

The first type is the easiest to recognize, since its form is fixed. Hughes differs only in that he breaks each line in two, creating a six-line stanza—for typographical convenience. At least half of Hughes's blues belong in this first category. The most prominent example of the second type is "Seven Moments of Love," the opening section of *Shakespeare in Harlem*. It is mostly in rhymed couplets, and subtitled "An Un-Sonnet Sequence in Blues" to underline the fact that these are not love sonnets but love blues (such as Shakespeare might have written had he been a Harlemite), and that they are blues even though not in the classic blues form. The best examples of the third type are "The Weary Blues," "Blues Fantasy," and "The Cat and the Saxophone," all in the opening section of *The Weary Blues*. The fourth type is to be found, for instance, in "Still Here" ("I've been scarred and battered. / My hopes the wind done scattered / . . . . But I don't care! / I'm still here!" [26]) and in Simple's accounts of his feet and genealogy in "Census" [27] and "Feet Live Their Own Life," [28] and of his "passed-around" childhood with its "nobody-home-that-belongs-to-you feeling" in "Empty Houses." [29] Indeed, many of the Simple stories could be described as blues in prose.

The blues poem, then, is one that, regardless of form, utilizes the themes, motifs, language, and imagery common to popular blues literature; and in the discussion that follows, no distinction will be made between the above four formal categories.

The bulk of Hughes's blues is to be found in *The Weary Blues, Fine Clothes to the Jew, Shakespeare in Harlem,* and *One-Way Ticket,* and even a running excursion through these books would suggest that Hughes was familiar with the vast body of popular blues literature of his day. As critic Alain Locke observed, Hughes's blues "in thought and style of expression are so close as scarcely to be distinguishable from the popular variety." [30] Close, but not quite the same; there are subtle differences. Unlike most of the popular variety, Hughes's blues are composed rather than improvised, and accordingly are more polished and structurally and thematically consistent. Also, the forced or half-rhymes which result sometimes from the singer's pronunciation, sometimes from the pressure of improvisation, are absent in Hughes. But Hughes's apparent gains are offset by his real losses, for since blues on paper are unassisted by performance, their auditory and visual dimensions are lost. The reader who would appreciate Hughes's blues fully must bring to them an active memory of the blues singer's stage presence, his gestures and groans, the peculiar timbre of his voice, and the audience's shouts and laughter, all of which so richly combine to deliver the blues on stage.

Hughes's blues are also somewhat less varied in imagery and more limited in subject matter. His repertory (collected poems) contains no topical or occasional blues,[31] no prison or chain gang blues, no gambling blues, and no blues about someone running his mouth (Ray Charles's second category). We find an occasional .44 or .32, but by and large the elaborate gun bores and weaponry of the popular blues are absent. The popular letter motif is rare ("Letter," [32] "Little Old Letter" [33]); and except possibly for the counterpoint of "Life is Fine," [34] there are no talking blues. Social protest is as rare in Hughes as in popular blues. In fact it is not until "The Backlash Blues" (1967) [35] that we encounter what might . properly be classified as social protest blues in Hughes's collected poetry.

In Hughes's repertory, as in the popular blues, there is no significant difference between blues by men and those by women. Blues related to work are usually by men, but other than that, themes and styles are the same for men and women.

Finally, Hughes's love blues have none of the powerful sexual imagery which is the unique stamp of the popular love blues. Popular love blues are filled with references to "pony" and "easy rider," to the "chauffeur with a brand new V-8 Ford" and other sophisticated agents of sweet mobility:

> I got a horse in Texas, pony all ready in Spain, [twice]
> I got a girl in Newport, got hair just like a mane.
>
> If you see my pony, please start her home, [twice]
> Babe, I ain't had no ridin' since my pony been gone.[36]

An ordinary towboat is here transfigured:

Well, let me be your towboat and I'll tow you 'cross the pond, [twice]
Well, I'll take you slow and easy, ooh well, it really wont take me long . . .

Now blow your whistle, daddy, when you want a little more speed, [twice]
Well, I am here to please you, ooh well, just tell me what you need.[37]

References to "jelly roll," "jelly bean," "biscuit roller," "honey-dripper," "coffee grinder" and other culinary paraphernalia bring the matter down home:

Bought me a coffee-grinder, got the best one I could find, [twice]
So he could grind my coffee, 'cause he has a brand new grind.

He's a deep sea diver with a stroke that can't go wrong, [twice]
He can touch the bottom, and his wind holds out so long.

He boiled my first cabbage, and he made it awful hot, [twice]
Then he put in the bacon and it overflowed the pot.[38]

Hughes has none of these fantastic vehicular or culinary sexual images, but by choice no doubt. The closest he comes is in the last stanza of "Ma Man":

Eagle-rockin',
Daddy, eagle-rock with me.
Eagle-rockin',
Come an' eagle-rock with me.
Honey baby,
Eagle-rockish as I kin be! [39]

However, love dominates his blues. Occasionally, happy love is celebrated, as in "Ma Man" (above):

When ma man looks at me
He knocks me off ma feet.
He's got those 'lectric-shockin' eyes an'
De way he shocks me sho is sweet.

Or as in "Minnie Sings Her Blues":

Jazz band, jazz band!
Ma man an' me dance.
When I cuddles up to him
No other gal's got a chance.[40]

On such occasions there is fun and laughter (Ray Charles's "having fun"). "Hey-Hey Blues," [41] "Song for a Banjo Dance," [42] "The Cat and the Saxophone," [43] and "Negro Dancers" [44] are full of love frolic and fun.

In situations (or moments) of happy love, lovers' quarrels may be mild and innocuous, as in "Morning After" [45] and "Hard Daddy." [46] But "Beale Street Love" describes a love (or moment) that is not so sunny:

Love
Is a brown man's fist
With hard knuckles
Crushing the lips,
Blackening the eyes—
Hit me again,
Says Clorinda.[47]

And the "Bad Man," [48] snarled in his own emotions ("I'm so bad I / Don't even want to be good"), beats his wife and his girl friend, then declares with some astonishment: "Don't know why I do it but / It keeps me from feelin' blue." These latter love situations, equally vividly presented in "Early Evening Quarrel," [49] are not entirely cheerful but still manageable. Here the poet's ear has caught not the gaiety and fulfillment of the happy loves but the sigh of resignation in a relationship that could be better but which, for better or for worse, is largely under control.

But the occasions of happy and not-so-happy love are few. Most of the time what the poet catches and expresses is a lament over unhappy or lost love. In Hughes, as in the popular blues, love is lost with great frequency—sometimes by death ("Gal's Cry for a

Dying Lover," [50] "Widow Woman," [51] "Lover's Return," [52]
"Monroe's Blues" [53]), but most often by desertion. The reasons for
desertion are rarely spelled out; what matters is the impact of
desertion on the deserted. Desertion and lost love invariably bring
pain; the lone cry of "good riddance" in "Only Woman Blues" [54] is
more than offset by repeated lovers' pleas not to be deserted or
mistreated ("In a Troubled Key," [55] "Love Again Blues" [56]). The
woman of "Midwinter Blues" [57] doesn't mind her man leaving,
just that he left right in the middle of winter "when the coal was
low." And that's a cruel thing to do: "if a man loves a woman / That
ain't no time to go." The "Workin' Man" [58] works all day with pick
and shovel, only to return at night to find his home "nothin' but a
hovel" and his woman "out in de street,— / Ain't nothin' but a
'hore." And the "Black Gal" [59] has given all she has to her
brownskin lover, but the first chance he gets he "goes an finds a
yaller gal." And so it goes.

The possibility or actuality of desertion or lost love frequently
threatens to explode into violence—violence to self or to loved one
or both. The subdued complaint of "Workin' Man" conceals the
trigger of violence, while in "Evil Woman" [60] and "In a Troubled
Key" the threat is explicit. Threats of suicide in particular are not
without humor: the gypsy of "Bad Luck Card" [61] is not content
with showing the lady her bad luck card; she recommends suicide:
"Gypsy says I'd kill ma self / If I was you." In "Lament Over
Love" [62] the wronged one is "goin' down to de river" and wants it
known she "ain't goin' there to swim." The lady in "Suicide" [63] is
"gonna buy a knife with / A blade ten inches long," and for a
moment she puzzles: "Shall I carve ma self or / That man that
done me wrong?" The dejected man of "Too Blue" [64] wonders if
he needs one bullet—or two: "As hard as my head is, / It would
probably take two." And the would-be suicide of "Life is Fine,"
possibly the most comical suicide in literature, jumps in the water
and finds it too cold, climbs a skyscraper and finds it too high, and,

surprised to find himself still alive, decides he was born not for
dying but for living:

> You may hear me holler,
> You may see me cry—
> But I'll be dogged, sweet baby,
> If you gonna see me die.
>
> *Life is fine!*
> *Fine as wine!*
> *Life is fine!* [65]

Threat of violence is only the most striking and predictable of an
assortment of responses which the pain of lost love generates. The
wronged lovers ruminate copiously on the nature of love. Love is a
hunter's net: once it enmeshes you you can't get out. "Love, Oh,
love is / Such a strange disease. / When it hurts yo' heart
you / Sho can't find no ease" ("Gypsy Man").[66] Once love gets to
you, nothing else will do. You may get up and pack your trunk and
ride ("Blues Fantasy"),[67] or lie down and indulge in "if-ing"
("Twilight Reverie," [68] "Supper Time," [69] "Bed Time" [70]). You
may wish you'd never been born ("Po' Boy Blues"),[71] or "buy a
rose bud / And plant it at ma back door, / So when I'm dead
they / Won't need no flowers from de store" ("Midwinter Blues").
Or you may call for blues, for "no other music / 'Ll ease ma
misery" ("Misery"),[72] resolve to "have mo' sense next time"
("Gypsy Man"), and admonish the young ones to do the same
("Listen Here Blues").[73] For while there is breath there will be a
next time: blues personas, in Hughes and elsewhere, are no-
toriously addicted to love. The grief-crushed widow resolves never
to have another man; then adds: "Yet you never can tell when
a / Woman like me is free!" ("Widow Woman"). Only one says she
will shut and lock her door "next time a man comes near me / . . .
Cause they treats me mean" ("Cora").[74] But even then we are not
so sure. Most are convinced that love is "like whiskey" or "like red,

red wine. / If you wants to be happy / You got to love all the time"
("Lament Over Love"). The essence of love may be apprehended
only by analogy, its power only by its effects: "It takes you and it
breaks you— / But you got to love again" ("Love Again Blues").
The only manageable truce with the overwhelming power of love,
they all say, is to love again.

But until love returns or is found again, the interim is a seem-
ingly interminable stretch, sleepless and alone "by myself in a double bed" ("Letter"). "A human gets lonesome if there ain't two"
("Bed Time"). The threats of violence and the fantasies and resolu-
tions gradually modulate into quietude and the long even plaint
which is by far the dominant mood of the blues as a genre:

> I went down to the corner.
> I stood there feelin' blue—
> I used to go *round* the corner,
> Babe, and call on you.
>
> Old lonesome corner!
> People pass by me—
> But none of them peoples
> Is who I want to see. [75]

The "left-lonesome blues" have taken over. "They tell me blues
and trouble walk hand in hand," sang Lonnie Johnson, and they
told him true. For when you're lonesome and no one cares about
you, "those sad old weary blues" are relentless, will follow you
wherever you go. This is the blues that possessed Hughes's original "Weary Blues" man at his sad raggy piano down on Lenox Avenue that night; that possesses the young man who left the sunny
South for the lonely wintry North ("Po' Boy Blues"), and the
ruined and friendless young girl who now "won't be nobody's
bride" ("A Ruined Gal"). [76] The streetwalker down on 31st Street
has the lonesome blues so bad she'd give her love away for no
money at all—only to be rebuffed: "when a two-bit woman / Gives
love away she's through" ("Midnight Chippie's Lament"). [77]

When jobs are hard to get, as in "Out of Work," or the work is

too hard (a variant), as in "Mississippi Levee," [78] you could find
yourself down and out and deserted by your friends ("Down
and Out"),[79] and you just might have to "gather up yo' fine
clothes / An' sell 'em to de Jew." Then may follow the mismated
shoes ("Bad Morning") [80]—and the Railroad Blues:

> De railroad bridge's
> A sad song in de air.
> Ever time de trains pass
> I wants to go somewhere.[81]

Or the Long-Hard-Road Blues or Bound-North Blues:

> Road's in front o' me,
> Nothin' to do but walk.
> Road's in front o' me,
> Walk . . . and walk . . . and walk.
> I'd like to meet a good friend
> To come along an' talk.[82]

Loveless and lonesome, or out of work, down and out, and walking the long hard road toward another chance, the blues echo
through your head, repeating their same essential message: *resignation* to present circumstance, *hope* for the future. Surely the sun
is gonna shine again in your backyard someday.

> Sun's gonna shine
> Somewhere
> Again.[83]

And when the sun does shine, you will let loose the loud Hey!
Hey!

> Cause I can HEY on water,
> I said HEY-HEY on beer—
> HEY on water
> And HEY-HEY on beer—
> But gimme good corn whiskey
> And I'll HEY-HEY-HEY—and cheer!

> Yee—ee-e-who—ooo-oo-o! [84]

The blues carry the cry of cheer as readily as the cry of pain, sometimes in the same breath and beat.

Hughes's blues provide in miniature what their larger original (popular blues) also provide: a profile of black folks, both in their parochial racial aspect and in their broader humanity. Racial attitudes expressed in the blues include the equation (derived from white attitudes) of blackness with ugliness ("Gal's Cry For a Dying Lover," "Evil Woman"); the preference for lighter skin over darker skin, and the exploitation of this preference by the lighter-skinned ("Gypsy Man," "Black Gal"). But by and large, the blues touch upon universal life experiences and emotions, echoing age-old cries: "I wonder is there nowhere a / Do-right man?" ("Early Evening Quarrel"); affirming age-old wisdoms: "A wandering man makes a wandering woman" ("Gypsy Man"). Most prominent, of course, is the unending battle of the sexes. Love is a protection against loneliness; but in love, as in other life experiences, things are not always what they seem. Things sometimes start out good, end up bad. Treachery in love and friendship sometimes forces one into self-protective caution verging on paranoia ("Lament Over Love," "Listen Here Blues," "Cora," "Payday," [85] "Down and Out," "Bound No'th Blues"). The emotions at the death of a loved one might be quite tangled, ambivalent ("Widow Woman," "Lover's Return"). And when in trouble you either cry by yourself or risk being ridiculed ("Midnight Chippie's Lament"). The pitfalls of life are reason for singing the blues. Blues turn wronged love into a song instead of into a knife ("In a Troubled Key"). And to the man who wonders if any but black folks ever feel lonesome and sad ("Daybreak"),[86] the answer is obvious: all humanity, rich and poor, black and white, red, yellow, and brown, have their share of adversity, and sing their own local version of the blues.

Action in Hughes's blues, as in the popular blues, is characteristically undramatic, understated, laced with irony and humor. The language alternates between plain, simple diction and striking visual imagery. The stoicism of the blues, of which much has been written, consists in the resolve not only to endure life but also to enjoy it; in the determination that "I'm-gonna-be-happy-anyhow-in-spite-of-this-world." [87] Or as Ralph Ellison stated it, the blues "at once express both the agony of life and the possibility of conquering it through sheer toughness of spirit." [88] "Sheer toughness of spirit": that is what Charles S. Johnson meant when he said that the blues carry "the curious story of disillusionment without a saving philosophy and yet without defeat." [89] The blues generate no consolations, no false hopes. The blues singer looks to no strength outside himself; he projects only a bald determination: I shall endure and I shall overcome. The power of transcendence is within.

That Hughes was able to capture and transmit this ethos so completely in his work must be counted among his greatest achievements. The achievement is even greater when we remember that blues was not as popular among black people (of Hughes's day or any day) as we would like to think. Indeed, outside its Southern rural homeland, blues was something of a cult. Hughes's devotion to it was certainly singular. The majority of black intellectuals and artists of his day, including, regrettably, the eminent James Weldon Johnson and Alain Locke whose sympathies were so deep and whose critical sights were so broad and piercing, despised blues even more than they despised jazz. At worst they regretted the nightclub associations of jazz; but the blues they considered downright artificial, vulgar, and obscene. To Johnson and Locke, great black folk music is the spirituals. [90]

Hughes recalls one occasion when he read his poems to a church audience. In the midst of it, the minister had a note delivered to him ordering him not to read any more blues in his pulpit. [91] Some blacks who despised blues could tolerate jazz partly because jazz was, for the most part, instrumental, whereas blues came with what they considered offensive lyrics, off-color jokes, and lewd gestures. Words are subject to censorship, but pure instrumental sound is not, at least not in the same way. What the voice cannot say, an instrument might say with impunity. Assertions, boasts, curses, and threats may be felt in the instrumental sound, but no one can be quite sure. For player and audience, then, instrumental jazz affords a certain immunity.

Of the few intellectuals and artists who thought highly of the blues, only Hughes devoted any considerable attention to imitating or incorporating them into his own work. Probably closest to Hughes in sensibility was Sterling Brown; but Sterling Brown worked mostly with ballads and epics. Aside from the few blues poems in *Southern Road* (1932) and any other uncollected pieces, Brown's treatment of the blues was, for the most part, analytical (academic in the most positive sense) rather than presentational. Nowhere in black literature of any period do we see the blues live and move as they live and move in Langston Hughes. In Hughes's blues we find the spirit of an age recreated and preserved in one of its great cultural forms.

Hughes's blues are significant in another way. As I said earlier, black music, especially the blues, had such an impact on Hughes's concept of life and art that he sought in his work to produce, as it were, a literary equivalent of black music. Blues is central to his artistic vision: the blues outlook of stoic endurance, and its style of understatement and ironic humor, suffuses not only his poetry but his prose and drama as well.

On the other side of the blues are spirituals and gospel. Blues could be regarded as spirituals secularized. Hughes's repertory of spirituals, sermons, and gospel is sparse, most of them in "Glory! Halleluiah!," the third section of *Fine Clothes to the Jew.* [92] Unlike James Weldon Johnson, Hughes was more fascinated with the literary possibilities of the secular forms (jazz, blues, ballads) than of the religious forms (sermons, spirituals, gospel). Indeed, compared to the sustained intensity of the traditional spirituals or the scope and sweep of Johnson's *God's Trombones,* Hughes's spirituals and sermons appear fragmentary. However, all the pain and prayer of the traditional spirituals are there. The fear is of judgment, the desire of heaven. Saints croon or shout from the amencorner: "Glory! Halleluiah! / De dawn's a-comin'!" ("Prayer Meeting"). Sinners moan and reckon up their sins (sometimes with a touch of hyperbole and secret satisfaction):

> I been stealin'
> Been tellin' lies,
> Had more women
> Than Pharaoh had wives.   ("Fire")

They fall "at de feet o' Jesus," pooling around those feet "sorrow like a sea." One worshipper fiercely shouts: "Listen to yo' prophets, / Little Jesus! / Listen to yo' saints!" ("Shout"). The brilliant imagery of the traditional folk sermon, which James Weldon Johnson transcribed so magnificently in *God's Trombones,* figures only very briefly in "Sunday Morning Prophecy":

> . . . and now
> When the rumble of death
> Rushes down the drain
> Pipe of eternity,
> And hell breaks out
> Into a thousand smiles,
> And the devil licks his chops
> Preparing to feast on life,
> And all the little devils
> Get out their bibs
> To devour the corrupt bones
> Of this world—
> Oh-ooo-oo-o!
> Then my friends!
> Oh, then! Oh, then!
> What will you do? . . .[93]

But even in these fragments of sermons, spirituals, and prayers, moans and hollers and shouts, Hughes succeeds in capturing some of the emotional intensity of the great religious folk tradition. We are afforded a brief glimpse into the nature of that tradition, its origins and uses, in "Communion":

> I was trying to figure out
> What it was all about
> But I could not figure out
> What it was all about
> So I gave up and went
> To take the sacrament
> And when I took it
> It felt good to shout! [94]

The shout is a plausible response to the ungraspable mystery of life, and not very different from the ecstatic secular shout of the "Hey-Hey Blues." Spirituals and blues are two sides of the same coin, two exhaust pipes leading out of the same engine. Each is an emotional outlet, the blues more private and personal, the spiritual more communal. The blues turn inward, finding strength in the self, strength in the sheer determination to survive, while the spiritual turns outward, finding someone (Jesus) to lean on. The anguish is equally excruciating, but in the spiritual it is compounded with guilt (and fear of hell). Guilt implies acceptance of at least limited responsibility for one's pain, a feeling of responsibility fostered, in this case, by the Christian doctrine of original sin. Guilt in this form is almost wholly absent from the blues, whether of Hughes or of the popular variety. Blues victims generally project responsibility outward onto someone else, omitting whatever part they may have played in bringing about their own pain. Both blues and spirituals end in hope—for the blues a sun-filled future, for the spirituals, heaven.

CHAPTER 3

Jazz, Jive, and Jam

Unlike classic blues, the jazz poem has no fixed form: it is a species of free verse which attempts to approximate some of the qualities of jazz. The dynamic energy of jazz is to be contrasted with the relatively low-keyed and generally elegiac tone of the blues. Blues is for the most part vocal and mellow, jazz for the most part instrumental and aggressive. The jazz poem attempts to capture that instrumental vigor.

In the free verse of Walt Whitman, and its modernist sequel in Pound, Eliot, and others, the language is formal and literary, with long, complex sentences and well-made phrases, or informal but not conversational; or, when it is conversational, it is in the idiom of the educated middle class. Jazz poetry, on the other hand, moves with the bouncy rhythms and exuberance that characterize the music. The sentences are casual and short-winded; the phrases are short, tumbling after one another in rapid succession:

> Dusk dark
> On Railroad Avenue.
> Lights in the fish joints,
> Lights in the pool rooms.
> A box-car some train

> Has forgotten
> In the middle of the
> Block.
> A player piano,
> A victrola.
>   942
>   Was the number.
> A boy
> Lounging on a corner.
> A passing girl
> With purple powdered skin. . . .[1]

The jazz poem derives from oral performance and music. Its relaxed attitude reflects the informal atmosphere in which the music thrives, and its open verse form is reminiscent of the improvisational latitude of the music. Its language—swift-paced, informal talk—aids the impression of spontaneity. The language is most often colloquial, sometimes the hip talk of the musicians, almost always the language of the common people, rarely the language of the academies.

Jazz poetry might be viewed as a stage in that search for native American rhythms begun by Walt Whitman and carried forward in the early 20th century by such poets as Vachel Lindsay and Carl Sandburg. Its ancestor on the black side is the dialect poetry of Paul Laurence Dunbar which was built on black speech rhythms of the rural South. Of Hughes's contemporaries, Lindsay especially had established a reputation as a jazz poet with his "General William Booth Enters into Heaven" (1913), a rhythmic adaptation of black folk sermons, with built-in leader-choral antiphony and the accompaniment of drums, banjos, flutes, and tambourines; and with his racist "The Congo: A Study of the Negro Race" (1914), which came with precise marginal notes on mood and musical accompaniment. "The Congo" is a rehearsal of fantastic events in black lands of the white imagination, and a panegyric on the white man's so-called "civilizing mission" in Africa.

THEN I had religion, THEN I had a vision.
I could not turn from their revel in derision.
THEN I SAW THE CONGO, CREEPING THROUGH THE BLACK,
CUTTING THROUGH THE FOREST WITH A GOLDEN
  TRACK. . . .

"Be careful what you do,
Or Mumbo-Jumbo, God of the Congo . . .
Mumbo-Jumbo will hoo-doo you,
Mumbo-Jumbo will hoo-doo you,
Mumbo-Jumbo will hoo-doo you. . . .

Boomlay, boomlay, boomlay, boom.
Boomlay, boomlay, boomlay, boom.
Boomlay, boomlay, boomlay, boom.
Boomlay, boomlay, boomlay,
BOOM." [2]

Much of the poem's strength is in its rhythmic energy, its repetitions and imitative sounds, the vivid detail in which the varied scenes are painted, and the terror of the experience which is so vitally captured and dramatized. In his ability to recount the experience, Lindsay's spiritual voyager is Coleridge's Ancient Mariner, Sindbad the Sailor, and a convert testifying at a Holy Roller church all in one. Hughes himself has acknowledged the debt he owes to Dunbar, Sandburg, and Lindsay,[3] among others. His "Song for a Banjo Dance"[4] could be read as a version of Dunbar's "A Negro Love Song." His "Harlem Night Club"[5] and "Jazz Band in a Parisian Cabaret" remind us of Sandburg's "Jazz Fantasia" (1920). And his *Ask Your Mama* is closely related in form and manner to Lindsay's "The Congo."

Dunbar's dialect poetry, and the dialect stories of Charles Waddell Chesnutt, together constituted the fullest flowering in black literature of a 19th-century tradition which was popularized by the white minstrel stage and by white writers of the Southern local color school such as George Washington Cable, Thomas Nelson Page, Joel Chandler Harris, and Irwin Russell. Both Chesnutt and

Dunbar attempted to turn dialect inside out, to purge it of its all too familiar stereotypes of the happy-go-lucky, chicken-stealing, comic Sambo, but with limited success (with Dunbar the less successful). Chesnutt's last published novel in 1905, and Dunbar's death in 1906, might be said to have brought to a close the 19th century in black literature. The next fifteen to twenty years saw a dramatic shift in black population from the rural South to the urban North; and as it turned out, the transition in literature from 19th to 20th century, and from dialect poetry to jazz poetry and blues, paralleled that Great Migration. As might be expected, the younger generation of writers took their cues from Dunbar and Chesnutt, but they soon discovered that dialect was too old and crumbly to survive a face lift. It was impossible to use dialect and avoid the stereotypes. But fortunately for them, their coming of age coincided with the boisterous jazz and blues age, and it was in the contemporary life, language, and music of the city, rather than in the South and the past, that they found what James Weldon Johnson has called "form[s] that will express the racial spirit by symbols from within rather than by symbols from without (such as the mere mutilation of English spelling and pronunciation)." [6]

The jazz poem was such a form; and while Hughes did not invent it, he carried it to a high level of development. He manages to suggest the frenetic energy of instrumental jazz in the breathless enumerations of "Railroad Avenue," "Jitney," [7] "Man into Men," [8] "Brass Spittoons," [9] and "Laughers," [10] and the complex interplay of instruments in the counterpoint of voices in "Mulatto," [11] "Closing Time," [12] and "The Cat and the Saxophone":

> EVERYBODY
> Half-pint,—
> Gin?
> No, make it
> LOVES MY BABY
> corn. You like
> liquor,

don't you, honey?
BUT MY BABY
Sure. Kiss me,
DON'T LOVE NOBODY
daddy.
BUT ME.
Say!
EVERYBODY
Yes?
WANTS MY BABY
I'm your
BUT MY BABY
sweetie, ain't I?
DON'T WANT NOBODY
Sure.
BUT
Then let's
ME,
do it!
SWEET ME.
Charleston,
mamma!
¦ 13

Of "The Cat and the Saxophone" Countee Cullen wrote: "This creation is a *tour de force* of its kind, but is it a poem?"—a question not to be asked.

In "Death in Harlem" [14] Hughes builds an extended jazz narrative on the structure of the black folk epic or toast, adding exhortative asides ("Do it, Arabella! / Honey baby, sock it!"). The setting is Dixie's, a Harlem basement nightclub. The Texas Kid, "a dumb little jigaboo from / Somewhere South," has a thick bill roll in his hands, and Arabella Johnson has her hands on him. Dixie's musician whips that piano. "Aw, play it, Miss Lucy! / Lawd! / Ain't you shame?" They drink and dance and laugh. "Everybody's happy. It's a spending crowd— / Big time sports and girls who know / Dixie's ain't no place for a crowd that's slow." Then Arabella goes to the "LADIES' ROOM" and comes back to find another good-time woman has taken her place. "(It was just as if somebody / Kicked her in the face)." She drew her pistol and the shots rang out. "Take me, / Jesus, take me / Home today." Bessie falls and Arabella is taken to jail. And the Texas Kid—he "picked up another woman and / Went to bed."

"Death in Harlem" is a record of one of the meanings of Harlem nightlife. Dixie's pleasure cellar is a den of death. Dixie is an eager Tom who wants money—bootleg money, sex money, blood money, any money. He rubs his hands and grins and bows as his white customers enter. In this nightspot the contraries meet and merge: black and white, poor and rich, pleasure and pain, laughter and death. The white presence presages death: the white women look at the blacks and think of rape, a rope, a flame. They dream of sex and violence, anticipating the sexual rivalry that will force the evening to a shuddering climax. Down south in Dixie it would have been death from a white mob; but up north at Dixie's it is death from the self-destructiveness of blacks, as it were activated by the white presence, actualizing the hidden white wish.

Death is so close to the heightened moments of life that it is almost impossible to avoid. Danger and death are expected and accepted parts of the evening's entertainment. The line, "Everybody's happy," describing the music and dancing, is intimately related to "Stand back folkses, let us / Have our fun"—where the fun is with guns and knives. The ambiguity of the evening's experience is summed up in the closing image of night slipping away like a reefer-man, an image that captures the compulsion, pleasure, pain, and final death of the experience—of the addiction, whether to drugs, which the reefer-man dispenses, or to life's reckless pleasures (liquor, music, sex, and money), which Dixie in his nightclub dispenses.

The story is elaborately but briskly told, detailed but terse, in the classic folk manner. In conception and delivery, "Death in

Harlem" is a literary child of the great epic cycles such as "The Signifying Monkey," "Shine and the Sinking of the Titanic," and
"Stagolee." The mastery which Hughes developed in this and
other jazz poems is to be fully utilized in *Montage of a Dream
Deferred* and *Ask Your Mama.*

Montage of a Dream Deferred (1951) is more carefully orchestrated than Hughes's earlier volumes because conceived as a unity,
as one continuous poem, although it is organized in sections and
subtitles just like the others, and uses single poems previously
published in periodicals. In *Montage* the days of our black lives are
telescoped into one day and one night. Montage is primarily a
technique of the motion picture, its camera eye sweeping swiftly
from scene to scene, juxtaposing disparate scenes in rapid succession or superimposing one scene (layer of film) over another until
the last fades into the next. In literature, montage provides a technical shortcut, a means of avoiding the sometimes long-winded
"logical" transitions demanded by the conventional story line.
Through montage, the reader/viewer is able to traverse vast spaces
and times (and consciousness) in a relatively brief moment.
Hughes in his prefatory note prepares the reader for this mode of
seeing:

> In terms of current Afro-American popular music and the sources
> from which it has progressed—jazz, ragtime, swing, blues, boogie-
> woogie, and be-bop—this poem on contemporary Harlem, like be-
> bop, is marked by conflicting changes, sudden nuances, sharp and
> impudent interjections, broken rhythms, and passages sometimes in
> the manner of the jam session, sometimes the popular song, punc
> tuated by the riffs, runs, breaks, and disc-tortions of the music of a
> community in transition. [15]

The theme is the dream deferred. The vehicle is primarily be-
bop but also boogie-woogie and other black music. And the mode

is montage, which has its musical equivalent in be-bop and its literary equivalent in free association (stream of consciousness). Bebop, montage, and free association parallel one another so closely in technique (rapid shifts) that the mode could be thought of as all three simultaneously. However, free association is used sparingly, as in the "Dig and Be Dug" section when talk of death leads to talk of war. (Free association will see full service in *Ask Your Mama*.) Some sections open and close with the musical motif (boogie or bop), and each is sprinkled with musical references and phrases, including the "nonsense syllables" or "scat singing" ("Oop-pop-a-da! / Skee! Daddle-de-do! / Be-bop!") which especially characterized bop. In "Dive" (p. 33), for instance, while there is no mention of music, it is the music that is picking up rhythm "faster . . . / faster," lending its speed to the nightlife on Lenox Avenue. Similarly, "Up-Beat" (p. 35) describes a speeding up of the beat as well as a possible metamorphosis of black youth—their emergence from the gutter, up from the dead into the quick—the kind of process by which the youngsters of "Flatted Fifths," "Jam Session," "Be-Bop Boys," and "Tag" are transformed from jail-birds into musical celebrities.

The poem could be viewed as a ritual drama, but without the stiffness that the term usually connotes. It is a vibrant seriocomic ceremony in which a community of voices is orchestrated from a multiset or multilevel stage, the speakers meanwhile engaged in their normal chores or pleasures. The setting is Harlem, with a close awareness of its connection with downtown Manhattan and its place as a magnetic mecca for refugees from the South. The time: the continuous present on which the burden of times past is heavy, with brief projections into the future. The poem opens in the morning and progresses through daytime into evening, into late night, and on to the following dawn. *Harlem, a microcosm of the black presence in America,* is the victim of an economic blight, relieved only sporadically by the wartime boom. This is hardly the joy-filled night-town of the 1920s. Money, or more precisely the lack of money, determines many of the human relationships presented to our view especially in the opening section. Money is the main riff, the musical current flowing steadily just below the surface and surfacing from time to time, bearing the theme of the dream deferred. A few situations transcend the terms and boundaries of the economic imperative, as in "Juke Box Love Song" (p. 10), where love unlocks and lets fly softness and beauty amidst the discordant, dissatisfied voices of poverty, creating a harmony that money could not by itself accomplish; in "Projection" (p. 26), where unity and peace are described in terms of a harmonious orchestration of disparate types; and in "College Formal" (p. 41), where the youthful couples, wrapped in love and melody, lend transcendence to the audience as a whole.

The deferred dream is examined through a variety of human agencies, of interlocking and recurring voices and motifs fragmented and scattered throughout the six sections of the poem. Much as in bebop, the pattern is one of constant reversals and contrasts. Frequently the poems are placed in thematic clusters, with poems within the cluster arranged in contrasting pairs. *Montage* does not move in a straight line; its component poems move off in invisible directions, reappear and touch, creating a complex tapestry or mosaic.

The dream theme itself is carried in the musical motifs. It is especially characterized by the rumble ("The boogie-woogie rumble / Of a dream deferred")—that rapid thumping and tumbling of notes which so powerfully drives to the bottom of the emotions, stirring feelings too deep to be touched by the normal successions of notes and common rhythms. The rumble is an atomic explosion of musical energy, an articulate confusion, a moment of epiphany, a flash of blinding light in which all things are suddenly made clear. The theme is sounded at strategic times, culminating in the final section where all the instruments beat out their ver-

Theme of dream

sions of the theme. The energy level is brilliantly high in the wind-up: music as structure and metaphor succeeds in holding the poem together and moving it to the end, creating continuity in depth. Music is preeminently the medium that can hold so many sides and dimensions, that can bring to the front similarities among things apparently dissimilar—the similarities between church music and jazz; between the lives of the good folk and of the good time folk; between the lives of pimps, whores, mothers, children, musicians, and the folks that sit on stoops—similarities even to the point of desperation where they all cry out, "Great God!" ("Sliver of Sermon," p. 56). Jazz, above all, is the music that can hold so much simultaneous motion, melody, and meaning.

The first section, "Boogie Segue to Bop," opens with the theme question: "You think / It's a happy beat?"—this rumble of the boogie-woogie and pata-pata of the feet of the dance? And toward the end of the book the question is posed again in what is to become its classic form: "What happens to a dream deferred?" ("Harlem," p. 71). Hughes first made the point in *The Weary Blues* ("Does a jazz band ever sob?") that it may all sound like a happy beat but it ain't. Behind and beneath the gaiety is some-thing sad and ominous, something that some day might explode. Hughes is usually explicit and direct, but often enough he chooses to deliver his insights and warnings veiled in hints or wrapped in questions: "I wonder where I'm gonna die, / Being neither white nor black"; [16] "Who but the Lord / can protect me?"; [17] "Or does it explode?" (p. 71). Or he gives an answer that momentarily deflects our attention from the question and amounts to no answer at all. For instance, to the question "You think / It's a happy beat?" he replies: "Sure, / I'm happy." Or, as in "Projection" (p. 26), he forecasts that the day black unity is achieved—what would hap-pen? According to the poem, nothing more momentous than Fa-ther Divine declaring: "Peace! / It's truly / wonderful!"—which is momentous enough but not quite the point. In each case the weight of the question demands something more, and the reader is thrown back upon his own resources, is forced to confront the deeper implications of the question.

After the opening question comes "Parade," hauling out the whole cast, a concentration of blackness shocking in its vastness and vivacity ("I never knew / that many Negroes / were on earth, / did you?"). Cops stand alert when so many blacks come together, anticipating the unity that does not yet exist—"Solid black, / Can't be right"—and would speed them out of sight if they could. A festive atmosphere prevails. Harlem has seen some colorful parades, starting back in Marcus Garvey's days. As with Father Divine's declaration, Hughes chooses to give the parade a human significance and in the black folk style, instead of a political/rhetorical significance. The parade, he says, is just "a chance to let / . . . the whole world see / . . . old black me!"—which is what *Montage* itself is, with its variegated presentation of Harlem and Harlemites.

The rest of the opening section progresses from childhood to youth to adulthood. The youngsters of "Children's Rhymes" and "Sister" are in process of discovering the world and learning to cope with it. In "Children's Rhymes" the adult voice serves as counterpoint and foil to the young voices. Times have changed, and innocent rhymes have given way to verses fraught with precocious knowledge.

> By what sends
> the white kids
> I ain't sent:
> I know I can't
> be President.

This early, the children already understand their racial situation and the ceiling placed on their aspirations. They can distinguish rhetoric from reality. White kids are fired by political and other ambitions; black kids can't afford to be. This early their dream is already deferred—they can hardly afford to dream. So young, and so cynical, "living 20 years in 10," as Hughes will put it in *Ask Your Mama*. The letter of the law and the promise of the Constitution to them is meaningless: "Liberty And Justice— / Huh—For All."

Cynicism and disillusionment with America is nothing new, of course, but perhaps not until the generation of the 1960s was it so pervasive and complete among black youth, and even among a significant portion of white youth. Hughes may be said to have anticipated it in "Children's Rhymes."

In "Sister" the tables are turned. Here it is youth that is innocent and age that is realistic or cynical. If Marie runs around with trash it is because she needs cash; and "decent folks" (the unmarried gentleman ideal) usually have none to give. Poverty is generated by the limited opportunities outlined in "Children's Rhymes." Things being as they are, black women—and men too, as the voice on the stoop reminds us—do the best they can. Black men and women are equally trapped.

The truth of the voice on the stoop is immediately tested in "Preference." The young man prefers older women because they give more and ask for less. Like Marie, he too is doing the best he can. But the young man of "Necessity" is not so lucky: he has to work, if only to pay his high rent.

The common problem is economic. Love and money are closely intertwined, and in "Question" and "Ultimatum," as in "Sister" and "Preference," the choice of partners and the nature of the relationship is determined by economics. The question of "Question" is: can a man in these circumstances both love his woman and feed her (the familial ideal)? And if he cannot, what happens to their relationship, and their family? In "Buddy" the young man is doing his best to save his mother from the question of "Question" and its predictable answer ("De-bop!"—the answer is in the music, an answer too painful for words) by giving her ten of his twelve dollars a week. But we know it won't last: he is left only two dollars a week

for clothes and carfare. In "Croon" and "New Yorkers" the economic situation is summed up: North or South, black folks "never
own no parts / of earth nor sky."

The scene now modulates into night, the phrases "in the dark"
("New Yorkers") and "early blue evening" ("Wonder") serving as
time indicators. "Easy Boogie" ushers in the nightlife and ends the
opening section. It's been a short day, but it's going to be a long
night. Daytime will not return until the closing section.

In summary, the opening poem, "Dream Boogie," poses the
question, and the rest of *Montage* attempts to answer it. In *Montage* we see some of the things that happen to a dream deferred.
"Parade" presents the people: this is Harlem, "I'm talking
about / Harlem to you" (p. 74). The rest of the poems in the section exhibit the institutional limitations to black aspirations and the
effects of economic deprivation on black life and love. As usual
with Hughes, there is no moralizing; each poem delivers the picture starkly and without comment.

The second section, "Dig and Be Dug," opens with a juxtaposition of art ("Movies") and life ("Not a Movie"). Movies spin nonstop on celluloid the American Dream—while the KKK beat up
one more black man who tried to make that Dream real. Because
of its divorce from reality, movie art is "crocodile art" evoking
"crocodile tears." Harlem sees it for what it is—and laughs "in all
the wrong places." What is serious to Hollywood is funny to black
folks and vice versa. "Hollywood / laughs at me": when black people appear in the movies, it is in the service of white fantasies (stereotypes). But Hollywood refuses to deal with the brutality of the
South or the economic constrictions on life on 133rd Street, which
is no laughing matter. On 133rd Street you may not have the KKK
at your back, but you have the police; and you still don't own a
thing. "Why should it be *my* dream / deferred / overlong?" ("Tell
Me").

"Neon Signs" is a roll call of the night spots where black music reigns, the genius of "re-bop / sound" in such sharp contrast to Hollywood's sterile crocodile art on the one hand, and to the dilapidated physical environment ("broken glass," "smears") of black night spots on the other. The poet's camera and microphone make the rounds, recording the scene and reporting the conversation. Survival savvy in this night world is "play it cool / And dig all jive." Know the environment and be at home in it, be part of its swing. Live and let live: "Dig And Be Dug / In Return" ("Motto"). Gambling ("Numbers") is one way to get some money, entertainment ("Dancer") is another. Both are subject to rare and uncertain chances. Especially with gambling, too much luck among the luckless can be worse than too little: "When I rolled three 7's / in a row / I was scared to walk out / with the dough" ("Situation"). Death stalks. One of the inset progressions is from birth ("What? So Soon?") through survival / life ("Motto") to death ("Dead in There"). "Advice" pinpoints the lesson:

> Folks, I'm telling you,
> birthing is hard
> and dying is mean—
> so get yourself
> a little loving
> in between.

Talk of death brings back memories of the war. "Green Memory" is one of several excursions into history. As the red blood rolled out the green money rolled in. Blood money, as it were, is all that Harlem has ever been permitted. *But* even for this alone, let the white folks fight another war, "or even two" if they wish; "the one to stop 'em won't be me" ("Relief"). The issue is survival.

Memories of the depression and war time clear the stage for "Ballad of the Landlord," which is one of the high points of *Montage*. First collected in *Jim Crow's Last Stand* (1943), this poem is likely to remain contemporary for a long time to come. It is not for nothing that as recently as 1965 the public school system of a major

American city dismissed a teacher for assigning "Ballad of the Landlord" to his class. [18]

In a few bold strokes Hughes paints a picture of a slum dwelling broken from roof to bottom step; of the callous landlord who will not make repairs but will evict if rent is not paid on time; and, most importantly, of the forces of law and order who are ranged on the landlord's side and who, like the landlord, equate the assertion of tenant rights with revolution, for the tenant's refusal to accept and pay for substandard and dangerous living conditions is a threat to a society which grows fat from tenant abuse. Their reprisal is swift and smooth: landlord, police, judge, and press have rehearsed and acted out this scenario so many times before.

The poem is tightly constructed, and in the black idiom. The first half follows the form of the conventional English folk ballad: quatrains of alternating tetrameter and trimeter lines, rhyming *abcb*. The last half is irregular, the short, broken lines recreating the curtness of the police arrest, the precipitousness with which the judge assigns a jail term, and the brevity with which the press dismisses the incident. The rhymes are conventional until we get to "land" and "man," "press" and "arrest," which rhyme as they would in black folk dialect.

In the first half of the poem a balance is maintained between landlord and tenant with claims and counterclaims, threats and counterthreats, "I" and "you." The landlord is comfortable issuing threats, but he can't take them; and he quickly upsets the balance of words by yelling for the police. His hysterical "Police! Police!" is in violent contrast to the even tone of the tenant's "Landlord, landlord." But, ironically, the landlord's power is as great as his terror. The tenant calls on the landlord twice and gets no action; the landlord calls on the police once and gets immediate action. Against the landlord's organized might, the tenant's fearless manhood is ineffectual; his individual resistance is hopeless. And it is to gather organizational strength that the orator of the next poem, "Corner Meeting," mounts his ladder. His message is contained in "Projection"—that were disparate black factions to unite and work together in their own self-interest, it would be "truly / wonderful," for then would black power emerge, and only then would the problems of the ghetto, symbolized by the slumlord, begin to find solutions.

Thus, this second section, which opened with the nighttime escapes from and makeshift solutions to the frustrations aired in the preceding section, closes with a vision of a dependable vehicle of redress: *black unity, the prerequisite for black power*. Hughes of course does not spell it all out. He does not need to.

The third section, "Early Bright," is the late night, hard bop section. Here are the hard-core night people in their milieu: the music makers, the "little cullud boys" whose early encounters with "bail" and "jail" ("Jam Session") and "fear" ("Flatted Fifths," "Tag") erupt into be-bop; black celebrities ("Mellow") into whose laps "white girls fall," defying the taboos; drug pushers who find the people no obstacle (survival savvy: "Live And Let Live," "Dig And Be Dug"); "the vice squad / with weary sadistic eyes" sniffing out the degenerates ("Cafe: 3 A.M."); drunkards, rounders, and assorted faces. Ironically, the "Be-Bop Boys" implore "Mecca / to achieve / six discs / with Decca"—which, among other things, is Hughes's recognition of the non-Western forces at work in the community.

The first half of the fourth section, "Vice Versa to Bach,"offers a thematic contrast to the preceding section. Here the poet touches on the world of the educated and middle class aspiring after white culture—Bach, not bop.

> See that lady
> Dressed so fine?
> She ain't got boogie-woogie
> On her mind—
>
> ("Lady's Boogie," p. 44)

But even they, he says, if they would listen, they too would hear
the music of a dream deferred even in the Bach.

> But if she was to listen
> I bet she'd hear,
> Way up in the treble
> The tingle of a tear.
>
> Be-Bach!
>
> ("Lady's Boogie")

The delicate treble "tingle" is at the opposite end of the musical
scale from the deep "rumble," but the dream, encompassing life itself, is broad enough to touch both. The music of the dream is
inescapable: it is heard by high and low, by blacks everywhere and
in all circumstances.

"Theme for English B" is one of Hughes's most nearly autobiographical poems. There is relatively little distance between him
and the experience recounted in the poem. The "college on the
hill above Harlem" is of course Columbia University, where he
spent an unsatisfactory year in 1921–22, and the poem evidently
grew out of an incident there. The poem reiterates one of his leading themes, first enunciated at the close of *The Weary Blues:* that
"I, too, am America." American identity of necessity embraces
equally the white and the black experience. Those two experiences
interpenetrate, are defined one by the other, even though neither
group relishes the idea. "Sometimes perhaps you don't want to be
a part of me. / Nor do I want to be a part of you. / But we are,
that's true."

The quarrel between black and white finds an echo in the
argument between the "black bourgeoisie" and the "common element" in "Low to High" and "High to Low." The "low" accuse the
"high" of turning their backs on them, the masses. The "high,"
who are "trying to uphold the race" in the eyes of white folks,
regard the masses as a liability because they "talk too loud, / cuss

too loud, / look too black, / don't get anywhere, / and sometimes it seems / you don't even care." The argument is a classic and familiar one. And Hughes in his usual way is content to dramatize it, with no comment, although his manner of presentation leaves no doubt where his sympathies are.

"Freedom Train" and "Deferred" constitute the climax of this section and are among the most strategic poems in *Montage*. Each is a poem of considerable scope, permitting the varied illustration of the essential theme. "Freedom Train" is a response to the patriotic train which toured the United States in 1947–48 carrying historical documents and mementoes. The Freedom Train symbolizes the promise of America. For the black man, freedom has so far been a fantasy; he has heard the word but never experienced the reality. Past experience makes him skeptical: this train might be just another piece of pompous propaganda—unreal, in contrast to the very real deaths of black soldiers who helped make and keep America free. In his inventory of the things which should not be found on a Freedom Train (segregated facilities, job discrimination, denial of franchise) the poet gives an accurate description of racial abuses, of the United States as it is. The Freedom Train is long enough to encompass past, present and future, from the grandmother in Atlanta trying to board the train and some white man yelling "Get back! / A Negra's got no business on the Freedom Track!," to the children in their innocent questioning trying to make sense of senseless Jim Crow.

The train as metaphor comes out of Afro-American secular and religious traditions: it is the heaven-bound train and chariot of the spirituals, the northbound train of the Underground Railroad, and the out-bound trains carrying unhappy lovers and restless wanderers to fresh scenes and new hopes in the blues. Further, as a mode of speedy and comfortable travel, impressive with its sharp whistle, grinding wheels, and many cars rolling along at a swift and noisy pace, the train joins place to place and people to people in a

vast and varied land, abbreviating space and time and consciousness and thereby serving as an intimation of America's ability to
fuse the many into one, as in its motto "E Pluribus Unum." But
that fusion cannot be complete, America's unity train cannot run
full steam until a "coal black man," his color and strength in unison
with earth's great energy source, is also free to drive that train.

The poem has the amplitude and rhetorical sweep of a folk sermon, with its familiar and effective parallelisms and forceful repetitions:

> No back door entrance to the Freedom Train,
> No signs FOR COLORED on the Freedom Train,
> No WHITE FOLKS ONLY on the Freedom Train.

The lead voice is the preacher's, with the congregation providing a
choral counterpoint in the lines, "I'm gonna check up on
this / Freedom Train," "But maybe they'll explain it on the / Freedom Train," "But, Mister, I thought it were the / Freedom Train!"
etc. The sermon-poem is delivered in a smooth, driving rhythm,
building up to a screaming crescendo in the italicized lines at the
end. Religion is not isolated from politics and daily life; on the contrary, the poem achieves a happy union of secular matter and
religious manner. Even the racial harmony envisioned at the end
is given as a goal achievable here on earth, not in a religious after-
world.

From the collective political dream of "Freedom Train" Hughes
turns to fragments of individual dreams, so intimately connected
with the political, in "Deferred." The poem opens with a sustained
discourse by three whose long-deferred dreams are now about to
be fulfilled, followed by a flurry of voices rapidly listing dreams
whose fulfillment is still deferred to some vague future time. The
dreams are low-keyed and not at all extraordinary, ranging from
the tangible and material (housewares, furniture, clothing, radio
and television sets) to the intangible (a place in heaven, a good

wife); from economic ambitions (to pass the civil service) to educational and cultural ambitions (leisure to study French, leisure to discover and enjoy Bach). Most of the dreams are of necessities and minor luxuries, of things which a little money and leisure would buy. For those who have nothing, the little things are everything.

The section closes with another excursion into history. John Brown, who died fighting to stop the dream being deferred any longer, is now as forgotten as the "unknown soldier" ("Shame on You"). To black people in particular—"Black people don't remember / any better than white"—Hughes says "shame on you." But here again he avoids direct statement, pretends he is saying something else: "If you're not alive and kicking, / shame on you." The same people who so readily forget John Brown so readily remember "World War II" as a time of fun—"What a grand time was the war!"—till the Echo asks: "Did / Somebody / Die?" True, the war brought relief, which was a good thing; but to call the war fun is the thoughtless side of "Green Memory" (p. 22). "Shame on you!"

In the fifth section, "Dream Deferred," the dream is viewed through the monocle of the religious experience. Religion is a major segment of the black experience in America, over the centuries providing breeding ground for some of the greatest black poetry and music, incubating revolts, and serving for consolation. Even pimps and whores reach a point where they are forced to cry out to God ("Sliver of Sermon"). Those who have made it, those whose dreams have come true and who now live downtown or in the suburbs, all miss Harlem, with its bitter, unfulfilled dreams, especially on sunny, summer, Sunday afternoons when the crowded sidewalks, stoops, and windows resound with cheerful chatter ("Passing"). Deracinated, isolated from the vital nourishment of their people and culture, their fulfilled dream has become a nightmare of "faces / Turned dead white" ("Nightmare

Boogie")—the faces of their now white neighborhoods. So that their dreams have not really come true since, unlike other ethnic groups, they are forced to abandon their own people in their movement upwards. Their dreams will not come true till they come true for the masses of black folk.

Amidst the disparate voices of the community gossiping and commenting on various matters, the money motif returns in "Dime," "Fact," and "Hope." The child asking for a dime—and "Granny aint got no dime"—will reappear at the close of *Ask Your Mama*, crying "Show fare, Mama. . . . / Show fare!," his young dream still deferred. "Hope" (p. 68) is one of Hughes's many epigrammatic successes, succinct little statements carrying fantastic power:

> He rose up on his dying bed
> and asked for fish.
> His wife looked it up in her dream book
> and played it.

This is one of Hughes's most pointed comments on the erosion of black emotions, the dehumanization of people by poverty. Here Hughes is at his coldest and most brutal. W. C. Handy once said of this poem that in four lines Hughes says "what it would have taken Shakespeare two acts and three scenes to say." [19]

One of the closing themes of the section is the relationship of the different ethnic groups in the urban community. "Subway Rush Hour" forces a type of brotherhood: black and white are crowded so close there is "no room for fear." "Brothers" stresses pan-African unity: the Afro-American, Afro-Caribbean, and African are brothers. And in "Likewise" Hughes declares that Jews are not alone to blame for the ghetto's ills, and that they are likewise brothers, especially since they too, with their history of persecution, must have heard that same music of a dream deferred. The hostilities between black and white, Jew and Gentile, are symptomized by the "cheap little rhymes" deplored in "Sliver."

The poet has taken us on a guided tour of microcosmic Harlem, day and night, past and present. And as a new day dawns and the poem moves into a summing up in the final section, he again poses the question and examines the possibilities:

> What happens to a dream deferred?
>
>> Does it dry up
>> like a raisin in the sun?
>> Or fester like a sore—
>> And then run?
>> Does it stink like rotten meat?
>> Or crust and sugar over—
>> like a syrupy sweet?
>>
>> Maybe it just sags
>> like a heavy load.
>>
>> *Or does it explode?*

("Harlem," p. 71)

The images are sensory, domestic, earthy, like blues images. The stress is on deterioration—drying, rotting, festering, souring—on loss of essential natural quality. The raisin has fallen from a fresh, juicy grape to a dehydrated but still edible raisin to a sun-baked and inedible dead bone of itself. The Afro-American is not unlike the raisin, for he is in a sense a dessicated trunk of his original African self, used and abandoned in the American wilderness with the stipulation that he rot and disappear. Like the raisin lying neglected in the scorching sun, the black man is treated as a thing of no consequence. But the raisin refuses the fate assigned to it, metamorphoses instead into a malignant living sore that will not heal or disappear. Like the raisin, a sore is but a little thing, inconsequential on the surface but in fact symptomatic of a serious disorder. Its stink is like the stink of the rotten meat sold to black folks in so many ghetto groceries; meat no longer suitable for human use, deathly. And while a syrupy sweet is not central to the diet as meat might be, still it is a rounding-off final pleasure (dessert) at the end of a meal, or a delicious surprise that a child looks forward to at Halloween or Christmas. But that final pleasure turns out to be a pain. Aged, spoiled candy leaves a sickly taste in the mouth; sweetness gone bad turns a treat into a trick.

The elements of the deferred dream are, like the raisin, sore, meat, and candy, little things of no great consequence in themselves. But their unrelieved accretion packs together considerable pressure. Their combined weight becomes too great to carry about indefinitely: not only does the weight increase from continued accumulation, but the longer it is carried the heavier it feels. The load sags from its own weight, and the carrier sags with it; and if he should drop it, it just might explode from all its strange, tortured, and compressed energies.

In short, a dream deferred can be a terrifying thing. Its greatest threat is its unpredictability, and for this reason the question format is especially fitting. Questions demand the reader's participation, corner and sweep him headlong to the final, inescapable conclusion.

Each object (raisin, sore, meat, candy, load) is seen from the outside and therefore not fully apprehended. Each conceals a mystery; each generates its own threat. The question starts with the relatively innocuous raisin and, aided by the relentless repetition of "Does it . . . ?" intensifies until the violent crescendo at the end. With the explosion comes the ultimate epiphany: that the deadly poison of the deferred dream, which had seemed so neatly localized (the raisin drying up in a corner harmless and unnoticed; the sore that hurt only the man that had it; the rotten meat and sour candy that poisoned only those that ate it), does in fact seep into the mainstream from which the larger society drinks. The load, so characterless except for its weight, conceals sticks of dynamite whose shattering power none can escape.

Rotten meat is a lynched black man rotting on the tree. A sweet

gone bad is all of the broken promises of Emancipation and Recon-
struction, of the Great Migration, integration and voter registra-
tion, of Black Studies and Equal Opportunity. It might even be
possible to identify each of the key images with a generation or historical period, but this is not necessary: the deferred dream appears in these and similar guises in every generation and in the experience of individuals as well as of the group. The poem is the
"Lenox Avenue Mural" of the closing section title, painted in bold
letters up high and billboard-size for all to see. To step into or
drive through Harlem is at once to be confronted with its message
or question. The closing line is Hughes's final answer / threat and
will return with some frequency in *The Panther and the Lash.*

Each of the five other poems of the final section takes the question and plays with it, incorporating variations of it from earlier
sections. All sorts of things are liable to happen "when a dream
gets kicked around." And, sure, they kick dreams around downtown, too, even on Wall Street, not to speak of Appalachia or the
Indian Reservations. But right now, one thing at a time, first
things first: "I'm talking about / Harlem to you!" ("Comment on
Curb," p. 74).

Ask Your Mama (1961) is another montage of a dream deferred,
but this time the controlling mechanism, the instrument of seeing
is not the camera eye but the free-wheeling mind and memory
(free association) of the poet. Accordingly, the shift from scene to
scene is much more rapid than in *Montage*. In *Montage* scene
shifts took place at the end of a poem; here they take place in the
middle of a sentence or end of a line. In place of the neat set pieces
of *Montage*, we find here an almost nonstop flow of recall, allusion,
and juxtaposition of distant objects, events, and ideas. In *Montage*
themes recurred in the form of single poems. Here the leading
motifs—Santa Claus and Christmas; white snow and dark shadows;

mother, grandmother, and grandfather; river and railroad; quarter (time, money, living space, breathing space, violent death—"a lynched tomorrow . . . tarred and feathered," drawn and quartered)—recur quite often as single words or phrases embedded in alien contexts. These together with the book's design—its album shape, pastel colored pages, abstract cubist illustrations, two-tone lettering, and the capital letters in which the whole poem is printed—underline the fact that *Ask Your Mama* is an avant-garde experiment. Remarkably, the linguistic idiom is not primarily black, though of course the title, rhythm, music, and ethos are. Chiefly as a result of its total immersion in free association, there is a distinct "disorganization" about *Ask Your Mama.* Compared to the electric clarity of his other books, *Ask Your Mama* is Hughes's one and only difficult book. It is his sop to academia, his answer to those readers who demand complex surfaces to puzzle over. This is the kind of poetry Hughes might have written all his life had he not had such a clear conception of his goals and of the light years of difference between formal complexity and literary worth.

Ask Your Mama is intended to be performed. Hughes wrote mood and musical accompaniment into one earlier volume, *The Negro Mother and Other Dramatic Recitations* (1931), and of course over the years he frequently read his poems to jazz accompaniment. *Ask Your Mama* is his most elaborate effort along this line, and a climax of the life-long intimacy between his poetry and black music. In reading poetry to music, he insisted that

the music should not only be background to the poetry, but should comment on it. I tell the musicians—and I've worked with several different modern and traditional groups—to improvise as much as they care to around what I read. Whatever they bring of themselves to the poetry is welcome to me. I merely suggest the mood of each piece as a general orientation. Then I listen to what they say in their playing, and that affects my own rhythms when I read. We listen to each other.[20]

The poetry of *Ask Your Mama* does indeed "listen" to jazz rhythms. The step-rhythm of the following, for instance, recreates the cumulative repetition of instrumental jazz:

> IN THE
> IN THE QUARTER
> IN THE QUARTER OF THE NEGROES [21]
>
> SINGERS
> SINGERS LIKE O-
> SINGERS LIKE ODETTA—AND THAT STATUE   (p. 41)
>
> DE-
> DELIGHT-
> DELIGHTED! INTRODUCE ME TO EARTHA   (p. 69)

In each example, the musician / poet returns again and again to the mother-note, reaches back into that vast source of the music's energy, and pulls, each time dragging out a larger chunk of that energy, and in the process driving his audience into ecstasy. In the trail-off of the finale, the movement is reversed:

> IN THE QUARTER OF THE NEGROES
> WHERE NEGROES SING SO WELL
> NEGROES SING SO WELL
> SING SO WELL
> SO WELL,
> WELL?   (p. 19)
>
> SHOW FARE, MAMA, PLEASE.
> SHOW FARE, MAMA. . . .
> SHOW FARE!   (p. 83)

The jazz instrumentalist's predilection for picking on a note or phrase and playing with it, repeating it over and over and over and weaving it into changes on a theme, thereby creating unexpected intensities, is paralleled in the above repetitions as well as in the many reduplications: "Nasser Nasser"; "Manger Manger";

GRANDPA, DID YOU HEAR THE
HEAR THE OLD FOLKS SAY HOW
HOW TALL HOW TALL THE CANE GREW
SAY HOW WHITE THE COTTON COTTON . . .   (p. 71)

The book's title comes from the sassy black tradition of the dozens, a form of verbal contest commonest among adolescents.[22] The contestants trade insults (mostly sexual) on relatives (mostly female). The dozens is a mean game because, as H. Rap Brown has said, "what you try to do is totally destroy somebody else with words. . . . The real aim of the Dozens was to get a dude so mad that he'd cry or get mad enough to fight."[23]

—Let's get off the subject of mothers, 'cause I
   just got off of yours.

—I did it to your mama on the railroad track,
   And when her ass went up the trains went back.

—Your mother is a doorknob, everybody gets a turn.

—Your mama has so many wrinkles in her head she has
   to screw her hat on.

—I saw your mother on a bench trying to screw a
   cock with a monkey wrench.

Compared to this brutal comedy, Hughes might seem like a gentle and inhibited player. But his gentleness is deceptive. As in his love blues, he has chosen to avoid the strong sexual imagery of the folk original; instead, he has adapted the form, transforming it from an adolescent game of abuse and bravado confined to the ghetto, into an adult weapon of offense and defense in the sophisticated combats of the national and interracial arena. He has lifted the dozens out of the school yard into the boardroom and onto the floor of the Congress. To the white neighbors who ring his bell and ask if he would recommend a maid, Hughes's black suburbanite replies: "Yes, your mama" (p 46). To the creditor's threat of legal action, the debtor retorts: "Tell your ma" (p. 62). And to the question, "Did I vote for Nixon? / I said, Voted for your mama" (p. 70). Even on the two occasions when the question is left hanging fire: "They asked me right at Christmas, / Would I marry Pocahontas?" (p. 32)—a variant of "would I marry a white woman?"; and "Asked me right at Christmas / Did I want to eat with white folks?" (p. 73), the retort is the same, "Ask your mama." Hughes twice approaches the suggestiveness of the popular dozens: "They asked me at the PTA / Is it true that Negroes—? [have the most fun? as he explains in his notes, p. 90] / I said, Ask your mama" (p. 58); "And they asked me right at Christmas / If my blackness, would it rub off? / I said, Ask your mama" (p. 8)—because in both cases your mama ought to know, seeing as how I've been her backdoor man from way back since slavery time.

To these questions Hughes might have added the standard one heard after every ghetto riot: "What do you people want?" And the answer would have been the same: "Ask your mama," which is less an answer than a question (your mama knows what we want, she's got what we want, and don't ask what is it?). Oppression, Hughes says, "makes of almost every answer a question, and of men of every race or religion questioners" (p. 87).

> IN THE QUARTER OF THE NEGROES
> ANSWER QUESTIONS ANSWER
> AND ANSWERS WITH A QUESTION   (p. 20)

Hughes is a relentless questioner. In *Montage* it was: "What happens to a dream deferred?" And for answer he offered a series of questions, with an ominous closer: "Or does it explode?" In *Ask Your Mama* the key question is contained in the musical accompaniment, the "Hesitation Blues": "How long must I wait? / Can I get it now? / . . . Or must I hesitate?" To this question the "gentleman in expensive shoes / Made from the hides of blacks" (p. 72), builder of twenty-story housing projects covered with "chocolate gangrenous icing," and representative of white American power, replies: "Just wait" (p. 29). His answer is transparent with irony: go slow, be patient, you can't have it now, just wait, he says; just wait, Hughes says (explicit in a later book), you got something coming, something "upon the breeze / As yet unfelt among magnolia trees." [24] Just wait:

> You're the one,
> Yes, you're the one
> Will have the blues. [25]

Hughes varies the question: "Tell me, pretty papa, / What time is it now?" And the frivolous non-answer: "Don't care what time it is— / Gonna love you anyhow" (p. 28). But it is late, very late. It is the "last quarter of Centennial / 100-years Emancipation"—and still I must hesitate, can't have it now, got to wait. Time ("how long must I wait?") and money (quarter; show fare) are the dominant images in *Ask Your Mama,* just as they were in *Montage of a Dream* (money) *Deferred* (time).

Appropriately, the book is dedicated to Louis Armstrong, "the greatest horn blower of them all." And musicians and singers— Dinah Washington, Charlie Parker, and Leontyne Price among them—constitute the majority of the celebrities presented or alluded to. As a black singer of white opera Leontyne represents a particular kind of bridge between black and white culture. In her the two cultures ("collard greens," "lieder") coexist. Her experience is the "cultural exchange" of the opening section. "Culture, they say, is a two-way street" (p. 9); and it should therefore be possible for whites who are so inclined to participate in black culture the way the Leontynes participate in white culture. However, important as such exchange is, it is in the final analysis peripheral to Hughes's particular concern, which is the black community, "the quarter of the Negroes," its life and its woes. The book may be viewed as a historical pageant, recreating, in its zig-zag manner, significant scenes of Afro-American history from the villages by the Congo, their integrity unsullied by the white presence (p. 36), down through slavery to the present day.

The "quarter of the Negroes" is beleaguered. Its doors are "doors of paper," fragile against white lawlessness. The "amorphous jack-o'-lanterns" of the Ku Klux Klan "won't wait for midnight / For fun to blow doors down" (p. 3). And their lawlessness is protected by the law, whether in its constitutional instruments ("filibuster versus veto," p. 7), or in its cynical ventriloquisms ("with all deliberate speed," p. 30). White violence goes back to earliest American history when "the Tom dogs of the cabin / The cocoa and the cane brake / The chain gang and the slave block" (p. 7) made black life a daily death. The river and the railroad, staples of the blues and spirituals, "have doors that face each way"—one for whites and one for blacks; but more fundamentally, one facing south, through which many were sold further down the river into harder labor territory, and one facing north toward freedom, following the routes of the Underground Railroad, the archetypal northward movement of the black experience, and of the Great Migration, its modern analogue.

The movement north receives the attention it deserves as one of the most important ongoing processes of Afro-American life. Hughes celebrates the Underground Railroad, together with its most flamboyant conductor, tough, irrepressible Harriet Tubman, "a woman with two pistols / On a train that lost no passengers / On the line whose route was freedom" (p. 26). He contrasts its destination and dignity (freedom) with the ghetto terminal of the Great Migration. The Underground Railroad was made possible by the existence of a sense of human community among certain whites (Quakers, Abolitionists), a sense of community which extended to blacks. Slaves fled "through the jungle of white danger / To the haven of white Quakers / Whose haymow was a manger

manger / Where the Christ child once had lain" (p. 27). Paradox-
ically, the danger was white, and so was the haven, each finding its
rationale in the same Christian religion. The Quakers were truly
their brothers' keepers; but now, with slavery abolished, the rulers
of the nation have assumed the office of brother's keeper, and they
perform it gracelessly, with neither charity nor warmth. The
depersonalized ghetto housing project, which is the haven they
have constructed for modern fugitives from the Southern terror, is
a mockery of that original Quaker haven, a mockery of the communal idea and African communal past:

> TRIBAL NOW NO LONGER ONE FOR ALL
> AND ALL FOR ONE NO LONGER
> EXCEPT IN MEMORIES OF HATE
> UMBILICAL IN SULPHUROUS CHOCOLATE
>
> (pp. 29–30)

Locked in the project and supported by welfare, it is no longer
possible for a man to be his brother's keeper, nor even keeper to
his child. Welfare "generosity" is a mockery of Quaker generosity,
for the welfare system is created to perpetuate poverty and destroy
dignity.

> SANTA CLAUS, FORGIVE ME,
> BUT BABIES BORN IN SHADOWS
> IN THE SHADOW OF THE WELFARE
> IF BORN PREMATURE
> BRING WELFARE CHECKS MUCH SOONER
> YET NO PRESENTS DOWN THE CHIMNEY (pp. 28–29)

Santa Claus, the snowy northern liberal father-figure who brings
gifts to children, brings no gifts to "chocolate babies" born "in the
shadow of the welfare." Rather, ghetto money enables white folks
to live in comfort and to afford gifts (play Santa Claus) for their
children at Christmas. The "million pools of quarters / . . .
Sucked in by fat jukeboxes" are "carted off by Brink's" (p. 28). And

children born "in the shadow of the welfare" grow old before their time and die rapid early deaths,

> LIVING 20 YEARS IN 10
> BETTER HURRY, BETTER HURRY
> BEFORE THE PRESENT BECOMES WHEN
>   AND YOU'RE 50
>   WHEN YOU'RE 40
>   40 WHEN YOU'RE 30
>   30 WHEN YOU'RE 20
>   20 WHEN YOU'RE 10   (pp. 30–31)

You may dream "your number's coming out," but the chances are most uncertain. "In the quarter of the Negroes," "Even when you're winning / There's no way not to lose" (p. 31). Hughes sums it all up in the couplet: "White folks' recession / Is colored folks' depression" (p. 32).

But those who have "made it," the few who have been showered by the "horn of plenty," those whose dreams have come true (and who will miss Harlem on sunny summer Sunday afternoons), live only a little less precariously in suburbia, surrounded by manicured lawns and suspicious neighbors. Hughes surrounds their names (famous athletes, entertainers) with dollars and cents (money talks). They are the ones who have managed

> TO MOVE OUT TO ST. ALBANS $ $ $ $ $ $ $
> WHERE THE GRASS IS GREENER $ $ $ $ $ $
> SCHOOLS ARE BETTER FOR THEIR CHILDREN $
> AND OTHER KIDS LESS MEANER THAN   ¢ ¢ ¢ ¢
> IN THE QUARTER OF THE NEGROES   ¢ ¢ ¢ ¢ ¢ (p. 42)

But racial attitudes pursue them there. They all achieved fame the hard way, and are known across the country and abroad.

> YET THEY ASKED ME OUT ON MY PATIO
> WHERE DID I GET MY MONEY?
> I SAID, FROM YOUR MAMA!   (p. 43)

However, even they do not want too many blacks to move into their neighborhood:

> HIGHLY INTEGRATED
> MEANS TOO MANY NEGROES
> EVEN FOR THE NEGROES—
> ESPECIALLY FOR THE FIRST ONES   (p. 44)

Those left behind "in the quarter of the Negroes," those who never owned "$40,000 houses," who can't even keep up payments on their furniture: these have-nots sometimes find consolation in religious ecstasy, celebrated in the "Gospel Cha-Cha" section. Religion is offered as a contrast to the comforts of the financially successful. It is what the successful do not need, but since it is also a part of the total culture which they miss when they move out of the black community, it hovers unacknowledged in the background of their nostalgia. It is no accident therefore that Hughes places "Gospel Cha-Cha" immediately after "Horn of Plenty," or that in *Montage,* "the ones who've crossed the line / to live downtown" miss Harlem most on sunny Sunday afternoons when the folks crowd the streets in their Sunday best and grandma can't get her gospel hymns on the radio because of the ball games.

"Gospel Cha-Cha" is an account of the syncretic religions of the black Americas. It is a dramatized fragment of a sermon, prayer, vision, testimony, and ritual possession all in one, starting with Haitian voodoo (cha-cha) and moving to the Holy Roller churches (gospel) of North America. The horse and its white tourist rider laboring up the mountain to the "citadelle" metamorphose into the statue of Toussaint L'Ouverture mounted on his stone horse, then into the possessed votary and the divine horseman that rides him in the voodoo ceremony, and finally into the black Christian reenacting Christ's journey lugging his heavy cross up the hill to Calvary. The believer arrives at the hill-top to find that Christ has already been crucified. Christ has already died for him; he does not now need to die, only to endure the pain. The ritual of atonement is complete when he suffers as Christ suffered, bearing his own cross through life. Of the three crucified on the hill, he says, "One / Was black as me"; and the one is Jesus himself rather than one of the two thieves, not only because that belief has some basis in history, but more importantly, because only a black Christ (or a syncretized, non racial Christ) could know the agonies of the black man in the New World and therefore serve for identification.

The matter of identification with a member of the trinity recurs at the end of the book:

> THE HEADS ON THESE TWO QUARTERS
> ARE *THIS* OR *THAT*
> OR *LESS* OR *MOST*—
> SINCE BUT TWO EXIST
> BEYOND THE HOLY GHOST.
> OF THESE THREE,
> IS ONE
> ME? (pp. 82–83)

These disparate and incongruent images are held together by the centripetal force of free association. In the passage immediately preceding, blacks are portrayed as making a way out of no way, "ten Negroes / Weaving metal from two quarters / Into cloth of dollars / For a suit of good-time wearing" (p. 82). The poet then makes an associational leap to the image of George Washington's head engraved on the two quarters, and from that to the segregated living quarters which characterize the nation. The mottos "In God We Trust" and "E Pluribus Unum" inscribed on the coin provide a bridge to the three-in-one principle of the Christian godhead, which parallels the ethnic multiplicity of the nation. Since whites and blacks occupy the poles of American consciousness, they could be identified with the first and second persons of the trinity, and all other groups with the ghostly third. More specifically, Washington, as "father of his country," is Father and Head in that trinity, and his white progeny partake of his primacy. Blacks in their lesser status are "this" and "less," whites "that" and "most." As a citizen, even if second-class, the black man ("me") is a child of Washington in his capacity as father of his country; and as a mulatto, he is the unacknowledged and disinherited son of Washington and Jefferson and other "Founding Fathers" and their white brothers. He is the "holy bastard," the "nigger Christ" who in "Christ in Alabama" [26] is rejected, cast out, crucified. The dream of "E Pluribus Unum"—that out of the welter of nationalities a single whole American nation might arise—is still deferred.

Around and through the black ghetto and even integrated suburbia whip the heady winds of change, carrying rumors of revolutions in faraway lands. "Ça ira! Ça ira!" cried the French Revolutionary crowds at the aristocrats on their way to the guillotine; and Hughes incorporates their cry into the "Hesitation Blues" (p. 13). Europe's colonial empires disintegrate, but their "ghosts cast shadows"—the shadows of neocolonialism. New nations rise in Africa and the Caribbean. African leaders, diplomats, and students flood the scene, bringing to the "quarter of the Negroes" ancestral memories:

> THERE, FORBID US TO REMEMBER,
> COMES AN AFRICAN IN MID-DECEMBER
> SENT BY THE STATE DEPARTMENT
> AMONG THE SHACKS TO MEET THE BLACKS   (p. 4)

The activities of communists and revolutionaries ("Ride, Red, Ride", pp. 12–15) on the international scene reverberate on the domestic scene. Conservative public opinion blames social unrest and the civil rights movement on communist agitators, New York niggers, and Yankee liberals:

> THOSE SIT-IN KIDS, HE SAID,
>   MUST BE RED!
> KENYATTA RED! CASTRO RED!
>   NKRUMAH RED!
> RALPH BUNCHE INVESTIGATED!   (p. 73)

Witch-hunt flames burn as fiercely in the House Un-American Activities Committee as they ever did in colonial New England.

> SANTA CLAUS, FORGIVE ME,
> BUT YOUR GIFT BOOKS ARE SUBVERSIVE,
> YOUR DOLLS ARE INTERRACIAL.
> YOU'LL BE CALLED BY EASTLAND.
> WHEN THEY ASK YOU IF YOU KNOW ME,
> DON'T TAKE THE FIFTH AMENDMENT.   (p. 14)

Martin Luther King and his followers, on their nonviolent boycotts, sit-ins, and freedom rides, are met head-on with violence. But King preaches love and dreams on his impossible dream: *

> THE REVEREND MARTIN LUTHER
> KING MOUNTS HIS UNICORN
> OBLIVIOUS TO BLOOD   (p. 70)

The unicorn is a figure of imagination and mythology said to be accessible only to virgins, the "pure at heart." It represents the vast faith which sustained Martin Luther King and his followers in their massive programs of civil disobedience. The unicorn is King's belief that the deferred dream could be made reality, that racial justice, brotherhood, and peace were possible in America. The poem precedes King's famous oration, "I Have a Dream," by two years, but of course King's program had been in operation since his Montgomery, Alabama bus boycott of 1955. When King in his idealism and innocence mounts his unicorn, he appears suspended in air, above reality, for his dream-horse is invisible, inaccessible to the multitude.

The image of the unicorn is deliberately ambiguous: King's idealism makes him a hero but also makes him blind to reality, "oblivious to blood." And, historically speaking, it was not long before he himself publicly admitted that his program was inadequate to demolish the stone walls of America's racist realities, and that his dream had turned into a nightmare.

King is not the only one in the poem who holds commerce with the unicorn, for his dream is but an articulation of his people's individual dreams and collective dream:

> IN THE QUARTER OF THE NEGROES
> WHERE NO SHADOW WALKS ALONE
> LITTLE MULES AND DONKEYS SHARE
> THEIR GRASS WITH UNICORNS   (p. 65)

Communal living in the original African style has disappeared among black people, but not completely. A considerable sense of relatedness, of community, survives, and the people even in their poverty share their material goods, their dreams, and their dream-producing drugs.

In and out of the scenes of turmoil glides the unobtrusive figure of Santa Claus, the liberal northerner. He is a philanthropist, a giver of gifts, and he gives to blacks as well as whites (his dolls are interracial). He is a nice fellow—except that he has no gifts for the children of the welfare poor (p. 29). Because he is so friendly-seeming to blacks, he is not well liked in the South. Yet, as holder and exerciser of American power, he is different from his Southern peers chiefly in his smoothness and sophistication. He welcomes black participation, but only a token participation which permits blacks no share of real power. Adam Clayton Powell, as paradigmatic black Congressman, loaded with seniority and an outstanding record as sponsor of important social legislation, nevertheless rides the American power chariot only as a chauffeur rides a limousine:

> IN THE QUARTER OF THE NEGROES
> RIDING IN A JAGUAR, SANTA CLAUS,
> SEEMS LIKE ONCE I MET YOU
> WITH ADAM POWELL FOR CHAUFFEUR
> AND YOUR HAIR WAS BLOWING BACK
> IN THE WIND.   (p. 15)

Santa Claus in his bohemian aspect, and his well-fed sons and daughters, come to black life as observers or limited participants, with romantic notions and protections, with boots far too deep for the shallow waters where they choose to wade:

> HIP BOOTS
> DEEP IN THE BLUES
> (AND I NEVER HAD A HIP BOOT ON). . . .
> DIAMONDS IN PAWN
> (AND I NEVER HAD A DIAMOND
> IN MY NATURAL LIFE)   (p. 12)

For blacks, there is no protection from the harshness of ghetto life, the harshness which explodes into blues and into revolutionary struggle. Santa's protective boots (American prosperity), like the shoes of the gentleman "who tips among the shadows / Soaking up the music," were made from the hides of blacks (p. 74).

The most poignant figure in *Ask Your Mama* is the Black Mother or Grandmother, she who watched helpless as her children were sold down the river (or as they meet early deaths or go to prison in the modern context):

> I LOOK AT THE STARS
> AND THEY LOOK AT THE STARS,
> AND THEY WONDER WHERE I BE
> AND I WONDER WHERE THEY BE   (p. 72)

Grandpa and Grandma are the Black Archives, the experiencers and rememberers of our oldest history. All questions ("Ask Your Mama") eventually filter back to them.

> GRANDPA, WHERE DID YOU MEET MY GRANDMA?
> AT MOTHER BETHEL'S IN THE MORNING?
> I'M ASKING, GRANDPA, ASKING. . . .
> GRANDPA, DID YOU HEAR THE
> HEAR THE OLD FOLKS SAY HOW
> HOW TALL HOW TALL THE CANE GREW
> SAY HOW WHITE THE COTTON COTTON
> SPEAK OF RICE DOWN IN THE MARSHLAND   (p. 71)

But all too often they and their history are lost in the shuffle, in the confusion of the dream deferred, in the revolutionary struggle:

> IN THE QUARTER OF THE NEGROES
> TU ABUELA,¿DÓNDE ESTÁ?
> LOST IN CASTRO'S BEARD
> TU ABUELA, ¿DÓNDE ESTÁ?
> BLOWN SKY HIGH BY MONT PELÉE?
> ¿DÓNDE ESTÁ? ¿DÓNDE ESTÁ?
> WAS SHE FLEEING WITH LUMUMBA?   (p. 14)

Wherever Grandma ("abuela") is, that is where the answers are. But Hughes tells us in his notes (p. 92) that "grandma lost her apron with all the answers in her pocket (perhaps consumed by fire)"—the fire that leaps "From the wing tip of a match tip / On the breath of Ornette Coleman" (p. 77). Ornette and the new black music, signifying the spirit of the age, deliver "consternation" (p. 6), burn "like dry ice against the ear" (p. 92). And this is the spirit which in its relentless progression produces freedom rides, sit-ins, riots and fires, the Black Panthers, and the Black Esthetic. History, in other words, has made Grandma's answers inadequate. Her answers were in her apron; and her apron, the badge of black servitude in white kitchens, has been consumed by the flaming spirit of the age.

Grandma's answers are unacceptable to the modern generation. Yet the adequate and proper answers are nowhere to be found. The dream of social and economic well-being remains a dream, almost as distant and fantastic as the dream "that the Negroes / Of the South have taken over— / Voted all the Dixiecrats / Right out of power" and reversed the racial hierarchy:

WEALTHY NEGROES HAVE WHITE SERVANTS,
WHITE SHARECROPPERS WORK THE BLACK PLANTATIONS,
AND COLORED CHILDREN HAVE WHITE MAMMIES:
    MAMMY FAUBUS
    MAMMY EASTLAND
    MAMMY PATTERSON.

DEAR, DEAR DARLING OLD WHITE MAMMIES—
SOMETIMES EVEN BURIED WITH OUR FAMILY!   (pp. 8–9)

This dream, with its variations, is a longstanding one in black literature,[27] and Hughes uses it again in his Simple tales.[28] The drastic
reversal of racial/social roles is as startling and effective as the
reversal of man and horse in Swift's *Gulliver's Travels:* it enables
the author to show how ridiculous the society's beliefs and behavior really are. But the fantasy does not last. A rude awakening soon
follows, and *Ask Your Mama* ends with the frustrated dream of
black youth (our future) still asking mama for "show fare," and
mama saying:

NO SHOW FARE, BABY—
NOT THESE DAYS   (p. 30)

"Ask your mama": and this is mama's final answer. Things didn't
get better, they got worse ("Not these days"). The dream is still
deferred.

CHAPTER 4

Or Does It Explode?

Amiri Baraka (LeRoi Jones) once defined the black writer's function as follows:

> The Black Artist's role in America is to aid in the destruction of America as he knows it. His role is to report and reflect so precisely the nature of the society, and of himself in that society, that other men will be moved by the exactness of his rendering and, if they are black men, grow strong through this moving, having seen their own strength, and weakness; and if they are white men, tremble, curse, and go mad, because they will be drenched with the filth of their evil.[1]

The statement is at once descriptive and prescriptive, not unlike Aristotle's *Poetics* which is both a description of the practice of leading Greek playwrights of his day and a recommendation or prescription to future playwrights. Except for the anticipated effect of the work of art on the audience (and such effect is always a theoretical ideal and difficult to measure), Baraka's statement accurately describes the main tradition of Afro-American writing from the slave narratives and abolitionist fiction to the novels of Wright, Himes, and Ellison, the essays of DuBois, Baldwin, and Cleaver, and the poetry and drama of the Black Consciousness era of the

1960s and 70s. Certainly, it describes Hughes's lifelong artistic theory and practice. We have already seen, in the blues and jazz poems, how precisely Hughes reports and reflects the nature of American society and the black man's life in it. His other poems, those not modeled on black musical forms, are informed by the same vision.

Hughes's "report" includes a picture of America as a cage, a zoo, a circus, a gory monster cannibal and a syphilitic whore, and the black man as deracinated, alienated, exiled, groping for reconnection with his African past. Africa is "time lost," surviving only in fragments and in dim racial memories felt, like the music that is its chief surrogate, in the blood and bones, in received culture not fully understood.[2] Hughes was more fortunate than most of his contemporaries in that he had actually visited the coastal areas of West Africa, a region rich in history for Afro-Americans. But the contact was brief—too brief to save his early evocations of Africa wholly from the romanticism which characterized, for instance, Countee Cullen's "Heritage" or Claude McKay's "In Bondage," "Outcast," and "Africa."

In any case, what is crucial is not so much Hughes's image of Africa as his image of America. In his early poems, Africa is for him a distant ideal, foil and backdrop for his portrait of the present reality that is America. America to him is a cold, joyless wilderness, Africa a carefree tropical paradise,[3] a land where it would be customary, for instance, to "work maybe a little today, rest a little tomorrow. Play awhile. Sing awhile. O, let's dance."[4] Uprooted from a natural environment of palms and forests and silver moons, blacks in America suffocate in a prison of skyscrapers and industrial smog.[5] And as lions, tigers, and elephants, nature's majestic creatures created to live free, are trapped and harnessed for entertainment and profit, so have the non-white peoples of the world been converted from human beings into natural resources in the Western "circus of civilization."[6]

Forced to play "the dumb clown of the world," the black man finds a limited victory in laughter,[7] hiding his "tears and sighs" (to use Dunbar's phrase) behind a mask that "grins and lies." [8] The comic exterior is the black entertainer's particular stereotype. Hughes himself muffles a blazing rage behind his genial mask. But in "Summer Night" and "Disillusion," in the solitude of privacy, the public mask is momentarily lifted, and we feel in full the anguish of the poet or his persona. Like the rest of his brethren trapped in this circus, he tosses weary and sleepless, his soul "empty as the silence." [9] The mask, the music, the wild laughter of Harlem's nights are but temporary escapes. And he longs for a return to the wholeness both of childhood and of the African past:

> I would be simple again,
> Simple and clean
> Like the earth,
> Like the rain. . . .[10]

In "Danse Africaine" we glimpse a possible ritual of at-one-ment, with the priestess, "night-veiled girl," whirling softly to the low beating of tom-toms, drawing her audience into the unifying circle of light.[11] In the overwhelming compulsion toward spiritual reunion with the fatherland, first expressed in *The Weary Blues* in "Dream Variation" and "Our Land," the two halves of Hughes's dream theme—the dream deferred and the dream as romantic fantasy—merge.

The "Proem," later titled "Negro," which introduces *The Weary Blues*, is both a catalogue of wrongs against the black man over the centuries and a celebration of the strength by which he has survived those wrongs. That strength, a strength rooted in hope where there is no visible basis for hope, is, as we have seen, the essence of the blues. Outside of the blues, its most profound expressions in Hughes's poetry are in "Mother to Son," "The Negro Mother," "I, Too," and "The Negro Speaks of Rivers."

MOTHER TO SON

Well, son, I'll tell you:
Life for me ain't been no crystal stair.
It's had tacks in it,
And splinters,
And boards torn up,
And places with no carpet on the floor—
Bare.
But all the time
I'se been a-climbin' on,
And reachin' landin's,
And turnin' corners,
And sometimes goin' in the dark
Where there ain't been no light.
So boy, don't you turn back.
Don't you set down on the steps
'Cause you finds it's kinder hard.
Don't you fall now—
For I'se still goin', honey,
I'se still climbin',
And life for me ain't been no crystal stair. [12]

"The Negro Mother" [13] is a narrative version (dramatic mono-logue) of the more compact and earlier "Mother to Son." Both poems share the metaphor of life as a journey, in particular a climbing up the ladder of success, or "up the great stairs" to heaven's golden gate. For the rich the stairs are crystal and smooth and the climb easy; for the poor the stairs are splintered and torn up and dark, not unlike the ghetto stairway of "Ballad of the Landlord," and the climb is slow and arduous. (Or: the rich ride up in elevators, but tenement dwellers must walk up.) To get to the top, one must keep moving, cannot stop and sit. "I *had* to keep on! No stopping for me." To stop is to become a sitter on stoops and stander on street corners (the ghetto versions of the beach bum), or to become a prostitute, pimp, hustler, or thief. To despair is, in short, to wither and die. And as one conscious of her destiny as bearer of "the seed of the Free," one therefore on whom the future depended, the Black Mother chose to keep climbing. This is her achievement, that she survived to bear and nourish new generations, a staggering achievement under the circumstances. It is from this perspective that we must view Hughes's later summoning of "Uncle Tom on his mighty knees," [14] or the mild mannered grandfather in Ellison's *Invisible Man* describing himself as a sophisticated saboteur and guerrilla. These men and women acquiesced in their own humiliation and kept climbing on in order to prepare the way for "the coming Free." Their reward is in their vision of the possibility of freedom for their children. They are conservers and transmitters of the national soul, an example of love, wisdom, perseverance, and triumph for the younger generations to emulate.

Both poems reflect the form of a church testimony, with the lesson: "It's a sin to give up. I'm pressing toward the mark." This along with the traditional religious image of the stairs, and the stark endurance, fuelled by the "dream like steel in my soul" and expressed in "A song and a prayer," show both poems as emerging from the same big sea as the traditional spirituals and blues.

I, TOO

I, too, sing America.

I am the darker brother.
They send me to eat in the kitchen
When company comes,
But I laugh,
And eat well,
And grow strong.

Tomorrow,
I'll sit at the table
When company comes.
Nobody'll dare
Say to me
"Eat in the kitchen,"
Then.

Besides,
They'll see how beautiful I am
And be ashamed,—

I, too, am America. [15]

"I, Too" is as stoical as it is affirmative. Hughes accepts the brotherhood of black and white as beyond question. In addition, white and mulatto are brothers by immediate blood. The "darker brother" is America's secret shame, the kitchen his secret kingdom. Banished from polite company, he laughs, transforming his "yeah" into a "nay," as the grandfather in *Invisible Man* advised. He bides his time, eats well and grows strong, confident in his own beauty, and confident that "tomorrow" he will share the table (of communion) with the others. The domestic context lends mythic depth to the poem; for what we are witnessing is the career of the young prince dispossessed and suppressed by his wicked relatives. The certainty of his return and reinstatement is foretold in the archetypes.

The poem seems in particular response to Walt Whitman's insistent singing of his American soil and genealogy:

My tongue, every atom of my blood, form'd from this
    soil, this air,
Born here of parents born here from parents the same,
    and their parents the same. . . . [16]

The black man's roots in American soil are as deep, indeed deeper than the roots of most whites. Therefore Hughes, too, celebrates America, but unlike Whitman, not the America that is but the America that is to come. The democratic vistas which Whitman saw all about him are, to Hughes, still distant on the horizon, yet to be.

THE NEGRO SPEAKS OF RIVERS

I've known rivers:
I've known rivers ancient as the world and older than the
    flow of human blood in human veins.

My soul has grown deep like the rivers.

I bathed in the Euphrates when dawns were young.
I built my hut near the Congo and it lulled me to sleep.
I looked upon the Nile and raised the pyramids above it.
I heard the singing of the Mississippi when Abe Lincoln
> went down to New Orleans, and I've seen its muddy
> bosom turn all golden in the sunset.

I've known rivers:
Ancient, dusky rivers.

My soul has grown deep like the rivers.[17]

"The Negro Speaks of Rivers" is perhaps the most profound of these poems of heritage and strength. Composed when Hughes was a mere 17 years old, and dedicated to W. E. B. DuBois, it is a sonorous evocation of transcendent essences so ancient as to appear timeless, predating human existence, longer than human memory. The rivers are part of God's body, and participate in his immortality. They are the earthly analogues of eternity: deep, continuous, mysterious. They are named in the order of their association with black history. The black man has drunk of their life-giving essences, and thereby borrowed their immortality. He and the rivers have become one. The magical transformation of the Mississippi from mud to gold by the sun's radiance is mirrored in the transformation of slaves into free men by Lincoln's Proclamation (and, in Hughes's poems, the transformation of shabby cabarets into gorgeous palaces, dancing girls into queens and priestesses by the spell of black music). As the rivers deepen with time, so does the black man's soul; as their waters ceaselessly flow, so will the black soul endure. The black man has seen the rise and fall of civilizations from the earliest times, seen the beauty and death-changes of the world over the thousands of years, and will survive even this America. The poem's meaning is related to Zora Neale Hurston's judgment of the mythic High John de Conquer, whom she held as a symbol of the triumphant spirit of black America: that John was of the "Be" class. "*Be* here when the ruthless man comes, and *be* here when he is gone." [18] In a time and place where black life is held cheap and the days of black men appear to be numbered, the poem is a majestic reminder of the strength and fullness of history, of the source of that life which transcends even ceaseless labor and burning crosses.

One of Hughes's fullest representations of this black strength is in his twelve-poem sequence on the life and times of Alberta K. Johnson, "Madam to You." [19] Madam Alberta Johnson is hewed out of solid rock, yet soft flesh and rollicking soul. She is a contemporary of Jesse B. Semple, and her life and times, like Simple's, are the stuff of the blues. She once owned a beauty parlor, then a barbecue stand, but the depression and a no-good man took care of those. Now she works as a domestic. She bears her losses bravely. Her spirit is resilient; she is strong, outspoken, determined not to be taken advantage of, determined to survive. The people she comes in contact with, each with his hustle, each aiming to exploit her, feel the lash of her tongue and recoil from the sharp edge of her resistance: the employer with her twelve-room house and spine-breaking cooking, ironing, scrubbing, baby-nursing, and dog-walking, who nevertheless professes concern ("You know, Alberta, / I love you so! / I said, Madam, / That may be true— / But I'll be dogged / If I love you!"); the rent man who wants his money but wouldn't make repairs; the telephone operator who wants payment for a collect call she says she didn't authorize; the social worker who knows very well you can't raise a foster child on four dollars a week, yet keeps coming around asking for a report ("Last time I told her, / Report, my eye! / Things is bad— / *You* figure out why"); the fortune teller, pretending a mystery, who wants another dollar and a half to read the other palm; Mr. Death himself who has come before his time (". . . Alberta / Ain't goin' with you today!"); and the census man who wants to change her name to suit his bureaucratic convenience ("I said, I don't / Give a damn! / Leave me and my name / Just like I am!"). Everyone of them is quickly put in his place. Hers is the same spirit which, years later, in response to similar pressures, issued in the sassy "Ask Your Mama" retorts. Nothing and no one will dominate her. With the printer she insists on her American identity, wants her business cards in American letters, not in Old English or Roman letters: "There's nothing foreign / To my pedigree: / Alberta K. Johnson— / American that's me." The minister by preaching sin strives in vain for hegemony over her mind: "He said, Sister / Have you back-slid? / I said, it felt good— / If I did." Not even love can rule or ruin her. She grew up the hard way, has had two husbands, and when she met a man who was "always giving / And never taking," who swore "All I want is you"—

> Right then and there
> I knowed we was through. . . .
>
> Nobody loves nobody
> For yourself alone.

The world is too harsh, her emotional equilibrium too hard-earned to permit the turbulence of love to disrupt it.

> I said, I don't want
> My heart to bust.

"Madam's Past History" offers us a glimpse of the total destitution blacks are required to suffer before they are considered in need. Just as in "Out of Work" the WPA turned down a man who had not lived in the city a year and a day, they turn down Alberta because she has insurance. Her reaction is much like his— not anger or bitterness or self-pity, but the sassy humor of the blues:

> I said,
> DON'T WORRY 'BOUT ME!
> Just like the song,
> Take care of yourself—
> And I'll get along

—as though the WPA and other social welfare agencies ever took care of anyone but themselves, which is part of the intended irony. Now she may be a domestic—but she is still "Madam." Her dignity will hold up, for it is not the position that makes the person.

"Madam and Her Madam" tears down the myth that the black woman ever had it easy because she could easily get a job (as a domestic) because of white folks' love for her. The employer is not mean, she just happens to have too much work for one domestic. Still she lives in the illusion that she is doing Alberta a favor, and is shocked to discover otherwise. Not only does Alberta speak up for herself, showing none of the false humility of the black servant stereotype which the employer no doubt expected, but she boldly rips off the employer's own sentimental-master mask.

The employer's false concern is echoed in the rent collector's polite "Howdy-do?" in "Madam and the Rent Man." Alberta is sharp, matches him word for word. She is polite ("What / Can I do for you?") when he is, but when he sheds his mask and talks tough, she does too, producing a rapid inventory of needed repairs comparable to that in "Ballad of the Landlord." But the rent man claims he is only an agent, not responsible; the owner is absent, distant, never there to accept responsibility.

The impersonal owner reappears in "Madam and the Phone Bill." To Alberta, the telephone operator is simply "Central," a disembodied voice representing an invisible empire. But she is not intimidated: she is concerned about what is central to her, not what is central to the phone company. In "Madam's Past History" the words important to her—the name plates over her business establishments—were capitalized; here it is the words important to the phone company that are capitalized. What is central to her is not to them, and vice versa. They don't care to hear about her private affairs, and she doesn't care to hear about their phone bill. As with the rent man, her wit matches her spunk. Her long monologue on Roscoe and his girl friends in Kansas City is a deliberate ploy, the traditional nigger jive used to confuse white folks, wear out their patience and force them to give up. And Alberta is a mean player.

Alberta's frivolous, gentle side is seen in "Madam's Calling Cards," "Madam and the Number Writer," and "Madam and the Fortune Teller." There is a comic incongruity in her desire for calling cards, but it is an understandable bit of compensation and wish-fulfillment which is common with poor folks. The scene with the fortune teller is a farce. This is a jive fortune teller, saying and doing all the wrong things. Alberta sees through her, offers to pay her "some mind," not some money. That contest is a draw; but when it comes to the number writer she loses out. This is the only time someone out-raps her. But with the number man she is light-hearted and relaxed; she knows he is not out to swindle her out of a lot of money. He is even willing to risk a dime himself. He is playful and she is game—and lets herself be taken. And in the end they find themselves in the same fix (they lost), and there is no hostility. Her irreverence (heaven as a place in which not only to gamble but to win continuously) is echoed in her flippant replies to Rev. Butler in "Madam and the Minister," an irreverence common enough in a culture in which the line between the religious and the secular is often quite thin.

Alberta K. Johnson is the kind of black woman so frequently portrayed as a simple-minded nonentity. What Hughes has done, in effect, is to turn the stereotype inside out. Alberta is bright, strong, knows who she is, and insists on her identity. Her middle initial, which stands for nothing but itself, is a symbol of her unique person. Her battle with the census-taker is a battle that black people, individually and collectively, have fought over and over: the battle over *names,* the battle for *self-definition.* The man came to take the census, but turns around and attempts to *censor,* define, and confer identities. He came to count her, ends up at-tempting to *discount* her. But neither her name nor her life will be subsumed under anyone else's control. She stands on her dignity, demands respect: she is "Madam" to him.

We would have to go to Hughes's prose to find (in Simple) a comparably complete and arresting portrait of a black man. In Hughes's poetry no man, and for that matter no other woman, is presented so memorably.

In describing America Hughes pays particular attention to the South, for the obvious reason that the black man's unfreedom is most starkly evident there. The South with its lynchings is, in his view, the measure of America. In "Magnolia Flowers" [20] the poet goes South looking for the region's storied beauty, but finds instead "a corner full of ugliness." That ugliness is delivered with devastating finality in his early poem "The South":

> The lazy, laughing South
> With blood on its mouth.
> The sunny-faced South,
>   Beast-strong,
>   Idiot-brained.
> The child-minded South
> Scratching in the dead fire's ashes
> For a Negro's bones.
>   Cotton and the moon,
>   Warmth, earth, warmth,
>   The sky, the sun, the stars,
>   The magnolia-scented South.
> Beautiful, like a woman,
> Seductive as a dark-eyed whore,
>   Passionate, cruel,
>   Honey-lipped, syphilitic—
>   That is the South.
> And I, who am black, would love her
> But she spits in my face.
> And I, who am black,

> Would give her many rare gifts
> But she turns her back upon me.
>   So now I seek the North—
>   The cold-faced North,
>   For she, they say,
>   Is a kinder mistress,
> And in her house my children
> May escape the spell of the South.[21]

The poem is a fierce portrait etched with fire. In its masculine aspect the South is bestial, sub-human, a predator and scavenger, and in its feminine aspect a degenerate *femme fatale*, a syphilitic whore. These are not Hughes's sad, gentle black prostitutes and pathetic black clowns but their malicious and deadly white counterparts. The masculine image elicits total repulsion, the feminine mixed attraction and repulsion. It is the seductive female principle that entangles the unwary black man, delivering him up finally to be hanged, maimed, and burned by the male of the species, as the community watches and cheers. The landscape too is innocently seductive, but those who yield to its sunshine and magnolia fragrance (which becomes the sickly-sweet smell of flowers on a coffin) will have to live under constant threat of destruction by the human predators who roam the region as their preserve and hunting ground. The "rotten meat" of the lynched body defaces the landscape. Nature's beauty is desecrated by the brutal acts committed within it.[22]

The poem's metaphors conform to history and experience. For the usual excuse for lynching a black man is that he raped a white woman.

> "No I didn't touch her
> White flesh ain't for me." [23]

Protestations of innocence are useless. A black man accused of molesting a white woman is as good as dead. The rope around his neck, the knife at his genitals, and the fire all over him is all the due process he could ever hope for. When the lynch fever seizes the mob, any excuse will do. They will lynch a black man for threatening a white man who not only works him too hard for too little pay, but in addition has raped his wife.[24] They will lynch a black man for speaking of freedom:

> Last week they lynched a colored boy.
> They hung him to a tree.
> That colored boy ain't said a thing
> But we all should be free.[25]

And they will lynch a black man for resisting their claims of racial superiority:

> They hit me in the head
> And knocked me down. . . .
>
> A cracker said, "Nigger,
> Look me in the face—
> And tell me you believe in
> The great white race." [26]

Whatever the excuse, ultimately blacks are lynched because they are powerless, because they have none but God to protect them:

> Way Down South in Dixie
>   (Bruised body high in air)
> I asked the white Lord Jesus
>   What was the use of prayer.[27]

And while this grisly ritual is taking place, the men, women, and children, "little lads, lynchers that were to be," as Claude McKay called them,[28] dance and cheer "in fiendish glee":

> Pull at the rope! Oh!
> Pull it high!
> Let the white folks live
> And the black boy die.
>
> Pull it, boys,
> With a bloody cry

> As the black boy spins
> And the white folks die. . . .[29]

Most lynchings are for rape. But it is common knowledge that in the South it is extremely rare that a black man has actually raped or attempted to rape a white woman. In the South, sexual contact between black men and white women, from slavery times to the present, has almost always been initiated by the white woman. And every black man in the South knows that if he is unlucky enough to become the object of a white woman's affections, he must leave town or die. When a white woman invites you to love, you are doomed. If you accept and it is found out, as it will sooner or later, she will cry rape, and you will be lynched. If you refuse, she will in humiliation and revenge cry rape, and you will be lynched.

The rape-and-lynch psychosis must be viewed in the context of the perverted sexual mythology whereby white Americans first reduced black people to subhumans, then invested them with a hypersexuality, forced access of white males to black females, blocked access of black males to white females, and proceeded to project white lust and puritan guilt onto black males and victimize them for the sins of white males. For Southern white men to publicly admit that in liaisons with black men, Southern white women are usually willing accomplices, most often the provocateurs, is for them to lose control of reality as they wish to know it. Instead, that secret knowledge drives them even more rabidly violent. It is this psychological cat and mouse game that gives a poem like "Silhouette" its ironic power:

> Southern gentle lady,
> Do not swoon.
> They've just hung a black man. . . .
> For the world to see
> How Dixie protects
> Its white womanhood.

> Southern gentle lady,
> Be good!
> Be good! [30]

The most prolonged and deeply moving of Hughes's lynch poems is "The Bitter River," [31] a dirge for two black youths lynched in Mississippi in 1942. Hughes conceives of the lynch terror as a bitter, poisonous river flowing through the South, a river at which black people have been forced to drink too long. Its water galls the taste, poisons the blood, and drowns black hopes. The "snake-like hiss of its stream" strangles black dreams. The bitter river reflects no stars, only the steel bars behind which are confined numberless innocents—the Scottsboro Boys, sharecroppers, and labor leaders. The bitter river makes nonsense of liberal rhetoric:

> "Work, education, patience
> Will bring a better day."
> The swirl of the bitter river
> Carries your "patience" away.

Patience is useless, the hope in work and education a slim and distant one. The poem ends in bitter complaint, weariness and gloom:

> I'm tired of the bitter river!
> Tired of the bars!

Hughes's most brilliant lynch poem is "Christ in Alabama," one of the four poems accompanying the title play in *Scottsboro Limited* (1932). The Scottsboro Boys, eight black youths falsely accused of rape on the forced testimony of a group of disreputable white women, were in jail awaiting a legal lynching. This was the occasion of Hughes's epigrammatic "Justice":

> That Justice is a blind goddess
> Is a thing to which we black are wise:
> Her bandage hides two festering sores
> That once perhaps were eyes. [32]

In the poem "Scottsboro" the youths are identified with Jesus
Christ, John Brown, Nat Turner, Gandhi, and other martyrs.
These men are not dead, Hughes declares, they are immortal; and
"Is it much to die when immortal feet / March with you down
Time's street . . . ?" [33] In "Christ in Alabama" Jesus is pictured as
a lynched black man:

> Christ is a nigger,
> Beaten and black:
> Oh, bare your back!
>
> Mary is His mother;
> Mammy of the South,
> Silence your mouth.
>
> God is His father:
> White Master above
> Grant Him your love.
>
> Most holy bastard
> Of the bleeding mouth,
>   Nigger Christ
>   On the cross
>   Of the South. [34]

"Christ is a nigger" in two senses: in the historical sense as a
brown-skinned Jew like other Jews of his day, with a brown-
skinned mother—both later adopted into the white West and
given a lily-white heavenly father; and in the symbolic sense of
Jesus as an alien presence, preaching an exacting spirituality, a
foreign religion as it were, much as the black man, with his different color and culture, is an alien presence in the South. Each is
a scapegoat sacrificed for the society's sins. In particular, the white
sin of lust has created a mongrel mulatto race ("most holy bastard")
with black slave mothers ("Mammy of the South") and white
slavemaster fathers ("White Master above"). And, once created,
this race is cast out, disinherited, crucified.

A later poem, "Bible Belt," amplifies and illuminates "Christ in
Alabama":

"Bible Belt"

It would be too bad if Jesus
Were to come back black.
There are so many churches
Where he could not pray
In the U.S.A.,
Where entrance to Negroes,
No matter how sanctified,
Is denied,
Where race, not religion,
Is glorified.
But say it—
You may be
Crucified. [35]

If they remembered Jesus in his historical identity ("nigger"), the
white people of the United States would not so readily call themselves Christians. Hughes recalls an occasion when students at the
University of North Carolina at Chapel Hill printed "Christ in
Alabama" on the front page of their newspaper on the day he was
scheduled to speak at the university. Some of the townspeople,
including the sheriff, suggested that the poet be run out of town:
"It's bad enough to call Christ a *bastard.* But when he calls him a
nigger, he's gone too far!" [36]

The cryptic simplicity of "Christ in Alabama" exhibits Hughes at
his best. Profound insight is carelessly draped in the most facile
diction and form, the most commonplace images. There is no dec-
oration or pedantry. The poem is so stark it could almost have
been written by a child. It reminds one of classic African sculpture,
with its bold lines and geometric precision. The poem evokes the
feeling that great art so often evokes: that it could not have been
done any other way. It commands both accessibility and depth.
Hughes is a master at clothing the complex and profound in simple
garb; and perhaps it is this more than any other quality that marks
him as a great poet.

Lynching is the ultimate weapon of the Southern terror; but

other bitter tributaries feed its bitter stream. What Hughes said of the people and town of Scottsboro may be said of many small towns of the South:

> Scottsboro's just a little place:
> No shame is writ across its face—
> Its court, too weak to stand against a mob,
> Its people's heart, too small to hold a sob. [37]

Sharecroppers, cotton pickers and other rural laborers, regardless of how hard they work, will remain in drastic poverty:

> The cotton's picked
> And the work is done
> Boss man takes the money
> And we get none,
>
> Leaves us hungry, ragged
> As we were before. [38]

And sooner or later many come to the conclusion that there is no reason to stay. Life anywhere else could hardly be worse:

> Cause it's hard for a jigaboo
> With a wife and children, too,
> To make a livin'
> Anywhere
> Today.
>
> But in West Texas where de sun
> Shines like de evil one,
> There ain't no reason
> For a man
> To stay! [39]

And therefore many buy a ticket and head north, not intending to return:

> I pick up my life
> And take it with me
> And I put it down in

Chicago, Detroit,
Buffalo, Scranton,
Any place that is
North and East—
And not Dixie. . . .

I am fed up
With Jim Crow laws,
People who are cruel
And afraid,
Who lynch and run,
Who are scared of me
And me of them.[40]

This is the Great Migration, and they come sometimes in a trickle, sometimes in an avalanche. And what do they find up north? As Hughes was to show in *Montage of a Dream Deferred,* the migrant discovers that he still can't own anything up north, but at least he is thankful that "there ain't no Ku Klux / on a 133rd." However, his gratitude will diminish considerably when he discovers police brutality.

Hughes equates the Northern police violence of "Third Degree" and "Who But the Lord?" with the Southern violence of "Ku Klux." The police have the same "faces like jack-o-lanterns" as the members of the KKK in *Ask Your Mama.*

KU KLUX

They took me out
To some lonesome place.
They said, "Do you believe
In the great white race?"

I said, "Mister,
To tell you the truth,
I'd believe in anything
If you'd just turn me loose."

The white man said, "Boy,
Can it be

You're a-standin' there
A-sassin' me?"

They hit me in the head
And knocked me down.
And then they kicked me
On the ground.

A cracker said, "Nigger,
Look me in the face—
And tell me you believe in
The great white race." [41]

Like Madam Alberta Johnson in "Madam and the Phone Bill," the narrator of "Ku Klux" is signifying and clowning around, sassing the white folks. He knows that anything he says will be used against him, and this knowledge gives him a certain freedom. He mocks his attackers' beliefs by saying he would believe in anything if they would just turn him loose; that is, he would accept their reading of reality only under duress. They are desperate to persuade him, but they also know it's useless. And the fact that he knows and says as much makes them even more frantic. The poem holds five hundred years of history in capsule, spotlighting the physical violence by which the West established and enforced the myth of its superiority over the rest of the world.

"Third Degree," a later poem, repeats the structure and drama of "Ku Klux."

THIRD DEGREE

Hit me! Jab me!
Make me say I did it.
Blood on my sport shirt
And my tan suede shoes.

Faces like jack-o-lanterns
In gray slouch hats.

Slug me! Beat me!
Scream jumps out

Like blow-torch.
Three kicks between the legs
That kill the kids
I'd make tomorrow.

Bars and floor skyrocket
And burst like Roman candles.

When you throw
Cold water on me,
I'll sign the
Paper. . . .[42]

"Ku Klux" is a leisurely account after the event; the victim has lived to tell his story, and can afford to mellow its memory with humor and sass. But in "Third Degree" the drama is more immediate, taking place in the present, and there is no room for humor. We are inside the victim looking out, feeling the blows and watching physical objects blurr and merge. The intensity of pain is suggested in the fire images: blow-torch, skyrocket, candles. As in "Ku Klux" the victim is defiant and his confession is forced.

It is perhaps no accident that organized white violence, actuated by the myths breeding sexual paranoia, so frequently focusses on black male genitals: lynch mobs shear them off; Southern sheriffs attacked them with electric cattle prods during the civil rights movement of the 1960s; and in "Third Degree," Northern white police attempt to crush them ("Three kicks between the legs / That kill the kids / I'd make tomorrow").

WHO BUT THE LORD?

I looked and I saw
That man they call the law.
He was coming
Down the street at me!
I had visions in my head
Of being laid out cold and dead,
Or else murdered
By the third degree.

I said, *O Lord, if you can,*
Save me from that man!
Don't let him make a pulp out of me!
But the Lord he was not quick.
The law raised up his stick
And beat the living hell
Out of me!

Now I do not understand
Why God don't protect a man
From police brutality.
Being poor and black,
I've no weapon to strike back
So who but the Lord
Can protect me? [43]

"Who But the Lord?" is the most humorous of the trio. Like "Ku Klux," a leisurely after-the-fact account, the poem establishes a comic equation between the Lord and the law. Both presume to protect, but in the course of the poem we learn that the law destroys and the Lord fails to protect. The victim had been taught to live in fear of God, but as it turns out, in the real world the law carries greater weight, is the one to be feared. The Lord may be Savior, but the law moves so much faster that one has to have something else for protection. The narrator's "I do not understand" is ironic, for he does; and his wisdom is in the knowledge that at least in dealing with police brutality God is but a weak wish, that black folks need some other real power to protect them.

The poem ends in one of those tense moments where Hughes leaves a question hanging fire. That his intention is not only to censure God and criticize black religiosity, but also to make a radical political statement, is confirmed in the ominous closer which he added to the version of the poem that appeared years later in *The Panther and the Lash*. To the question: who but the Lord can protect me? the rejoinder is a subterranean "We'll see." [44]

Taken together, these three key poems on white physical brutality reveal Hughes as sharing the sentiment, quite common among blacks, that as long as you're south of the Canadian border, you're south; that Mississippi is in New York.

Through the four decades of his career Hughes's poetry reflected public concerns, borrowing insights from the spirit of each era. The 1930s and 60s were the particular decades of radicals and extremists, and for Hughes each was an ideological and rhetorical decade, the 30s perhaps more so than the 60s: the difference was between the fire and enthusiasm of a young man in his thirties and the weariness and disappointment of an old man in his sixties who finds his dreams still deferred.

Some of Hughes's political poetry of the 30s was collected in two pamphlets: *Scottsboro Limited* (1932) and *A New Song* (1938). Both are party-line statements calling for revolution, calling on black and white workers to sink their racial antagonisms and band together to overthrow their common enemy, the capitalist ruling class and its agents.

Open Letter to the South

> Let us forget what Booker T. said,
> "Separate as the fingers."
>
> Let us become instead, you and I,
> One single hand
> That can united rise
> To smash the old dead dogmas of the past—
> To kill the lies of color
> That keep the rich enthroned
> And drive us to the time-clock and the plow
> Helpless, stupid, scattered, and alone—as now—
> Race against race,
> Because one is black,
> Another white of face. [45]

The union is to be forged under the communist banner. In the verse play "Scottsboro Limited" the Communist Party offers aid, and the eight youths accept: "Who else is there to help us out o'

this?" The Communist Party made a *cause célèbre* of the Scottsboro case. In the strength of this new alliance, the youths declare:

> Now out of the darkness
> The new Red Negro will come:
> That's me!
> No death in the chair! [46]

The "New Negro" of the 20s has become the "Red Negro" of the
30s. The onset of the depression, which brought early death to all
the high optimism of the Harlem Renaissance, made the alliance of
the black struggle with the communist labor movement, in history
as well as in Hughes's poetry, almost inevitable. *A New Song* was
published by the International Workers Order, with an introduction by Michael Gold, editor of *New Masses* magazine. In it
Hughes champions the cause of the oppressed of all races—blacks,
Indians, poor whites, and new immigrants—against "the same old
stupid plan / Of dog eat dog, of mighty crush the weak." [47] In
"Justice" (p. 11), reprinted from *Scottsboro*, it is no longer "we
black" but "we poor" who know that American justice is not
merely blindfolded but horribly eyeless. The derelict in "Park
Bench" (p. 12) who threatens to invade wealthy Park Avenue is not
necessarily black, nor is the militant of "Pride" (p. 16). The
people—and their enemies—come from all races; the division is
class, not race. The "Kids Who Die" are murdered with the aid of
the pseudoscience of "the gentlemen with Dr. in front of their
names, / White and black, / Who make surveys and write books"
(p. 18). The powerful proletarian chants and ballads ("Chant for
May Day," "Chant for Tom Mooney," "Ballad of Ozie Powell,"
"Ballads of Lenin," "Song of Spain") are rendered in the multina-
tional voices of workers the world over. The workers are of one
mind, their voices are strident, and they are determined to push
the world forward into a future better than the past.

> The past has been
> A mint of blood and sorrow—

That must not be
True of tomorrow.   ("History," p. 19)

The "New Song" of the title is a song of unity and revolt:

Revolt! Arise!

The Black
And White World
Shall be one!
The Worker's World!   (p. 25)

Hughes's ideological interest in communism may indeed
have commenced with the Scottsboro case in 1931; however, his
sympathies were radical and his voice defiant years before that, as
exemplified in "God to Hungry Child" (1925):

Hungry child,
I didn't make this world for you.
You didn't buy any stock in my railroad,
You didn't invest in my corporation.
Where are your shares in standard oil?
I made the world for the rich
And the will-be-rich
And the have-always-been-rich.
Not for you,
Hungry child.[48]

Or in "Johannesburg Mines" (1928):

In the Johannesburg mines
There are 240,000 natives working.

What kind of poem
Would you make out of that?

240,000 natives working
In the Johannesburg mines.[49]

Nor did his Marxist vision subside with the Nazi-Soviet Pact of
1939 and the onset of World War II. The exposure of poverty and
oppression and the call for world-wide revolution in *Scottsboro*

Limited and *A New Song* are duplicated and reinforced not only in
his uncollected poetry of the same period, e.g., "Advertisement
for the Waldorf-Astoria," [50] "Goodbye, Christ," "Good Morning,
Revolution," "The Same," "Air Raid Over Harlem," and "White
Man," but also in such later works as the series of laudatory essays
on the Soviet Union in his weekly column in the *Chicago Defender*
of June, July, and August of 1946, and on China in "The Revolutionary Armies of China—1949." However, by 1943, when his next
two pamphlets of political poetry, *Jim Crow's Last Stand* and
Freedom's Plow, were published, Hughes had indeed beat a tac-
tical retreat—*but only in his collected works*—from the broad-
based multiracial Marxist workers' platform, to concentrate once
more on black people's particular American dream, without
specifying an ideology or method for fulfilling that dream. In these
two later pamphlets he focusses most closely on America's avowed
principles and the contradiction between those principles and the
oppression of blacks. The dominant mood is bewilderment, the
tone is hurt. The black man who speaks in "The Black Man
Speaks" just "can't see / Why Democracy means / Everybody but
me." The question is all the more urgent in a time of war (1943):

> If we're fighting to create
> A free world tomorrow,
> Why not end *right now*
> Old Jim Crow's sorrow? [51]

Roosevelt's "Four Freedoms" should be made a reality here at
home:

> Freedom's not just
> To be won Over There.
> It means Freedom at home, too—
> Now—*right here!* [52]

And Freedom is immortal, will not be destroyed by burning
books, imprisoning Nehru, or lynching black men. [53]

In *Jim Crow* and *Freedom's Plow* Hughes takes America's democratic rhetoric seriously. Nowhere is he more patently patriotic.
These poems pick up where "I, too, sing America" left off. They
are protest poems in the classic sense, addressed to white
America, and not so much to their hearts as to their heads. The
poet attempts to *reason* with white folks. He urges them to return
America to first principles. There might even be no need to go
hunting for foreign ideologies. The blueprint is right here at home,
it's just a matter of building upon it:

> The plan and the pattern is here,
> Woven from the beginning
> Into the warp and woof of America.[54]

But until this is done, he urges black folks to hold on to the plow
and never let go. This, he says, is the song the slaves sang long ago:
"Keep Your Hand on the Plow! Hold On!" This is the invariable
message of the spirituals and blues, the meaning of black history
thus far: no solution at hand, only endurance, a continuing
struggle.

But the dream may not be deferred indefinitely without reper-
cussions. In "Roland Hayes Beaten" (1949) Hughes warned that
black people will not always be patient and nonviolent, that the
dream will explode. *The Panther and the Lash* (1967) is a poetic
record of the beginning of that explosion. When such a dream is
deferred overlong, paramilitary groups such as the Black Panthers
are liable to appear, followed by the usual white backlash—and the
scene is set for violent clashes. This is the meaning of the book's
title.

The Panther and the Lash is subtitled "Poems of Our Times";
and it is a testimony to Hughes's deep insight and enduring quality
that of the 70 poems in the collection, 28 (or over a third) are
reprints from earlier works, are poems of other times which speak
just as directly to the high-strung 60s. "Christ in Alabama" reflects

America as accurately in 1967 as in 1932. Not much has changed in the black situation, nor in Hughes's perception of it. His vision was from the beginning pan-African in scope, with the black man in America closest to home and squarely in the center. Africa at first inhabited the vague, outer reaches of that vision-scope, until the proletarian 30s; then, starting in the late 50s and 60s, modern communications and international politics dramatically transformed time, distance, and visibility, bringing Africa so much closer and providing the details and drama which make Africa so much more real in *Ask Your Mama* and *The Panther and the Lash*, than, for instance, in *The Weary Blues* or *One-Way Ticket*. The transformation of time, distance, and visibility had a great deal to do with the black consciousness revolution of the 1960s, which in turn set the stage for the reemergence in his collected poems of Hughes's own Third World consciousness and his vision of the possibility of world-wide revolution—although this possibility is rendered in more deliberately circumspect terms than in his radical poetry of the 30s.

In *The Panther and the Lash,* as elsewhere, Hughes is a poet of his age, up to date, viewing the same black life through the lenses of the particular day. Whatever the era, his lenses are usually well fitted and focussed. He knows what he is looking for, and he captures it with astonishing clarity, in all its beauty, sordidness, or violence.

The Panther and the Lash is a book of the tense and violent 60s—in its title, in the occasional topicality of its verse, and in its Third World awareness. It is dominated by public issues. In it Hughes brings together some of his best political poems, with the result that the book is more consistently, directly, and bitingly political than any of his earlier poetry volumes, not counting the pamphlets of the 30s. There is no sweetness here. The energetic proletarian optimism of *Scottsboro Limited* and *A New Song*, which by 1943 had given way to the bewilderment and disappointment of *Jim Crow's Last Stand* and *Freedom's Plow*, has by the mid-60s soured into a full-bodied disillusionment and bitterness. And yet Hughes has not repudiated the dream. For although he says in "Oppression" that dreams are now no longer available to the dreamers, "Nor songs / To the singers," he hastens to add that "the dream / Will come back, / And the song break its jail." [55] And in "Dream Dust" (p. 93) he urges his readers to gather out of the broken pieces of their dreams "One handful of dream-dust / Not for sale." "Hold Fast To Dreams," he titled a speech around the same period. [56]

No, he has not given up the dream, but he is beginning to look elsewhere (away from white America, whether workers or liberal Northerners) for sources for fulfilling it. And while the means is not specified, the complex out of which that means is likely to develop is broadly hinted at. The hope (distant, but nevertheless a hope) is in the emerging modern powers of the African homeland, and in China; in other words, in a gathering of Third World forces, all of whom have suffered oppression from the white man. There is a threat in Hughes's voice, a threat which disappeared from his collected poetry after the 1930s, and the frequency and strength of that threat in *The Panther and the Lash* is supported by that Third World hope.

"The Backlash Blues" (p. 8), the one clearly political blues in his collected poems, warns that nonwhites are the majority of the world's peoples; and when they join together, as they are about to, then, Mister Backlash,

> You're the one,
> Yes, you're the one
> Will have the blues.

The youngster of "Junior Addict" (p. 12), suffering from poverty and ignorance, and rapidly destroying himself with drugs, has no way of knowing that there is about to emerge a saving "sunrise out of Africa." And the poet calls out to the African nations to do their "emerging" quickly and get to the job at hand:

> Quick, sunrise, come!
> Sunrise out of Africa,
> Quick, come!
> Sunrise, please come!
> Come! Come!

Hughes envisages revenge and redress, this time from a powerful China, for the four little girls killed in Birmingham, Alabama, in September 1963 when their church was bombed by white terrorists. For centuries China made explosives, but used them for entertainment (fireworks). Europeans borrowed China's explosives, harnessed them to weapons of death and conquered the world with them. Now history has run full circle. China, borrowing modern technology from the West, has now harnessed those same explosives for death, although China's power is as yet unfelt, least of all in Dixie. But not for long. China too is building a nuclear arsenal; and on the Day of Judgment (the day of the nuclear destruction of the world) these four little girls will have their revenge ("Birmingham Sunday," pp. 46–47).

The threats in "Who But the Lord" ("We'll see," p. 16) and in "Office Building: Evening" ("But just wait, chile. . . ," p. 40), are less pointed and therefore perhaps even more ominous. China and Africa are distant threats, but these others may prove to be something more immediate, something on a local or even a personal scale but equally devastating and final. "Who But the Lord" is in its original 1949 version—except for the added threat, "We'll see." God has not protected black folks from police brutality. Somebody surely will; but who? If we wait long enough, it will be the avenging forces of the Third World. But before that, right now, on a local scale, it might be the Panthers, or their successors. Right now, the Panthers are all brashness and youth. Their "fist is clenched / Today— / To strike your face" ("Militant," p. 39). Desperate in their boldness, they hide nothing, wear "no disguise" ("Black Panther," p. 19). But their successors are likely to be more sophisticated—and deadly. The threat renews itself daily.

Finally, the greatest threat is simply in the people themselves, the black masses, in their continued existence, their refusal to disappear. The Pilgrims of Jamestown made the fatal error, and black people are here, a hard-rock reality. The sons of former slave owners may wish them away all they want, but these "Ghosts of 1619" (p. 26) will continue to haunt them, to "rape, rob, steal, / Sit-in, stand-in, stall-in, vote-in," until it's either liberation or genocide, freedom or death. Hughes sums it all up in "Final Call" (p. 20). To pipe the rats away, he suggests sending for the Pied Piper and other men of power; and he proceeds with a fantastic roll call of persons and shades, of all those who might, however vaguely, be connected with the case: the dead as well as the living, here and abroad; figures of history and figures of myth; black people and white people; miracle workers and makers of laws, declarations, and decrees; preachers and politicians; monarchs and rebels and revolutionaries; artists and freedom fighters; "old John Brown who knew slavery couldn't last," and "Uncle Tom on his mighty knees" (for even the Uncle cried "Freedom Now!" as best he knew how—*that* was his way of crying "Freedom Now!"—and as though his archetypal greatness does not loom large enough, he is described as having "mighty knees"). The one obvious omission is Booker T. Washington, and it is not clear why. Even Adam Clayton Powell, a Congressman-fugitive from New York State law, might come in "on a non-subpoena day" (a line weighted with all the ambiguity, all the sorrow and jest of the blues; a line as bitterly ironic as the man's career). The rats are the real rats infesting the ghetto, therefore poverty; but they are also the black masses, those same ghosts of 1619 whom the children of former slaveholders so desperately wish some pied piper would pipe away. The rats symbolize America's problems in general, and the poet is engaged in malicious fun (although this is humor that, as in the blues, cuts both ways): white America will try everything, however far-fetched or fantastic, except the one and only remedy that would work. The poem is, among other things, a poem about national bad faith and lack of commitment, about "experts" and their cartoon theories and programs. It is a majestic and stately poem, anticipating those militant poems of the late 6os and 7os which will find their strength in forceful repetition, their shrillness a mark of the stresses and dynamic energies of their times. It is a dangerous poem.

First comes the prolonged crash and roar:

> SEND FOR THE PIED PIPER AND LET HIM PIPE THE RATS
>   AWAY.
> SEND FOR ROBIN HOOD TO CLINCH THE ANTI-POVERTY
>   CAMPAIGN.
> SEND FOR THE FAIRY QUEEN. . . .
> SEND FOR. . . .
> SEND FOR. . . .
> SEND FOR. . . .

Then, silence. And then, the quiet last line, its triumphant humility accentuated by the parenthesis: "(And if nobody comes, send for me.)"

For all its calm, that closing line is in the sassy tradition of the dozens: If nobody comes, send for your mother. She's the pied piper. Your mama will pipe the rats away. It is also a boast: If no one else can, I can. Me, I'll take care of business. If I can't do it, it can't be done. The line also carries the ironic humor and ambiguity of the blues: Well, I can't do it either, and then too I can. If you'd listen to me (Langston Hughes, *vox populi*) you'd know how it could be done.

As a public poet, Hughes normally uses the personal pronoun to weld himself tightly to his people, making his voice their voice, their joys and sorrows his joys and sorrows: "I am a Negro: / Black

as the night is black / . . . . I brushed the boots of Washington";
"I, too, sing America. / . . . They send me to eat in the
kitchen / When company comes"; "O white strong ones, / Why do
you torture me?" But in the closing line of "Final Call," and in a
number of other places, Hughes uses the personal pronoun not to
merge but rather to disengage himself from the generality. We
find this "movement away," usually with "me" as its pronoun-sig-
nature, in the title "Stokely Malcolm Me" (p. 94), or in the line
"The land that's mine—the poor man's, Indian's Negro's, ME—"
("Let America Be America Again"). In *Ask Your Mama* it appears
in a half-comic, half-defiant phrase:

> LOVELY LENA MARIAN LOUIS PEARLIE MAE
> GEORGE S. SCHUYLER MOLTO BENE
> COME WHAT MAY LANGSTON HUGHES. . . .[57]

(He will not let a false modesty write him out of the rolls of the
celebrities). In each of these examples the poet's reference to himself is tossed in carelessly like an afterthought, not unlike a
painter's signature tucked away in a corner of his canvas. "Me" is
Hughes's way of establishing, publicly, a private, personal relationship to the emotion or action at hand. It is his way of being a
public voice without ceasing to be a flesh-and-blood member of
the community; his way of being a spokesman without becoming
an oracle. This occasional effort to disengage himself from the
crowd and to momentarily relish his individuality ("our individual
dark-skinned selves") is a salutary one. It is not egotism—on the
contrary: I may be all black men, but not all the time, even in
verse. Sometimes I just got to be me, just *me*, Langston Hughes!

CHAPTER 5

The Dream Keeper

The deferred dream was overwhelming, yet not even its great weight could crush the purely lyric impulse totally. The world of beauty and lyricism may have been distant from Hughes's daily life and the concerns of his art, as he claims in "My Adventures as a Social Poet," but, all the same, he made frequent and pleasurable excursions into that world. Especially in his early years he maintains a respectable balance between social and lyric poems. Of his first five books, only *Fine Clothes to the Jew* and *The Negro Mother* are entirely social and/or modeled on black folk forms.[1] Lyric poetry with no immediate social or political content occupies most of *Dear Lovely Death* (1931) and roughly a half of *The Weary Blues* (1926) and of *The Dream Keeper* (1932) (although two-thirds of the latter were reprints). But after that it was three or four lyric poems per volume, except for *Fields of Wonder* (1947), which was almost entirely lyric.

The most prominent feature of Hughes's lyric verse is its brilliance of imagery. Hughes makes frequent use of poetic conceits as we find them in Shakespeare, the Metaphysical Poets, and Emily Dickinson, and of the brief and bright flashes that characterize Japanese haiku and the early 20th century Imagists. The lyric poem is the particular vehicle of the dream as romantic fantasy and wish fulfillment ("love, roses, and moonlight"). And in *The Weary Blues* the dreamers include the lovers of the "Black Pierrot" section, seeking relatedness; the sailors of "Water Front Streets" who seek adventure in faraway lands; and the wretched bits of humanity in "Shadows in the Sun" who endure as best they can life's heavy foot that crushes all of their dreams.[2] "Pierrot" is a ballad of desertion and elopement. "A Black Pierrot" and "Songs to the Dark Virgin" are in the surrealistic, imagistic mode: in the one, the rejected lover weeps "until the red dawn / Dripped blood over the eastern hills," his "once gay-colored soul / Shrunken like a balloon without air"; and in the other, the lover conceives of himself in three stages—as a shattered jewel falling humbly at his loved one's feet, as a silken garment wrapping her body close, and as a leaping flame enveloping and annihilating her. "Ardella," "Poem: To the Black Beloved," and "When Sue Wears Red" are lyrical celebrations of female beauty.

> I would liken you
> To a night without stars
> Were it not for your eyes.
> I would liken you
> To a sleep without dreams
> Were it not for your songs.
>
> ("Ardella")

"When Sue Wears Red" is perhaps the most powerful of Hughes's love poems:

> When Susanna Jones wears red
> Her face is like an ancient cameo
> Turned brown by the ages.
> Come with a blast of trumpets,
>   Jesus!
>
> When Susanna Jones wears red
> A queen from some time-dead Egyptian night
> Walks once again.

Blow trumpets, Jesus!

And the beauty of Susanna Jones in red
Burns in my heart a love-fire sharp like pain.

Sweet silver trumpets,
    Jesus!

Like "The Negro Speaks of Rivers," which it rivals in brilliance, this too is an early poem, written while Hughes was in high school, a poetically mature 17. And just as that poem fuses into one timeless flow the soul-deep rivers of the black experience through the ages, so does this reincarnate in one woman the feminine beauty and majesty of the ages. The poem derives its power from its vision of eternity and from the holler and shout of religious enthusiasm ("Come with a blast of trumpets, Jesus!"). In addition, it has its literary antecedents in Dunbar's "The Colored Band" and "When Malindy Sings": [3] Malindy, whose voice in "Come to Jesus" sets sinners' hearts atremble and compels their feet Christ-ward; Malindy, whose "Swing Low, Sweet Chariot" echoes "from de valley to de hill / . . . Th'oo de bresh of angels' wings, / Sof' an' sweet." In both poets the vision is of transfiguration through art/magic: through Sue's red dress, a type of magic mantle, which resurrects in her the queens of other ages; through the Colored Band's syncopated rhythms in response to which "de hea't goes into bus'ness fu' to he'p erlong de eah"; and through the mesmeric power of Malindy's down-home voice.

The sailors and cabin boys of "Water Front Streets" pursue their dreams of romance on the waters and faraway lands. Abandoning the constricted life "between the hills," they haul off to sea carrying "beauties in their hearts." The waterfront streets themselves are unbeautiful, but their denizens are in touch with the sea, which is a vehicle of the dream, the sea on which "dream ships sail away / To where the spring is wondrous rare / And life is gay," to where the sunset is like God's hemorrhage "coughed across the sky." And in that land of romance the young sailor, like the long-headed jazzers and other habitués of Harlem nights, lives for the moment, bearing "his own strength / And his own laughter, / His own today / And his own hereafter." His sojourn on land is a circus of wine, women, and laughter, "and nothing hereafter." It is at sea that his soul flowers and is fulfilled.

The sea itself is acutely characterized: it is "a wilderness of waves, / A desert of water" endlessly dipping and diving, rising and rolling, all day and all night. It will not stand still; tranquility is not in its nature. And when it is calm, it is ominously calm—"It is not good / For water / To be so still that way"—reminding us of its double nature as a gateway to dreams fulfilled and a destroyer. The sea is "strong / Like God's hand" and holds "a wide, deep death." Not even the sea's own children understand its fascination, they only feel in their marrows that they belong to it. So that when the old seaman dies and is buried "high on a windy hill," his "sea-soul" refuses the weight and confinement of earth and reverts to the freedom of the sea:

> Put no tombstone at my head,
> For here I do not make my bed.
> Strew no flowers on my grave,
> I've gone back to the wind and wave.
> Do not, do not weep for me.
> For I am happy with my sea.
>
> ("Death of an Old Seaman")

From the gypsies and seafarers it is only a half-step to "Shadows in the Sun," a series of vignettes of broken and forgotten humanity, bits of human clay hardly more than shadows. Through each the poet discovers and exposes the cord that binds him and the reader to all mankind. Something in each which he can "neither hear nor feel nor see . . . nor understand" reaches for him like a magnet, compelling sympathy and identification, bringing communion. So that the poet—and the reader—becomes in turn the beggar boy playing "upon his flute a wild free tune / As if Fate had not bled him with her knife"; the "troubled woman / Bowed by / Weariness and pain / Like an autumn flower / In the frozen rain"; the suicide who could not resist the call of water ("The calm, / Cool face of the river / Asked me for a kiss"); the sick woman lying under "a sheet of pain . . . between two lovers— / Life and Death"; the aged Mexican woman who sits on the ground "day in, day round . . . selling her scanty wares"; the young bride dead; and the man who loved and lost his friend ("I loved my friend. / He went away from me. / There's nothing more to say").

To the poet and the reader, and to the lovers, sailors, gypsies, and other bits of unfulfilled humanity, the vast mysterious figure of "The Dream Keeper" stretches out his arms and calls:

> Bring me all of your dreams,
> You dreamers.
> Bring me all of your
> Heart melodies
> That I may wrap them
> In a blue cloud-cloth
> Away from the too rough fingers
> Of the world.

There is consolation in the dream, for when all else is lost, the dream is the one thing that can be saved, sacred, personal, and inviolate. And the poet is an articulator, protector, and transmitter of the dream. He too is The Dream Keeper.

Hughes's nature poems share the power of imagery of his other lyric verse. In "Poème D'Automne" [4] the trees are "dressed in scarlet gold / Like young courtesans / Waiting for their lovers," and their lovers, the winter winds, first strip and then attack their bare bodies with "sharp, sleet-stung / Caresses of the cold." The "March Moon," [5] though more distant, fares no better: the winds strip away her cloud-garments and abandon her naked and shameless.

Hughes holds a carnival to wild nature in *Fields of Wonder*. This book is unique among his works in that it is almost all sweetness, with hardly a discordant note. Even the poems on Harlem are tender and wistful. Images flame and burst like stars upon the page. The book is a literary heaven, "the place where / Happiness is / Everywhere" and animals and birds and stones sing and salute each other.[6] Here, one might say, the poet is at peace with himself and the world. He is what Jean Toomer once called himself: Earth-Being.[7] Here are earth-songs of an earth-being, celebrating nature and all living creatures, the stars, sun and moon, and the changing seasons; the spring sprouting of plants and flowers, the rain and the rainbow; bird, snake, and snail; the global dew; the cycles of birth, life, death, and rebirth, the ineffable powers of night, sleep, love, and desire.

The influence of Emily Dickinson is very strong in such poems as "Heaven," "Snail," "Border Line," "Luck," "Walls," "Personal," "Gifts" ("To some people / Love is given. / To others— / Only heaven," p. 19); and the influence of Imagism and haiku in "One," "Montmartre," "Fragments," "Motherland," "Big Sur" ("Great lonely hills. / Great mountains. / Mighty touchstones of song," p. 5). One is reminded of Pound's "In a Station of the Metro" by Hughes's characterization of "Gypsy Melodies" as

> Songs that break
> And scatter
> Out of the moon:
> Rockets of joy
> Dimmed too soon   (p. 24)

All the same, these poems are not mere imitations but imaginative and fresh originals.

The most intriguingly mystical poem in the collection is "A House in Taos" (pp. 73–75), in which a weary trinity, "you, she, and I . . . smitten by beauty," seek the wilderness, "waiting for nothingness." And they pray to the cosmic forces to sweep

"Through the red, white, yellow skins / Of our bodies," watering and mellowing their barren hearts and whipping their divided racial souls into "one snarl of souls," into human unity and divine oneness.

Brilliant and unusual imagery is also what makes Hughes's poems on so common a subject as death so engaging. His habit is through the use of metaphors to draw parallels between death and human activity, objectifying and defining death into its niche in the cycle of existence. He looks on death with a cold, detached poetic eye. His basic definition is the common one of death as change:

> Dear lovely Death
> That taketh all things under wing—
> Never to kill—
> Only to change
> Into some other thing. . . .
> Dear lovely Death,
> Change is thy other name.[8]

Death is "a drum / Beating for ever / Till the last worms come / To answer its call," till atoms, stars, time, and space have come and danced themselves to exhaustion and are no more.[9] Death's call is magnetic, powerful, and inescapable as the music: when the drum beats, willy-nilly, the body responds. Death is like an absent mother for whom the child longs and waits: "I'm waiting for ma mammy,— / She is Death." [10] It is "a nothingness / From where / No soul returns." [11] It is "a tower / To which the soul ascends / To spend a meditative hour— / That never ends." [12]

For the musicians and hedonists, death is the cessation of music and fun: life for them is

> The shivering of
> A great drum
> Beaten with swift sticks
> Then at the closing hour

> The lights go out
> And there is no music at all
> And death becomes
> An empty cabaret
> And eternity an unblown saxophone
> And yesterday
> A glass of gin
> Drunk long
> Ago. [13]

As for the grave, it is the "Cheapest boarding house; / Some of these days / We'll all board there." [14] It is "that sleeping place, / Long resting place, / No stretching place, / That never-get-up-no-more / Place." [15] And beyond death is eternity, where "I, / Who am nobody, / Will become Infinity, / Even perhaps / Divinity." [16]

In the same unintimidated spirit, Hughes's people die nonchalant, doing whatever they love to do best. Some ask to be accompanied by their favorite music. One requests the "St. Louis Blues" and "St. James Infirmary": "I want some fine music / Up there in the sky." [17] Another wants "a stormy song" to drown the rattle of his dying breath:

> Beat the drums of tragedy for me,
> And let the white violins whir thin and slow,
> But blow one blaring trumpet note of sun
> To go with me
>   to the darkness
>   where I go. [18]

The cabaret girl dying quietly on Welfare Island regrets just one thing—that she did not die as she lived, "drunk and rowdy and gay . . . / where the band's a-playin' / Noisy and loud." [19] Old seamen who have "weathered / A thousand storms, / Two wars, / And submarines / From here to there," set out on yet another voyage, not knowing and not caring whether this one is "To the Nevermore— / Perhaps— / Or just another / Trip." [20]

And when they die, all they want is to be buried with their sea, to be one forever with their element.[21]

Aside from "Death in Harlem," Hughes's most exuberant death poem is "Sylvester's Dying Bed."[22] Great lover that he is, Sylvester is surrounded, in his hyperbolic imagination, by "All de womens in town / . . . Sweet gals . . . a-moanin' / . . . And a hundred pretty mamas" crying and begging him not to die: "Daddy! / Honey! Baby! . . . / You can't leave us here!" So he decides to love them all one more time. "I's still Sweet Papa 'Vester, / Yes, sir! Long as life do last!" But life doesn't last much longer; and as he reaches up to hug them, "de Lawd put out de light," and all is darkness, his dying simultaneous with the symbolic moment of consummated love. Hughes's people carry their love of life into death.

Hughes's lyric poetry is no doubt of secondary importance in his work; yet, as usually happens with the minor work of great artists, this minor (lyric) poetry is high enough in quality and great enough in quantity to have sustained the reputation of a lesser poet.

A brief word about Hughes's prose works which, though perhaps not of secondary importance in his overall *opus*, are nevertheless peripheral to the present study. His prose is of a piece with his poetry. His essays and speeches over the years reiterate and reinforce the esthetic first advanced in "The Negro Artist and the Racial Mountain." His first novel, *Not Without Laughter* (1930), contrasts the blues-filled life of itinerant minstrel man Jimboy, who in his wanderings neglects his wife and son, with the upward-bound austerity of his wife's sister Tempy, both against the background of family poverty. Jimboy's son, Sandy, seems destined for one or the other of these worlds; but his aunt Harriett's success on the concert circuit as a blues queen, and her assumption of moral and financial responsibility for him, rescues him from

Tempy's joyless household and ensures that he would indeed acquire education and money—but "not without laughter." In Sandy's future Hughes envisions a life in which it would not be necessary to abandon the folk culture in order to progress; a life in which one could be comfortable and middle class and still affirm the black heritage.

True to its title, Hughes's first collection of short stories, *The Ways of White Folks* (1934), focusses on what to black folks are the strange, contradictory, and absurd customs and attitudes of white folks. As one character puts it, "the ways of white folks, I mean some white folks, is too much for me. I reckon they must be a few good ones, but most of 'em ain't good—leastwise they don't treat me good. And Lawd knows, I ain't never done nothin' to 'em, nothin' a-tall." [23] Hughes is gently vicious (his usual manner); his wit is razor-sharp, and it cuts precisely and deeply. The areas probed include the white "cult of primitivism" during the Harlem Renaissance ("Rejuvenation Through Joy"); the ironies of white patronage of blacks ("Slave on the Block," "The Blues I'm Playing," "Poor Little Black Fellow"); lynching ("Home"); and the bitter complex of interracial love, miscegenation and passing ("A Good Job Gone," "Mother and Child," "Red-Headed Baby," "Passing," "Father and Son"). "Passing," which consists of a son's letter to his mother explaining why he had to pretend not to know her when they passed each other in the street, is an almost clinical dissection of the tragedy of the mulatto. Characteristically, Hughes is sympathetic without being sentimental, ironic without being frivolous. There is a cold, brutal adherence to the facts, with a concise intimation of the complex emotions of the parties involved. Hughes dramatizes the attitudes of those who could and did pass as effectively in these five brief pages as some full-length novels on the subject.

His second and third collections of short stories, *Laughing to Keep From Crying* (1952) and *Something In Common* (1963) (the latter consisting mostly of reprints from the former), take up some of the same themes. Black folks can be just as strange in their ways as white folks. White folks and black folks do indeed have something in common, and they need not travel all the way to Hong Kong to find out, as the characters of that title story did.

Hughes's best known prose is his Tales of Simple. Originating as a regular column in the *Chicago Defender* in 1943, Jesse B. Semple's conversations with Ananias Boyd finally grew to fill four volumes: *Simple Speaks His Mind* (1950), *Simple Takes a Wife* (1953), *Simple Stakes a Claim* (1957), and *Simple's Uncle Sam* (1965), plus a volume of selections, *The Best of Simple* (1961). These conversations, reported by Boyd, are witty, rich in folkways and folk humor. The language is sometimes uneven (possibly due to the tyranny of newspaper deadlines), wavering between formal English and black urban dialect. Simple's life is the stuff of the urban blues: he grew up poor in the South, made a bad marriage, left his wife, and migrated North. Now he is a Harlemite, living in a furnished room and carrying on the usual battles with difficult landladies, trying to save money to pay for his divorce, patronizing Paddy's bar and rapping with his buddies there, including Boyd. We are exposed to Simple's life and loves in cumulative detail, and to his views on a broad range of subjects, the same subjects which preoccupied Hughes during the same period. In fact, the Tales of Simple closely parallel Hughes's poetry of the 40s, 50s and 60s.

Simple's views are those of the average Harlemite, the simple folk; to a large extent they are also Hughes's views. Simple's interlocutor, Boyd, is not so much an antagonist as a foil, a wall against which ideas are bounced, a dialectical proposition. It takes two to make conversation, and if you don't want a chorus or a dirge, you need a dissenting voice, however mild. Boyd plays devil's advocate; he is, firstly, a listener and recorder, and secondly, a stand-in for all those who insist that every truth must have two sides. He articulates the conventional, often conservative opinion on all things; but he doesn't push it. It's Simple's scene, not his. His function is to disagree just long enough to drive Simple to his swift anecdotes and witty but pithy conclusions. With Boyd, Hughes is running a game and fooling no one (intending to fool no one)—no more than Plato fools us with Socrates' respondents. In both writers the respondent is a protodramatic device to provide the main character an audience and the reader a bit of human excitement. Simple/Socrates is the preordained winner of every argument; but the argument is presented, not as a dry socio-philosophical treatise, but as a human drama.

There is no real difference of opinion between Simple and Boyd. Simple speaks for Boyd about as often as he speaks for Hughes and the black masses, which is most of the time. Those who say that Boyd is Hughes's alter ego but Simple is not, miss the picture. Boyd is Hughes's alter ego, but so is Simple; Hughes's identity embraces both. For, though college educated, Boyd is, like Hughes, not a member of the "black bourgeoisie" in the classic sense (the "black bourgeoisie" do not hang out in "low-down" Harlem bars). Like Hughes, Boyd is the writer as social enquirer, as recorder and recaller of the lives of the folk (this is the only view of Boyd we are permitted to see, a functional and deliberately incomplete view); and Simple is a representative of the folk of whom this breed of writer is a part. The writer (Boyd) and the folk (Simple) are aspects of Hughes's own identity. They belong harmoniously together. And where there is no opposition, there is no choice to be made. They are one.

In another sense, Simple is a dreamer-idealist-Quixote, Boyd his realist-Sancho Panza. This would seem the primary sense in which these dialogues were influenced by Hughes's reading of Cervantes.[24] Simple and the Don are the ones who insist that the ideal and the real can and should be one. Their dream is so powerful, its logic so implacable that it attains the status of a force of nature. They themselves are larger than life, heroic, dwarfing the

Boyds and Sancho Panzas—those loyal, sane, and quite necessary reminders of our human limitations and common mortality. But still, limited as men are, they dare not lose the vision of the Simple/Quixotes, or they will perish in the narrow prison of the quotidian. In myth and story, and in real life, it is the Simples and Quixotes, the stretchers of possibility, not the Boyds and Sancho Panzas, the literalists, who command our profoundest allegiance. *Simple's Uncle Sam*, the last of the series, closes with Boyd prostrate before Simple's overwhelming dream—Hughes's deferred dream that will not die—crying a deep Amen: "Dream on, dreamer . . . dream on."

The Tales of Simple are about as difficult to classify as Jean Toomer's *Cane*. They have been variously designated as short stories, sketches, novels, humor, epic, and the like. Perhaps a term like "editorial fiction" or "documentary fiction" captures more accurately their central charcter, namely, a fictionalized commentary both on Afro-American life and culture and on American public affairs from a black perspective.

Hughes's drama includes nine full-length plays, two one-act plays, four gospel musicals, a Christmas cantata, four opera librettos, and one screenplay. In addition, over forty of his poems and lyrics have been set to music and performed by well-known artists. His drama is a cut of the same rich fabric as his poetry and fiction. The themes are variations of the same abiding one, presented, again, with the aid of the vast resources of Afro-American musical, religious, and comic traditions. On occasion, Hughes tells the same story in two genres, as in *Mulatto* (drama, 1931) and "Father and Son" (short story, 1934); *Tambourines to Glory* (drama, 1949; novel, 1958); *Simple Takes a Wife* (documentary fiction, 1953) and *Simply Heavenly* (drama, 1956). But even these do not give us any immediate sense of redundancy; each is freshly adapted to its genre.

CHAPTER 6

Hughes and the Evolution of Consciousness in Black Poetry

W. E. B. DuBois's formulation of the dilemma of the black artist was one of the earliest and is still, perhaps, the most lucid. As he stated it, the black artist's problem was in deciding whether to reflect "the beauty revealed to him . . . the soul-beauty of a race which his larger audience despised," or to "articulate the message of another people." [1] As Afro-American history is in part the history of a people caught between two conflicting worlds, and of their efforts to reconcile those worlds, to bring to an end their "double-consciousness" by merging their African and American selves into a single, undivided whole, so is Afro-American literary history in part a record of the black writer's choices between revealing the soul-beauty of his own people and articulating the message of another people; so is it the history of his efforts to bring to an end the very need for choice by somehow bringing the two things together.

The literary beauty revealed to the black writer is contained in his oral folk tradition with its vast universe of themes and images and its smooth and complex strategies of delivery. The "message of another people," on the other hand, is carried in the forms and attitudes, themes and styles and sensibilities of white American and European culture and literature. In another sense, the black writer's problem is as much one of medium as of ethos: his problem is how to actualize the oral tradition in written form, how to recreate the vital force, the sights and sounds and smells of the performance-event on dumb, flat, one-dimensional paper. This problem of *media transfer* is one which the black musician, for instance, does not have, for his art operates within the continuum of the oral medium. The black writer's problem is further complicated by the fact that he has no long written tradition of his own to emulate; and for him to abandon the effort to translate into written form that oral medium which is the full reservoir of his culture would be to annihilate his identity and become a zombie, a programmed vehicle for "the message of another people."

Hardly any black writer of any generation has found it easy, or even possible, to avoid making a choice. And as might be expected, the choices have been neither uniform nor consistent in any era. In every generation, some writers have chosen to reveal the soul-beauty of their own people, some to carry the message of another people. Sometimes the writer vacillates, yielding to the one imperative at one time or in one work, to the other in another, or attempting to answer to both imperatives at the same time and in the same works. Or the writer may undercut the self-acceptance evident in his works with actions and pronouncements indicating reservations and self-doubt.

One of the most radical and complete examples of self-acceptance is to be found among the writers and critics associated with the Black Consciousness Movement of the late 1960s and the 70s. Many of these writers not only disavowed the expectations of the larger audience but refused to recognize the presence of that audience altogether. To them the larger audience is of no account whatever, being made up of "unpeople," as Don L. Lee once called them.[2] These writers not only chose to reveal the soul-

MATTER: theme, subject, concerns, sensibility, universe; *implied ethics:* what is considered good/evil, moral/immoral, e.g., a black man killing a white man in revenge or self-defense, as in Richard Wright's "Long Black Song" or "Big Boy Leaves Home"	black people and the things important to them	white people and the things important to them; racially unidentified characters; "universal" themes
MANNER: form, style, technique, treatment, point of view; grammar, diction, idiom; *implied esthetic:* what is considered beautiful/ugly, e.g., gospel shout, field holler, toast, dozens, as in "Signifying Monkey" or Hughes's *Ask Your Mama*	black oral folk tradition as model	white middle class American or European literary tradition as model
AUDIENCE: readers, listeners, viewers; those to whom the work is specifically addressed (if it is); those to whom it might appeal	blacks; "bohemian" whites; "radical" whites; "liberal" whites	whites; "respectable" blacks; "black bourgeoisie"; "colored middle class"

beauty of their people, but to reveal it solely to their people. To them, white readers, listeners, and viewers were at best eavesdroppers, at worst hustlers, profiteers, and spies.

Hughes's solution was a little different. He chose to reveal the soul-beauty of his people, but to reveal it for all who cared to see.

He neither succumbed to the expectations of the larger audience, nor disregarded their presence. He saw his audience as inclusive rather than exclusive, cutting across the lines of race. The literary grazing pasture that was his work was, he said, not trimmed to suit every breed of cattle; and as it turned out (as he anticipated), those who found that pasture palatable to their taste came from both races, as did those who did not.

A cursory look at black poets' responses to this problem through the centuries would help place Hughes's choice in perspective. The major components of the dilemma-choice, once again, are as shown in the table on the preceding page.

It might be well to start off by saying that before the Harlem Renaissance there was no black audience to speak of. This fact no doubt influenced the choices of matter and manner, but it is only one of a complex of factors. Black poets of the 18th and 19th centuries modeled themselves on the mainstream secular and religious verse of their day; and except for Frances Harper and Paul Laurence Dunbar and a few others who in writing dialect verse were emulating a white convention which was itself based on black oral tradition, these early poets made no attempt to utilize black oral techniques or folk verse forms. Eighteenth century poet Phillis Wheatley wrote on "universal" subjects, mostly death. When she mentions black people at all, it is to deprecate them. She was captured in West Africa as a child and sold into slavery in Boston. In her poems she celebrates her abduction and conversion to Christianity:

> 'Twas mercy brought me from my Pagan land,
> Taught my benighted soul to understand
> That there's a God, that there's a Saviour too. . . .[3]

> 'Twas not long since I left my native shore
> The land of errors, and Egyptian gloom:
> Father of mercy, 'twas thy gracious hand
> Brought me in safety from those dark abodes. . . .[4]

In her poem "To the Right Honourable William, Earl of Dart-
mouth, His Majesty's Principal Secretary of State for North
America," surely one of the most (unintentionally?) ironic poems
in black literature, she pleads for freedom for British settlers, cit-
ing as her unique credential her own servitude which has taught
her how stifling is lack of freedom. But she does not ask for
freedom for herself or her brethren:

> Should you, my lord, while you peruse my song,
> Wonder from whence my love of Freedom sprung,
> Whence flow these wishes for the common good,
> By feeling hearts alone best understood,
> I, young in life, by seeming cruel fate
> Was snatch'd from Afric's fancy'd happy seat:
> What pangs excruciating must molest,
> What sorrows labour in my parent's breast?
> Steel'd was that soul and by no misery mov'd
> That from a father seiz'd his babe belov'd:
> Such, such my case. And can I then but pray
> Others may never feel tyrannic sway? [5]

Her fellow slave poet and contemporary Jupiter Hammon also celebrates his conversion and echoes the slaveholder's favorite
biblical text counseling absolute obedience of servants to masters:

> MASTER: Come my servant, follow me,
>   According to thy place;
>   And surely God will be with thee,
>   And send thee heav'nly grace. . . .
>
> SERVANT: Dear Master, that's my whole delight,
>   Thy pleasure for to do;
>   As far as grace and truth's in sight,
>   Thus far I'll surely go. [6]

The achievement of these two poets in the eyes of their white
contemporaries was that they could write at all, and it is not too
surprising that they did not reflect the primary concerns of their

black contemporaries, namely, their overwhelming thirst for freedom. The most prominent slave poet of the 19th century, George Moses Horton, reflected those concerns. His voice is personal and muted:

> Alas! and am I born for this,
>   To wear this slavish chain? . . .
>
> How long have I in bondage lain,
>   And languished to be free!
> Alas! and must I still complain—
>   Deprived of liberty.
>
> Oh, Heaven! and is there no relief
>   This side the silent grave—
> To soothe the pain—to quell the grief
>   And anguish of a slave? . . .[7]

But oracular voices, weighted with sorrow and fury, finally exploded on the scene with the works of James Whitfield, James Madison Bell, Frances Harper, and Albery Whitman. Whitfield's "America" is an exemplary indictment:

> America, it is to thee
> Thou boasted land of liberty
> It is to thee I raise my song
> Thou land of blood, and crime, and wrong. . . .[8]

Frances Harper's black concern is evident in such poems as "The Slave Auction," "The Slave Mother," and the smooth, melodic "Bury Me in a Free Land." In her epic *Moses, A Story of the Nile* (1869), she points a lesson of responsible leadership for educated and privileged blacks: Moses, their prototype, abandons the princely ease of Pharaoh's palace to "lead his captive race to freedom."

> . . . . I go to join
> The fortunes of my race, and to put aside
> All other bright advantages, save

The approval of my conscience and the mood
Of rightly doing. . . .
I feel an earnest purpose binding all
My soul unto a strong resolve, which bids
Me put aside all other ends and aims,
Until the hour shall come when God—the God
Our fathers loved and worshipped—shall break our chains,
And lead our willing feet to freedom.[9]

Her dialect *Sketches of Southern Life* foreshadows Dunbar's sweeping presentation of the genre.

Frances Harper, Paul Laurence Dunbar, and Charles Waddell Chesnutt (working in prose fiction) might be said to represent a stage of transition in manner from accepted mainstream conventions to black folk tradition. True, the dialect which these writers used was first molded into a popular literary vehicle by Southern white writers, who did not neglect to carry over from minstrelsy the standard stereotypes of the comic, dishonest, idiotic black. Yet, despite its origins and associations, plantation dialect at its best, as in the hands of Dunbar and Chesnutt, was expressive of the black experience in the black style. It constituted an example of the literary possibilities both of black matter (common black folk) and black manner (black folk forms, language, and humor), possibilities which would be realized to a great extent in the next generation in the work of Jean Toomer, Rudolph Fisher, Langston Hughes, Zora Neale Hurston, Sterling Brown, James Weldon Johnson of *God's Trombones*, and Claude McKay in his novels.

It is mainly on looking back from the vantage point of our own era that one might be inclined to blame Dunbar for not seeing the transformational possibilities of plantation dialect, and for so stubbornly preferring his poems in standard English. The example of the Scottish Robert Burns notwithstanding, Dunbar was anxious to be recognized as a "serious" poet in the accepted mainstream tradition, not as exclusively or even primarily a practitioner of what was widely regarded as a deviant literary form. In "Misapprehension," "Prometheus" and "The Poet" he laments the preference of critics and audiences for his dialect poetry and their indifference to his standard English poems: he sang of life and love in all their complexity and fury, in serious, "good" English—"But ah, the world, it turned to praise / A jingle in a broken tongue." [10]

The pattern of praising the dialect poetry was set by William Dean Howells, whose review of Dunbar's second book, *Majors and Minors,* in the June 27, 1896, issue of *Harpers Weekly,* catapulted Dunbar into national fame. The standard English poems, observed Howells, were conventional and faceless, whereas the dialect poems spoke "with a direct and fresh authority," expressing the "race-life from within the race." With this pronouncement Howells defined Dunbar into literary fame but also into a literary corner (some would call it ghetto) from which Dunbar tried in vain to emerge; for subsequent critics, glad to be rid of the responsibility of making original assessments, simply echoed Howells. The irony, however, is that, regrettable as the neglect of Dunbar's standard English poems by his contemporaries might be, Howells's judgment was, in the main, just. For besides a handful of really exceptional poems on the order of "We Wear the Mask," "Sympathy," "Life," and "Dawn," Dunbar's standard English poems, comprising roughly two-thirds of his vast corpus, are for the most part undistinguished—no match for the high energy, sweeping movement, colorful drama, fresh and striking imagery, and humor of "Angelina," "The Colored Band," "The Party," "The Rivals," "Possum," "When Malindy Sings," "Temptation," "In the Morning," "How Lucy Backslid," "At Candle-Lightin' Time," "An Ante-Bellum Sermon," "A Negro Love Song," "A Death Song" and other dialect poems of great intensity. The real problem with the dialect poetry, certainly from the point of view of black readers of the Harlem Renaissance and after, is that Dunbar does not transcend often enough the negative stereotypes he inherited from the minstrel and plantation schools. All too often he differs from his predecessors chiefly in his technical excellence, in the auditory accuracy and metrical smoothness of his verse, rather than in the equally crucial matters of sensibility and viewpoint. This fact is glaringly apparent in such poems as "Chrismus on the Plantation" (the loyal, contented slave); "The Deserted Plantation" (ex-slave mourning the passing of the "good old days" of slavery); "A Corn Song" (the sentimental, tear-shedding master); "Accountability" (black dishonesty, hypocrisy, and theft); and "A Coquette Conquered" (black women's supposed easy morals). These latter are no doubt some of the poems James Weldon Johnson had in mind as he sought to explain why the younger generation of black poets turned their backs on Dunbar's pioneer work in dialect.[11]

Dunbar's career is a striking illustration of the acuteness of "double-consciousness." That he chose to write in both standard English and dialect is testimony to his recognition of the conflicting demands on his art, the demands of a mainstream esthetic on the one hand, and of a black folk esthetic on the other. But he merely provides a separate outlet for each, makes no real effort to reconcile them. His eminent contemporary, Charles Waddell Chesnutt, does not succeed in reconciling or fusing them either, but his experiment is perhaps more sophisticated. In *The Conjure Woman* (1899) Chesnutt adopted the structure and procedure of Joel Chandler Harris's Uncle Remus tales: a two-tiered story, with a white narrator in the outer story representing the mainstream sensibility and speaking in standard English, and an aged ex-slave who tells the humorous and fantastic dialect tales that constitute the core of the work. The standard stereotypes are there; the situation is made to order. But as the reader proceeds, he gradually discovers that, far from pandering to the convention, Chesnutt is turning the characters and situations upside down and inside out; and that, far from glorifying the institution of slavery as Harris declared his Remus tales would do, Chesnutt instead provides a subtle but scathing indictment.

And yet Chesnutt may have been *too* subtle. The book is addressed to a white audience; and in keeping with Chesnutt's avowed objective, it is a subterranean attack on their emotions, an effort to undermine their prejudice by leading them out, "imperceptibly, unconsciously, step by step, to the desired state of feeling." [12] In Uncle Julius's tales the experience of slavery is recreated in all its raw and bitter brutality; but if the reactions of the white couple to whom the tales are told are any guide to the reactions of the larger white audience to whom the book is addressed, then Chesnutt may be said to have failed in his objective. For at the end of each story the narrator's wife evinces no more than a mild susceptibility to the overwhelming indictment; and her husband reacts with a self-protective skepticism, ignoring the moral significance of the story and reassuring himself with trifling circumstantial evidence that Julius invented the story in an effort to achieve some material goal, e.g., to sell him a lame horse, to get his lazy grandson reemployed, to obtain an unused cabin for his church, and so on. The narrator is influenced only to the extent that he submits to what he perceives as Julius's material needs. He finds each tale amusing, and is condescending and patronizing toward the old man. But he misses, or refuses to acknowledge or permit his behavior to be influenced by, the deeper significance of the story.

The reaction of Chesnutt's white audience was probably no different. Accustomed to the "darky stories" of the plantation school, they may be presumed to have identified so closely with the white narrator as to miss the quite radical socio-political import of Chesnutt's story cycle. The double-tiered narrative frame, with its separation of sensibilities, serves to distance and refract the experience away from the audience, to muffle the thunder in the clouds, to deflect the lightning from where it might otherwise have struck full force. The aloofness and banality of the narrator's alien voice, the shallowness of his understanding or the cynicism of his pretended lack of understanding, and, above all, his failure to commit himself to significant right action—all this may constitute an intended criticism by the author, but criticism that was almost certain to be lost on the majority of his readers.

All in all, then, Chesnutt's and Dunbar's experiments are of the same kind. Each attempts to reveal the soul-beauty of his race, and at the same time to carry the message of another people. To do this, each is forced to "play white," to masquerade as an outsider part of the time; and as a result, the authenticity of the black world of Dunbar's dialect poetry is tainted by the white sensibility (stereotypes) to which it is married, while Chesnutt, by installing a liberal white Northerner as the controlling narrative voice in *The Conjure Woman,* at one and the same time both attacks the white sensibility and pacifies it, thereby blunting the thrust of his dialect tales.

Reservations, apologies, ambivalence, and racial self-doubt also mark the careers of many of the leading poets of the Harlem Renaissance. For instance, James Weldon Johnson, while on the one hand delivering himself totally to the black folk experience, affirming and recreating it with such authority in "O Black and Unknown Bards" (1917), in his two *Books of American Negro Spirituals* (1925, 1926), and in *God's Trombones* (1927), at the same time reminds himself and warns his readers repeatedly that black folk forms are "lower forms of art" which at best give "evidence of a power that will some day be applied to the higher forms," "the more formal and serious" forms of western culture.[13] This, sadly, is nothing less than a reiteration of the "universal" / "white" equation.

Jean Toomer's response was a bit different. By his own account the product of "seven blood mixtures," the nagging concern of his life was the harmonization of the different strains of his heritage, the forging of a self in which "no single element in me" would be

subdued to any other.[14] However, a year among the black peasantry of Georgia stimulated the black strain to gigantic growth, and
it burst forth in the profound and colorful tapestry of *Cane* (1923).
A harmonious kaleidoscope of prose sketches, poems, prose-
poems, and semidramatic dialogue rendered in an unusual blend
of black usage and Joycean wordsmithry, *Cane* in its form, structure, and idiom is unique in American literature. Its apprehension
and delivery of the black folk world was unmatched in the literature of its day except by Hughes's poetry and Johnson's *God's
Trombones,* and it remains still unsurpassed. But it was not long
before its author relapsed into the no man's land of identity that
was neither black nor white, "just American"—an identity which
might, as in Toomer's case, embrace several races but which nevertheless was forced to count for nothing. Toomer left New York
and settled in Chicago, married a white woman, declared himself
not black, refused permission for his work to appear in a black anthology, and disappeared into the great anonymity of the white
race. Toomer's history stands as a paradigm of an important segment of the black experience.

The vacillations of Johnson and Toomer are replayed in the career of Claude McKay. McKay began his career as a dialect poet in
the manner of Dunbar and Burns. Shortly after the publication of
his first two books, *Songs of Jamaica* (1912) and *Constab' Ballads*
(1912), McKay left his native Jamaica for higher education in the
United States. As it turned out, the transfer from that authentic
rural folk environment was accompanied by a subtle metamorphosis, a corresponding transfer in sensibility. As his next two
books, *Spring in New Hampshire* (1920) and *Harlem Shadows*
(1922) were to reveal, McKay had turned his back on the folk
rhythms and dialect of his early work instead of refining and per-
fecting them, and for his mature work had adopted the antiquated
European sonnet form and with it the archaic diction, inverted
syntax, and tyrannic rhyme scheme of Elizabethan poetics. Into

this constricted form McKay proceeded to pour all the venom and rage possible in a blackness drowning in an ocean of whiteness. Each of his protest sonnets just about explodes from the page. "If We Must Die" is one of the most explosive poems in black literature; and few poems can match the sheer energy of "Baptism," the stark cruelty of "The Lynching," the massive righteousness of "To the White Fiends," or the mixed nostalgia, resolution, and sorrow of "In Bondage," "Outcast," and "Enslaved." The white world was hardly ever more volubly rejected than in "America," "The White City," and "The White House." Like his own "pagan isms," these poems roar and crash and clatter about us, sweeping us irresistibly along with their power. The best of McKay's poetry exudes strength, more so because of the brief space of fourteen lines out of which it is forced. His poetry invites declamation, and once we begin we forget how old-fashioned and far away it all is; we become the poem.

The paradox, however, is that McKay's attacks on the white world are carried out in one of that culture's most entrenched and conservative poetic forms. McKay's words deny the white world, but his form, style, language, and poetic attitude tend to affirm it. Perhaps nowhere in black literature is the tension between content and form, or matter and manner, so sharp. And yet McKay largely succeeds in harnessing the content to the form, the matter to the manner. It is the mark of his achievement that he is able to work that fragile sonnet frame into a vehicle of dynamite.

After *Harlem Shadows* McKay moved to Europe and turned his literary gifts almost exclusively to prose fiction. Once again, a physical transfer signalled a shift in emphasis and viewpoint, for in the series of novels written during his twelve-year sojourn in Europe he returned to the life experiences, philosophy, and language of black peasantry and urban lower classes—matter and manner which he had so conspicuously excluded from his mature verse. His deviation, as it turned out, had been temporary—unless his conversion to Catholicism in 1944, four years before his death, may be read as still another deviation, for after his conversion he wrote virtually nothing but panegyrics to the Catholic world view.

In their shifts, dodges, retractions, and returns, Johnson, Toomer, and McKay might be said to inhabit the center strips of the black sensibility spectrum during the Harlem Renaissance. At one end of that spectrum was Langston Hughes, producing art whose matter and manner were relentlessly rooted in the black folk experience, and serving as the norm of happy self-acceptance; and at the other end, at the extreme of self-rejection, was, as indicated in the opening chapter, William Stanley Braithwaite, and not too far from him, Countee Cullen. Much like Phillis Wheatley, Braithwaite never permitted the vital traditions or serious concerns of his people to "violate" the "pure," "rare" lyricism of his "raceless-universal" verse. Samples:

> In a sunken pool
> Lies a jewel,—
> If Christ was a fool
> Saint Francis was cruel.[15]

> Heart free, hand free,
>   Blue above, brown under,
> All the world to me
>   Is a place of wonder.
> Sun shine, moon shine,
>   Stars, and winds a-blowing,
> All into this heart of mine
>   Flowing, flowing, flowing! [16]

James Weldon Johnson, trying hard not to offend, described Braithwaite's poetry as "marked by delicate beauty, often tinged by mysticism or whimsy." [17] Without benefit of euphemism, Braithwaite's poetry might better be described as effete and vacuous.

Again, James Weldon Johnson once wrote that "it is natural,

indeed inevitable, to juxtapose Hughes and Cullen," [18] and he was right (he usually was). Like Braithwaite, Countee Cullen was concerned with being "universal." He wanted to be "a poet, not a Negro poet." Accordingly, he chose English Romantic poet John Keats as his prime model, and no doubt partly because of this his poetry is self-centered, death-obsessed, weak and effeminate in the worst Keatsian tradition. Not unlike Toomer, Cullen wrestled with his racial identity all his life and, judging from his poetry, never quite came to terms with it. The self-pity which is at the core of his poetry is perhaps best expressed in his best known poem, "Yet Do I Marvel," [19] which marvels that God would "make a poet black and bid him sing"—as though being a poet was incompatible with being black. Cullen marvels that anyone could be expected to carry simultaneously the burdens of oppression and presumed inferiority and of artistic creativity. In his mind, at least in this poem, the two things are mutually exclusive; which makes one wonder whether he had ever really *listened* to the spirituals, ballads, blues, jazz, or folklore, had ever really grasped their quality and significance. James Weldon Johnson obviously had, despite his reservations, and this is why his "O Black and Unknown Bards," possibly Cullen's model, focusses with such clarity on black musical / literary creativity, defines it and celebrates it. Johnson rejoices in black grandeur; Cullen whines and complains.

In "The Shroud of Color," [20] one of his major poems, Cullen attempts to exorcise self-hate. The poet (or his persona) would rather die than continue to live black and despised:

> "Lord, being dark," I said, "I cannot bear
> The further touch of earth, the scented air;
> Lord, being dark, forewilled to that despair
> My color shrouds me in, I am as dirt
> Beneath my brother's heel . . ."

He asks for death. His God, bent on saving him, shows him a series of visions, each underlining the lesson of endurance in all

nature, all nature thriving amidst conflict and destruction and affirming life, none wishing for death. For each vision the poet in-
vents an excuse to exclude himself—as a special case—from that
cycle of existence. The fourth and final vision is of Africa, first free,
then subdued into brutal slavery, and of slaves enduring the apparently unendurable, the race surviving in spite of everything.

> And somehow it was borne upon my brain
> How being dark, and living through the pain
> Of it, is courage more than angels have.

This is true heroism, brought home to him at last, the heroism in
his own backyard, within his own race, within him.

> The cries of all dark people near or far
> Were billowed over me, a mighty surge
> Of suffering in which my puny grief must merge
> And lose itself; I had no further claim to urge
> For death.

So at last embracing that black heritage and merging his individual
suffering with that of his group, the poet finds strength to live and
to keep alive his dream of freedom and brotherhood on the one
hand, and of artistic creativity on the other. "My spirit has come
home, that sailed the doubtful seas! / . . . My sight was clear; I
looked and saw the rising sun."

But the peace forged with self and heritage is an uneasy one.
The self-pity and death-wish that dominate Cullen's first book,
Color, persist in subsequent works. Even his love poems are
gloomy and morbid. If Cullen had had the good sense to look to his
own folk tradition for models, as Hughes and some others of his
contemporaries did, he might have absorbed and reproduced
some of that strength and laughter by which the race had learned
to live with adversity.

Excluding *Ballad of the Brown Girl* (1927), which is a single
poem, each of Cullen's first three books is arranged in sections,

always including a section titled "Color." This cordoning off of his racial poems into a corner, along with his "universalist" opinions, evidently drew criticism from some of his contemporaries, and he lashed back at them in "To Certain Critics":

> I'll bear your censure as your praise,
> For never shall the clan
> Confine my singing to its ways
> Beyond the ways of man.[21]

Race or color is only a part of his concerns, separate and apart from his presumably larger Greco-Roman concerns. He grants it a hearing, assigns it a corner. His "Uncle Jim" is also revealing:

> "White folks is white," says uncle Jim;
> "A platitude," I sneer.
> And then I tell him so is milk
> And the froth upon his beer.[22]

And years later, lying in the grass with a friend, he wonders why "My mind should stray the Grecian urn / To muse on uncle Jim."

In "After a Visit" [23] Cullen recounts the experience of meeting with a group of Irish poets gathered at Padraic Colum's, their souls soaked in Irish mythology and folklore and their brains aflame with Irish nationalism. Cullen pays them eloquent tribute but shows no grasp of the significance of Irish cultural nationalism, nor of the example it might provide for black cultural nationalism. He has had the experience but missed the meaning. He bemoans merely a personal "apostasy," in that these poets are taut with literary activity whereas he has been lax for two years. But he does not see a possible apostasy in his failure to turn to good literary account his own folk heritage—an apostasy which at least partially explains why so much of his poetry is uninspired, deracinated, derivative, imperfectly grafted onto an alien trunk.

In contrast to Cullen, Hughes's poetry is centrally grounded in and derives its vital nourishment from the black folk heritage. His "racial" poems are not segregated into a corner. For Hughes, life, love, happiness, sorrow, death—all the so-called universals which Cullen supposedly explores in his non-"color" poems—are not separable from nor incompatible with racial identity or its assertion. The "universal" consists of "particulars"—any particulars; and Hughes finds in black life and culture the particulars—the substance, language, form, social and historical setting, backdrop, and atmosphere—for treatment of these universal themes, just as Irish, British, Russian, German, Chinese, and Japanese writers derive their particulars from the life and culture of their nation.

It could perhaps be argued that what Cullen dramatizes in his "color" poems (indeed, that the whole meaning of his career) is precisely that schizophrenia which DuBois dubbed the "double-consciousness." This indeed is so. And yet one cannot but regret that Cullen, whose superior gifts gleam so brightly through the stitches in his verse, almost invariably deals with his subjects in a morbid and regressive manner, with so much self-pity and so little strength or laughter, and to the end offers the reader no stable sense of black identity or black pride.

The leading poets of the post-Renaissance middle generation are Melvin Tolson,[24] Robert Hayden, and Gwendolyn Brooks. Like some of their predecessors, these poets have attempted at one and the same time to reveal the beauty of their own people and to carry the message of another people. The bulk of their works stands uneasily in the turbulent contested middle ground between two cultures. Their concern with black life is unquestionable; but on the whole they do not take sufficient advantage of the technical resources of their culture.

Tolson's first book, *Rendezvous with America* (1944), is characterized by strident Whitmanesque evocations:

America?
An international river with a legion of tributaries!
A magnificent cosmorama with myriad patterns and colors!
A giant forest with loin-roots in a hundred lands!
A cosmopolitan orchestra with a thousand instruments playing
                America! . . . .
And the termites of anti-Semitism busy themselves
And the Ku Klux Klan marches with rope and faggot
And the money-changers plunder the Temple of Democracy. . . .
And the con men try to jimmy the Constitution. . . .
And the People groan in the *tribulum* of tyranny.[25]

But in his subsequent works the broad genial spirit and language of
cultural democracy is overtaken and annihilated by a narrow academic impulse. Tolson's major works, *Libretto for the Republic of
Liberia* (1953) and *Harlem Gallery* (1965) are, among other things,
tedious exercises in recalling the personalities and incidents of European literature, history, mythology, philosophy, and religion,
with a passing nod to non-Western cultures. Each of these works is
a compendium of esoteric learning; each is obsessively pedantic,
wilfully obscure, allusive to the point of lunacy or frivolity, unnec-
essarily and artificially difficult. Tolson seems determined to out-
Eliot Eliot and out-Pound Pound:

The Harlem Gallery, an Afric pepper bird,
    awakes me at a people's dusk of dawn.
The age altars its image, a dog's hind leg,
    and hazards the moment of truth in pawn.
        The Lord of the House of Flies,
        jaundice-eyed, synapses purled,
    wries before the tumultuous canvas,
            The Second of May—
                by Goya:
            the dagger of Madrid
                vs.
            the scimitar of Murat.
    In Africa, in Asia, on the Day

of Barricades, alarm birds bedevil the Great White World,
a Buridan's ass—not Balaam's—between no oats and hay.

Sometimes a Roscius as tragedian,
sometimes a Kean as clown,
without Sir Henry's flap to shield my neck,
I travel, from oasis to oasis, man's Saharic up-and-down.[26]

This is the way *Harlem Gallery* opens, and this is the way it creaks
and crawls to the end, some 150 pages later. Tolson's wit and wisdom, which is considerable, is buried in this impossible jargon.
Like *Cane, Harlem Gallery* is an experimental work, not least of all
in its language. But where Toomer succeeds in creating a language
that is plastic, malleable, dynamic, Tolson's language comes out
rigid, petrified, static. There is relief, but it is brief and occasional:

O spiritual, work-song, ragtime, blues, jazz—
consorts of
the march, quadrille, polka, and waltz!
. . . .
I was born in Bitchville, Lousyana.
A son of Ham, I had to scram!
I was born in Bitchville, Lousyana;
so I ain't worth a T.B. damn! [27]

In the voice of his folk poet-hero, Hideho Heights, "the poet
laureate of Lenox Avenue" (a lifelike portrait of Langston Hughes),
Tolson treats the reader to fragments of ballads, raps, tall tales, and
the story of John Henry:

The night John Henry is born an ax
of lightning splits the sky,
and a hammer of thunder pounds the earth,
and the eagles and panthers cry! . . . .

Some say he was born in Georgia—O Lord!
Some say in Alabam.
But it's writ on the rock at the Big Bend Tunnel:
"Lousyana was my home. So scram!" [28]

Hideho Heights, just come from a jam session, sings Louis Armstrong a high ode, "a one-way ticket / to Immortality":

> *Old Satchmo's*
> *gravelly voice and tapping foot and crazy notes*
> *set my soul on fire.*
> *If I climbed*
> *the seventy-seven steps of the Seventh*
> *Heaven, Satchmo's high C would carry me higher!*
> *Are you hip to this, Harlem? Are you hip?*
> *On Judgment Day, Gabriel will say*
> *after he blows his horn:*
> *"I'd be the greatest trumpeter in the Universe,*
> *if old Satchmo had never been born!"* [29]

Beyond this, a few fragments of blues blared out of a juke box, and a spiritual "Homerized" by "Doctor Nkomo, / with Lionelbar-rymorean gestures." [30] These renditions of the folk sensibility are brilliant flashes, but far too brief and infrequent.

Tolson's *Libretto for the Republic of Liberia*, consisting of 29 pages of poetry with 16 pages of notes, is except for brevity just as tortured and difficult as *Harlem Gallery*. Both works demand prolonged devotion—and a roomful of dictionaries and encyclopedias; and few scholars, not to speak of general readers, can muster up such devotion. Consequently, both works are likely to remain *unread classics* for some time. Many will acknowledge their complexity and sophistication, but few will attempt to read them and fewer will understand them. Which raises a number of significant questions. If Tolson's convoluted syntax, esoteric learning and obscurity constitute such a formidable barrier to even the best educated readers of whatever race, how important or relevant are these works to the Afro-American people who are so obviously the center of the author's concerns? Tolson, for instance, describes *Harlem Gallery* as the chronicle of "a people's New World odyssey / from chattel to Esquire." [31] But to whom is the chronicle addressed? To a small inner circle of academics? Or to the broader populace whose story it is supposed to tell? Who can read and understand it? Granted, the terms "chronicle" and "libretto" are not to be taken literally; but, however broadly regarded, the fact remains that what Tolson has created is a chronicle in a cipher, a coded libretto. Should not the people, at least those literate among them, be able to read their own story with some ease, or understand the words celebrating their nationhood? The question of lucidity and meaning is crucial in any consideration of the relevance or centrality of a work of art to a given culture. The measure of an author must take in the matter of *accessibility* of his work. If a work is largely inaccessible, if a major portion of its presumed audience cannot read or understand it, it remains largely meaningless to that audience and peripheral to their culture, unless perhaps as a negative example.

Robert Hayden in his "Middle Passage" [32] recreates some of the horror and meaning of the slave experience, and incidentally demonstrates with excellence some of the poetic uses of history. His "Runagate Runagate" [33] is equally effective, incorporating spirituals and folklore and black idiom into a kaleidoscope of the Underground Railroad and other flights from slavery to freedom. Harriet Tubman is presented as the mean sister she was—when "fear starts a-murbling" she levels her pistol: "Dead folks can't jaybird-talk, she says; / you keep on going now or die, she says." Mean ole Harriet. If you mean to be free, you got to be mean like Harriet. No wonder in nineteen excursions she never lost a passenger. "Mean mean mean to be free." This towering figure in Afro-American history deserves and in this poem receives the highest possible tribute.

But the black style and language of "Runagate Runagate" is all too rare in Hayden's poetry. His "Homage to the Empress of the Blues" (a poem for Bessie Smith), "Summertime and the Living. . . ," "Night, Death, Mississippi," "El-Hajj Malik El-Shabazz"

(Malcolm X), and other poems of the black experience, are written in standard academic English with no black flavor. But this is a phenomenon which, as we have seen, is not unusual in black poetry. And the problem of language is less important than the overall problem of sensibility and viewpoint. For instance, in his *Selected Poems* (1966) Hayden repeatedly affirms the Baha'i faith to which he belongs, as in "Dawnbreaker," "From the Corpse Woodpiles, From the Ashes," and "Baha'u'llah in the Garden of Ridwan," but denigrates Afro-American religions, religious leaders, and believers, as in "Idol," "Incense of the Lucky Virgin," "Witch Doctor," "Mourning Poem for the Queen of Sunday," and "A Ballad of Remembrance." To religions and rituals of which he is not an initiate or which he does not understand, Hayden hands down an indictment. And since religion is a controlling element in any culture, one can only infer that his overall attitude to his own Afro-American culture is correspondingly negative. In "Idol," he associates the Aztec goddess Coatlicue exclusively with blood-curdling brutality, infanticide, and cannibalism:

> Wail of the newborn, cry of the dying,
> sirenscream of agonies;
>   taloned shriek, gong and cymbal of wreckage,
> drumbeat of bloodblackened praise;
>   soundless drumthrob of the heart wrenched
> from the living breast,
>   of the raw meaty heart quivering in copal
> smoke its praise.[34]

In "A Ballad of Remembrance," [35] a cliché-ridden travesty of the African heritage, terror, decadence, death, "contrived illuminations," "contrived ghosts" is all that the poet can make of the gorgeous parades and masquerades of New Orleans Mardi Gras. And he cowers in fear—till Mark Van Doren, "meditative, ironic, / richly human," the Great White Father to whom the poem is addressed, arrives and rescues him "from the hoodoo of that dance . . . that schizoid city . . . with death / in its jaws like gold teeth and archaic cusswords," enabling him to speak "with my true voice again." For Hayden, black tradition at its most mystical and profound is horror and chaos; white tradition is "humanism." What irony! Phillis Wheatley could perhaps be excused on account of her epoch and milieu. But Robert Hayden . . . ?

Gwendolyn Brooks is the most direct link between the middle generation and the poets of the late 1960s and the 70s. The younger generation reveres her as an Older Sister, and a number of them, most notably Don L. Lee, matured under her tutelage, especially as members of the Organization of Black American Culture (OBAC) workshop in Chicago, which she helped found. Until her own protegés, at once subjects and principals in the consciousness revolution of the 60s, began to influence her, Gwendolyn Brooks was very much a writer of what Don Lee (not necessarily referring to her work) once contemptuously described as "that which is now (& yesterday) considered poetry, i.e., whi-te poetry." [36] Her recent works, *In the Mecca* (1968), *Riot* (1969), *Family Pictures* (1970), and the three "Sermons on the Warpland" (1968–69), bear testimony to her metamorphosis. Of her development as a person, and of the differences between her earlier and later career, she herself has written: "It frightens me to realize that, if I had died before the age of fity, I would have died a 'Negro' fraction." [37]

Gwendolyn Brooks in her earlier period is rather like Tolson in that while her main subject matter is black, her style is for the most part academic and mannered. She is often difficult, though not as difficult as Tolson. Like Tolson, she sometimes dons a Greek mask, as in her titles "The Anniad" (Iliad, Aeneid) and *The Bean Eaters* (Lotus Eaters), which in the Afro-American context come off as precious and affected. Much of the time her language is unflavored academic English ("Consumption's spiritless expectoration; / An indignant robin's resolute donation / Pinching a track through apathy and din"),[38] occasionally emerging in awkward word coinages ("goldly," "bigly," "dim dears").[39] It is revealing that in preparing her *Selected Poems* (1963) she chose to omit (from *A Street in Bronzeville*) those poems which were strongest in Afro-American idiom: "Hattie Scott" (a five-poem sequence), "Queen of the Blues," and "Ballad of Pearl May Lee."

On the whole, the work of this earlier period is uneven. Much of it is governed by traditional western metrics, with regular stanzas and rhyme schemes, archaic diction, and inverted syntax. There is a tension between matter and manner which even her superior imagination and word mastery does not quite manage to resolve— a tension between her running theme of the life of the poor, her domestic settings and culinary images on the one hand, and her grand literary pose on the other. She hovers uneasily between imitation and parody, sometimes achieving bathos. "The Anniad," for example, is a narrative, in elevated language, concerning the adolescent dreams and mature love life of a "thaumaturgic lass [of] unembroidered brown" and her "man of tan." If it were less grim-faced, one might be inclined to call it an unsuccessful parody, rather than what it more readily appears to be—a serious attempt to engage European epic and romance traditions in this alien context. The poet's generally indeterminate tone, and her ambivalent attitude towards her characters, are well illustrated in "The Sundays of Satin-Legs Smith" and "The Anniad": with the former, she ranges from scorn and disapprobation to admiration; with the latter, she is too dispassionate for satire, but not distant enough to escape sentimentality.

All the same, passages of great beauty shine through in the early work. Her word-play is sometimes superbly felicitous:

> He never shall sally to Sally
> Nor soil any roofs of the town.[40]

> Not that success, for him, is sure, infallible.
> But never has he been afraid to reach.

His lesions are legion.
But reaching is his rule.[41]

She is a master of cadence and the elegant phrase. Of Satin-Legs Smith and his women (his personality revealed in his women) she writes:

Her affable extremes are like sweet bombs
About him, whom no middle grace or good
Could gratify. He had no education
In the quiet arts of compromise. He would
Not understand your counsels on control, nor
Thank you for your late trouble.[42]

And of their sexual union:

Her body is like new brown bread
Under the Woolworth mignonette.
Her body is a honey bowl
Whose waiting honey is deep and hot.
Her body is like summer earth,
Receptive, soft, and absolute . . .[43]

By the time Gwendolyn Brooks gets to *In the Mecca* her voice is sure, fresh, original. She strains neither for imitation nor for parody; the ghosts of Western literature have receded, been exorcised. There are no equivocations, no cautious hide-and-seek:

Way-out Morgan is collecting guns
in a tiny fourth-floor room.
He is not hungry, ever, though sinfully lean.
He flourishes, ever, on porridge or pat of bean
pudding or wiener soup—fills fearsomely
on visions of Death-to-the-Hordes-of-the-White-Men!
Death!
(This is the Maxim painted in big black
above a bed bought at a Champlain rummage sale.)
Remembering three local-and-legal beatings, he
rubs his hands in glee,
does Way-out Morgan. Remembering his Sister

> mob-raped in Mississippi, Way-out Morgan
> smacks sweet his lips and adds another gun
> and listens to Blackness stern and blunt and beautiful,
> organ-rich Blackness telling a terrible story.
> Way-out Morgan
> predicts the Day of Debt-pay shall begin,
> the Day of Demon-diamond,
> of blood in mouths and body-mouths,
> of flesh-rip in the Forum of Justice at last!
> Remembering mates in the Mississippi River,
> mates with black bodies once majestic, Way-out
> postpones a yellow woman in his bed, postpones
> wetnesses and little cries and stomachings—
> to consider Ruin. [44]

Her language is still a metaphoric, "invented" language, not colloquial, not rooted in Afro-American idiom, but far less difficult, less
artificially mannered and pretty. Her mode of thought and articulation has become like a diamond—hard, sharp, brilliant.

> The Black Philosopher says
> "Our chains are in the keep of the Keeper
> in a labeled cabinet
> on the second shelf by the cookies,
> sonatas, the arabesques. . . .
> There's a rattle, sometimes.
> You do not hear it who mind only
> cookies and crunch them.
> You do not hear the remarkable music—'A
> Death Song For You Before You Die.'
> If you could hear it
> you would make music too.
> The *black*blues." [45]

She has abandoned the habit of syntactic jugglery, made her vices
over into virtues. The measured cadence is still there, but now it
dances free and unimpeded with the free verse, no longer tied to
the will of metric and rhyme patterns. In her later work Gwendo-

lyn Brooks is possessed by a furious eloquence. She speaks in tongues, and her utterances are oracular—controlled, but controlled within an immense poetic universe, not within the claustrophobic cubicles of her earlier work. In "Speech to the Young. Speech to the Progress-Toward," she admonishes her children:

> Say to them,
> say to the down-keepers,
> the sun-slappers,
> the self-soilers,
> the harmony-hushers,
> "Even if you are not ready for day
> it cannot always be night."
> You will be right.
> For that is the hard home-run.
>
> And remember:
> live not for Battles Won.
> Live not for The-End-of-the-Song.
> Live in the along.[46]

By any reckoning, not least of all by her own reckoning, Gwendolyn Brooks must be counted fortunate to have lived long enough and had the strength and humility to participate as creature and creator in the black transformation of the 60s and 70s.

If the middle generation, or, more specifically, these three leading poets of the middle generation, did not learn enough from Hughes and the oral tradition, the younger generation, happily, did. In addition, the younger generation has been influenced by the white avant-garde movements of this century, via Amiri Baraka (LeRoi Jones). Baraka is the pathfinder and chief theoretician of the black arts renaissance of the late 1960s and the 70s, and a figure of seminal importance in contemporary Afro-American thought. He began his career in the late 50s as a Beat Generation poet, especially influenced by German philosophy and the European symbolists, surrealists, and dadaists, and by the idiosyncratic, pictographic verse experiments of E. E. Cummings and William Carlos Williams. Besides European influences, the Beat poets, white and black (Bob Kaufman and Ted Joans were the other leading black poets among the Beats), were heavily indebted to Langston Hughes and Afro-American oral tradition, and to the free verse of Walt Whitman and the jazz poetry of Vachel Lindsay and Carl Sandburg. Adopting saxophonist Charlie Parker as their patron saint, they popularized the poetry-and-jazz convention which Hughes had practiced quietly for decades, establishing cultic coffee houses in New York and San Francisco where they read their works to musical accompaniment.

Like much Beat poetry, Baraka's early work is characterized by the bohemian posturings and narcissistic navel-gazing of the artist-as-outsider-martyr, accompanied by verbal obscenities-as-rebellion ("throwing America's shit in its face," as it were). The work is largely autobiographical and confessional, death-obsessed, sex-obsessed, pervaded by a fashionable existential despair. In contrast to Allen Ginsberg, the prime poetic voice of the movement, who hurled fiery jeremiads at a bellicose and materialist America ("Moloch! Solitude! Filth! Ugliness! Ashcans and unobtainable dollars! . . . / Moloch whose mind is pure machinery! Moloch whose blood is running money! Moloch whose fingers are ten armies!"),[47] Baraka's early voice was muted and introspective, concerned with self-definition:

> . . . . It's impos-
> sible to be an artist and a bread
> winner at the same time.[48]
>
> If I think myself
> strong, then I am
> not true to the misery
> in my life. . . . If

> I think myself ugly
> & go to the mirror, smiling,
> at the inaccuracy . . . I think
> how very wise I am.[49]

He reaches for reconnection with his African past, and for an inclusive definition of black identity, but abandons that effort in frustration:

> African blues
> does not know me. Their steps, in sands
> of their own
> land. . . . Does
> not feel
> what I am. . . . Those
> heads, I call
> my "people."
>   (And who are they. People. To concern
> myself, ugly man. . . . My color
> is not theirs. Lighter, white man
> talk. They shy away. My own
> dead souls, my, so called
> people. Africa
> is a foreign place. You are
> as any other sad man here
> american.[50]

It is instructive to compare "Notes for a Speech," quoted above, with Hughes's "Afro-American Fragment," [51] a comparably early poem. In that poem, Hughes concludes that though time-distanced and not fully understood, Africa is nevertheless a potent reality in the Afro-American soul-psyche, a conclusion which carries an implicit optimism, an expectation of conscious rediscovery and recovery of the African heritage in the future.

During these early years, Baraka's rage, for which he is to become quite famous, is not yet public, is still concealed, repressed, and limitedly personal. But already he is aware of its intensity and potential vastness:

> There is something
> in me so cruel, so
> silent. It hesitates
> to sit on the grass
> with the young white
> > virgins
> of my time. The blood-
> letter, clothed in what
> it is. [52]

A few years later, that "something" emerges like a shark from the blurred and murky depths of the sea-soul into the surface transparency in "Black Dada Nihilismus":

> . . . A cult of death,
>
> need of the simple striking arm under
> the streetlamp. The cutters, from under
> their rented earth. Come up, black dada
>
> nihilismus. Rape the white girls. Rape
> their fathers. Cut the mothers' throats. [53]

What is envisioned is a ritual bloodletting against all that is false and dead, specifically white Christian civilization. The racial desire for revenge against the accumulated injuries of centuries has merged with a cosmic sense of religious duty to cleanse the earth of pollution and return it to primal innocence. To fulfill this dual vision an alliance must be forged with all those antagonistic to the West, and the strength must be tapped from the spiritual heritage of the oppressed, their gods, philosophies, and world-view providing an alternative order to replace the West's. And so the poet makes a pledge and offers a prayer to Damballah as arch-god representative of the African peoples:

> (may a lost god damballah, rest or save us
> against the murders we intend
> against his lost white children
> black dada nihilismus [54]

The conflict which began with "something . . . cruel" in the heart and activated in the "simple striking arm" of one man, has grown to encompass worlds. Later, the poet will name it a "jihad," a holy war of believers against infidels, of men against beasts, of nature against freaks ("This is a soulless beast, Jacoub. . . . Where the soul's print should be, there is only a cellulose pouch of disgusting habits").[55] It is a war of the forces of righteousness against the forces of evil, of God against the Devil:

> And so Brothers and Sisters, these beasts are still loose in the world.
> Still they spit their hideous cries. There are beasts in our world,
> Brothers and Sisters. There are beasts in our world. Let us find them
> and slay them. Let us lock them in their caves. Let us declare the
> Holy War. The Jihad. Or we cannot deserve to live. Izm-el-Azam.
> Izm-el-Azam. Izm-el-Azam. Izm-el-Azam. . . .[56]

It is this vision, first given in sketchy outline in "Black Dada Nihilismus," of an armaggeddon in which the present oppressive world order would be destroyed and a new world erected in its ashes, that propels Jones onto that perilous journey of phoenixlike self-consumption and regeneration from which he would emerge as Imamu Amiri Baraka, artist, priest, ideologue, formulator and disseminator of a Black Value System and a Black Esthetic, pan-African nationalist. The purgation process may be viewed in all its squalor and splendor in the Off-Broadway plays of his year of miracles, 1964: *Dutchman, The Slave, The Toilet, The Baptism. J-E-L-L-O* and *Experimental Death Unit #1*, plays of the same year, stand at the end of the transition-bridge, when the metamorphosis is virtually complete.

Baraka's metamorphosis distantly echoes Malcolm X's earlier transfiguration from hustler to teacher, pimp to preacher, sinner to savior. His journey follows the path blazed with such flaming passion by Malcolm, who more than any other single individual was responsible for the revolution in black consciousness in the 60s. Baraka is to become a Malcolm X of the arts, the Master's surrogate, a self-conscious disseminator and actualizer of Malcolm's teachings, just as in the 1920s Langston Hughes, though perhaps only half-consciously, served as the articulator and prime exemplar in the arts of the nationalist ideals of Marcus Garvey.

As would be expected, then, the productions of Baraka's second period are radically different from those of the first. Gone is the immoderate reverence for Western culture, and the self-abnegation that complemented it:

> I would take up painting
> if I cd think of a way to do it
> better than Leonardo. Than Bosch.
> Than Hogarth. Than Kline.[57]

In its place is a violent hatred for things white. He dismisses his early work as "a cloud of abstraction and disjointedness, that was just whiteness. European influence, etc., just as the concept of hopelessness and despair, from the dead minds the dying morality of Europe." [58] The self-conscious doubts as to his personal ugliness or beauty are drowned in the overwhelming assurance which swept black America in the 60s of the collective beauty of black people: "We are all beautiful (except white / people, they are full of, and made of / shit)"; [59] "Back home the black women are all beautiful, / . . . Even with all that grease / in their heads." [60] Black art should hold among its priorities the exorcising of self-doubt so the beauty can shine through. The black artist should "change the images his people identify with, by aserting Black feeling, Black mind, Black judgment." [61] "And if the beautiful see themselves, they will love themselves." [62] Earlier equivocations regarding heritage have been replaced by confidence and pride in an African identity:

> We are beautiful people
> with african imaginations
> full of masks and dances and swelling chants

with african eyes, and noses, and arms,
though we sprawl in grey chains in a place
full of winters, when what we want is sun.

We have been captured,
brothers. And we labor
to make our getaway, into
the ancient image, into a new

correspondence with ourselves
and our black family. We need magic
now we need the spells, to raise up
return, destroy, and create. What will be

the sacred words? [63]

Baraka calls for a political, revolutionary theatre that would "Accuse and Attack anything that can be accused and attacked" [64]—white liberals, white racists, white world-owners ("these dim-witted fatbellied white guys who somehow believe that the rest of the world is here for them to slobber on"); [65] black liberals, black Uncle Toms, black academics with white minds, black folks with white values. He wants an instrumental art, an art-weapon that would help slay them.

We want "poems that kill."
Assassin poems, Poems that shoot
guns. Poems that wrestle cops into alleys
and take their weapons leaving them dead
with tongues pulled out and sent to Ireland. Knockoff
poems for dope selling wops or slick halfwhite
politicians [66]

He counsels the impoverished masses, with no access to "unobtainable dollars," to take by force whatever they need from white people:

you cant steal nothin from a white man, he's already stole it he owes you anything you want, even his life. All the stores will open if you will say the magic words. The magic words are: Up against the wall mother fucker this is a stick up! Or: Smash the window at night (these are magic actions) smash the windows daytime, anytime, together, let's smash the window drag the shit from in there. No money down. No time to pay.[67]

And he calls all black people to come together, to come back home unto themselves, to know and love themselves and one another, to unite and build up their black nation within the white American nation (the black nation has always been there, dormant, inactive, needing to be activated and strengthened), their black nation that would eventually topple and supersede the white nation:

> Time to get
> together
> time to be one strong fast black energy space
>   one pulsating positive magnetism, rising
> time to get up and
> be
> come
> be
> come. . . .
> the black man is the future of the world. . . .
>
> niggers come out, brothers are we
>   with you and your sons your daughters are ours
>   and we are the same, all the blackness from one black allah
>   when the world is clear you'll be with us
>   come out niggers come out
>   come out niggers come out
>
> It's nation time eye ime
>   it's nation ti eye ime
>   chant with bells and drum
>   its nation time
>
> It's nation time, get up santa claus   (repeat)
>   it's nation time, build it
>   get up muffet dragger
>   get up rastus for real to be rasta farari
>   ras jua
>   get up got here bow

It's Nation
Time! [68]

In almost every instance, Baraka practiced what he preached. His own plays, and his work at the short-lived Black Arts Theatre in Harlem (1965) and, later, at his Spirit House in Newark, helped to touch off a renaissance in black drama and other arts, resulting in the rise of small black community theatres across the nation and the emergence of a mass of new theatrical talent, including playwrights Ben Caldwell, Ron Milner, N. R. Davidson, and most notably Ed Bullins, the most prolific and sophisticated of them, who served as resident playwright at the New Lafayette Theatre in Harlem for the duration of its life, 1967–72. Baraka's poetry similarly inspired a galaxy of new talent, among them Larry Neal, Don Lee, Sonia Sanchez, Nikki Giovanni, Marvin X, Askia Muhammed Touré, and South African poet-in-exile Keorapetse Kgositsile.

Like other political thinkers and activists of his generation and of generations before him, Baraka is not always clear or consistent in his ideas on black nationhood. Under pressure of public events and his own practical experience, his ideas have continued to evolve, divide, re-form and combine with a welter of other visions of nationalism and definitions of black power. [69] But on the whole, it would appear that the black nation as he sees it *in practice* would be activated with the acquisition of control of the political, social, and economic institutions in predominantly black communities, proceeding from that base to the exercise of power in the national and international arenas. The struggle for black power in America and the struggle for full liberation from neocolonialism on the African mainland would complement and somehow benefit each other.

Clearly, the black struggle, however well conceived or ill-defined, is no easy task, and Baraka has no illusions that it is. His intense local organizational work has wrought no spectacular changes in his hometown of Newark, New Jersey, but it has helped win a measure of political and economic power for the black community there—a necessary first half-step in the direction of his vast goal. And the struggle continues.

In his later poetry Baraka refers to his past from time to time as a reminder to himself and his readers of a loss of self that should never be repeated.

> Shacked up with a fat jew girl. Talking about
> Shakespeare, I didn't hear
> you brother. . . . And rode was rode
> by the cows and intelligent snakes of the age. . . .
> I strode with them, played with them, thought myself
> one with them, and jews were talking through
> my mouth. . . .[70]

When he was still groping for himself in *The Dead Lecturer* (1964), he had wondered just "who will they mean . . . / When they say, 'It is Roi / who is dead?' "[71] Now he knows who he is and what legacy he wishes to leave behind him; but he also acknowledges, with humility, that the past is indelible, can never be totally effaced, that his transformation is incomplete, that no human transformation can be complete:

> When I die, the consciousness I carry I will to
> black people. May they pick me apart and take the
> useful parts, the sweet meat of my feelings. And leave
> the bitter bullshit rotten white parts
> alone.[72]

Baraka's voice is duplicated and amplified by the younger black poets who came to maturity in his tight and potent shadow in the late 60s. These poets are, along with Baraka, direct inheritors of Hughes's legacy. They work on the same principle Hughes did, now brought up to date and in process of being codified. Most of their work, too, is "racial in theme and treatment, derived from the life [they] know." In their work, they too "try to grasp and hold

some of the meanings and rhythms of jazz" as well as of rhythm
and blues ("soul"), of black preaching and street-corner oratory,
and of the new spirit-music of John Coltrane, Pharaoh Sanders,
and Sun-Ra. It is this generation that coined the phrase "Black
Esthetic," and they attempt to practice it, thereby answering
Hughes's early call in "The Negro Artist and the Racial Mountain."
They are, like Hughes, products of the oral tradition, deriving
their strength from the same sources. Their tone is of course more
militant, more defiant, with a clearly stated rejection of Western
values. Hughes was a believer in the American Dream; he just
wanted it fulfilled for blacks. But the literary generation of the late
60s and the 70s at best views the American Dream with cynicism.
Most of them do not believe that any healthy black dreams could
be fulfilled within the American system as presently established.
Where Hughes's work only implied the existence of a black nation
within the nation, the younger writers ardently proclaim it. "The
white man's heaven is the Black man's hell"; [73] and they urge their
people to withdraw their energies from the white nation (hell for
the black man) and invest them in building up the black nation.

Most of the younger writers have been influenced by the
teachings of Elijah Muhammad and his Nation of Islam, and Elijah
was influenced by Marcus Garvey, who in turn was influenced by
Booker T. Washington, especially in his economic program, which
the Muslims adopted. Muslim influence has been either direct,
through membership, as in the case of Marvin X, or indirect,
through dissemination by Malcolm X.

Like Hughes, the younger writers dramatize and expose black
life in all its wretchedness and exultant beauty; but *exhortation* is
their primary domain. Their voice is urgent, their threat specific,
their promise near. They call for all kinds of necessary and immediate action: come together, black people, come together; change;
stop knifing each other on Saturday nights; stop shooting each
other for the CIA; kill the real enemy for a change; change; stop

wasting the wealth you don't have on liquor, the health you do
have on dope; stop chasing white women and start loving your own
black women; change; get the white out of your hair and out of
your head; learn, baby, learn; stop talking revolution and start
doing something to bring about change; stop rapping and start
working; unite or die. . . .

> change-up
> let's go for ourselves
> both cheeks are broken now.
> change-up,
> move past the corner bar,
> let yr / spirit lift u above that quick high.
> change-up,
> that tooth pick you're sucking on was
> once a log.
> change-up,
> and yr / children will look at u differently
> than we looked at our parents. [74]

Many of the younger poets reject the blues—not indeed the
music but the posture of resignation and longsuffering. They acknowledge the oppressive circumstances which gave birth to the
blues, but argue that blues must now be replaced with a consciously political, *engagé* art—a view not unlike Hughes's,
especially during his heavily Marxist period in the 1930s. Ron
Karenga stated it this way:

It [art] must not teach us resignation. For all our art must contribute
to revolutionary change and if it does not, it is invalid.
    Therefore, we say the blues are invalid; for they teach resignation,
in a word acceptance of reality—and we have come to change reality.
. . . Perhaps people will object violently to the idea that the blues
are invalid, but one should understand that they are not invalid historically. They will always represent a very beautiful, musical and
psychological achievement of our people; but today they are not functional because they do not commit us to the struggle of today and tomorrow, but keep us in the past. And whatever we do, we cannot

remain in the past, for we have too much at stake in the present. And we find our future much too rewarding to be rejected.[75]

No more blues, writes Sonia Sanchez; "blues ain't culture / they sounds of / oppression /against the white man's / shit. . . . no mo / blue / trains running on this track / they all been de / railed." [76] And David Nelson:

> Ain't no time for Blues now
>> Blues have played and played out
> Ain't no time for Blues cause Blues is
>> Slow an' sad an' we need somethin'
>> Fast an' happy an' mad!!!!! . . . .
>
> Ain't no time for Blues now
>> Blues was for waking and enduring and suffering
> We need a new BLACK thing.[77]

"Blues exhibited illusions of manhood," writes Don Lee.

>> we ain't blue, we are black.
>> we ain't blue, we are black.
>>> (all the blues did was
>>> make me cry).[78]

His mother had advised him: "Don't Cry, Scream," and he does—

> scream-eeeeeeeeeeeeeee-ing
> SCREAM-EEEeeeeeeeeeee-ing   loud &
> SCREAM-EEEEEEEEEEEEEE-ing   long with
>   feeling—[79]

attempting to approximate the frantic energy, the "man images" of John Coltrane's revolutionary new music, itself a reflection of the "fast an' happy an' mad" tempo of the 60s.

The younger writers have appropriated the mythic power which Western symbology imputes to blackness, and the minstrel and other stereotypes have turned these inside out and transformed them into a salve for blacks, a poisoned spear against whites:

The Black artist must teach the White Eyes their deaths, and teach the black man how to bring those deaths about.

> We are unfair, and unfair.
> We are black magicians, black art
> s we make in black labs of the heart.

> The fair are
> fair, and death
> ly white.

> The day will not save them
> and we own
> the night. [80]

Finally, the younger poets have developed a new school of poetry reading, a style of delivery that brings together black preaching and oratory to the accompaniment of drums, jazz, or gospel music. The performance usually follows the classic leader-chorus pattern which is endemic to African and Afro-American music: the leader recites at rapid-fire pace, and those in the chorus dance, sing, chant, echo, shout, mock, and exhort. The words can be heard and understood, but the words soon cease to be more important than the concert of voices and music and the intense electricity of the performance as a whole.

Besides Baraka himself, the best known performers in this style are the four-man Harlem group, The Last Poets, both the original and subsequent groups of that name. Even though Baraka and a number of others were reading poetry in this style before they came into being, The Last Poets may be said to have popularized and established it, especially on phonodisc, television, and film. Of the poems first heard in this style, David Nelson's "Die Nigga" [81] and Omar ben Hassen's "Niggers Are Scared of Revolution" [82] are classics—in print, on stage, or on phonodisc. Their popularity heralded the production of similar recordings, most notably Gil Scott-Heron's "The Revolution Will Not Be Televised," [83] and

Nikki Giovanni's Warrior's Boast, "Ego Tripping," [84] both of which became popular record hits.

If Hughes were alive, he would surely be pleased at this development, for it is a fulfillment of his own lifelong dream of fusing his poetry with black music—although his own readings, with or without musical accompaniment, were by comparison sedate and uninvolved. The emergence of the "preacher style" of poetry reading is a testimony to the vigor of the folk traditions of which both Hughes and the younger poets are a part.

But no account of the black arts renaissance of the 1960s would be creditable without an acknowledgment of the indispensable role played by black publisher Dudley Randall and his Detroit-based Broadside Press. Himself an older poet of note, Mr. Randall originated his outfit for the printing of single-poem broadsides. But history made him into a "man of destiny," the right man with the right idea in the right place at the right time: he was flexible and imaginative enough to move rapidly from single-poem broadsides to small pamphlets of powerful, expressive poetry inexpensively produced and relatively easy to market. The general ferment in black communities across the nation provided him with an almost inexhaustible supply of good material and a new awakened public hungry for good black literature. A distribution system within the black community—bookshops, community cultural centers, and the poets themselves peddling their books at lectures and readings and street corners, all independent of the established distribution networks controlled by the large white publishing houses—demonstrated something of the possibilities of black-controlled publishing of black literature. Virtually all of the young black poets who gained national reputations and national followings between 1967 and 1972 were first and sometimes exclusively published by Broadside Press. This black control of black publishing, minimal as it has been in the case of Broadside Press (and its offshoot, Don Lee's Third World Press), has been of incalculable importance in insulating the movement from the pressure-demands of the "larger audience," thus making possible a degree of autonomous development unprecedented in the history of Afro-American literature.

All told, then, the similarities between Hughes and the younger generation are far greater than their differences. The angle of vision has shifted somewhat, but the target is the same: the liberation of black people from oppression, the restoration of the full humanity of black people in their own eyes. This is the goal to which Hughes's art and the art of the younger writers is dedicated. Hughes is one parent they know they need not be ashamed of. He is their well-thought father, they his well-taught children.

CHAPTER 7

Conclusion

Langston Hughes is quite possibly the most grossly misjudged poet of major importance in America. The American literary establishment, their lenses ground to formal complexity and trained on "mainstream" culture, when they acknowledge Hughes's existence at all, typically view him as a poor misguided soul laboring in an unrewarding "ethnic province," searching for an illusory "racial art." Hughes is dismissed as too simple, too quaintly humorous, unserious, unreflective, parochial, limited in scope, without a metaphysic and without profundity. And his least helpful critics have not all been white, either (it could be argued—or could it, really?—that whites are strangers to the oral tradition which Hughes represents). Two black critics of our own era will serve to illustrate what has so far been the dominant trend in Hughes criticism.

James Baldwin, reviewing Hughes's *Selected Poems* when it was published in 1959, declared himself "depressed" that Hughes "has done so little with . . . his genuine gifts." [1] "A more disciplined poet," he suggests, "would have thrown into the wastebasket . . . almost all of the last section"—a section consisting of eleven poems, including "I, Too," "Freedom Train," "Freedom's Plow," and "The Negro Mother," four of Hughes's best!

Baldwin is perturbed by Hughes's impersonality, by the distance he so frequently chooses to place between himself and the black life experiences he depicts. Hughes, he says, takes "refuge . . . in a fake simplicity in order to avoid the very difficult simplicity of the experience." One is tempted to dismiss this as just another of the meaningless paradoxes for which Baldwin is so famous. But no; for support, he cites the poem "Third Degree": [2]

> And one sometimes has the impression, as in a poem like "Third Degree"—which is about the beating up of a Negro boy in a police station—that Hughes has to hold the experience outside him in order to be able to write at all. And certainly this is understandable. Nevertheless, the poetic trick, so to speak, is to be within the experience and outside it at the same time—and the poem fails.

What is the "very difficult simplicity of the experience" which Hughes fails to capture? What makes the dramatic simplicity of his treatment of the experience "fake"? How do we know when a poet is "within the experience and outside it at the same time," and how does that differ either from the poet's placement in "Third Degree" or from the probable effects of that poem on the reader?

Baldwin's statement is much less astonishing when we remember that he is very much a writer of the autobiographical-confessional school, that in his own work he permits himself little or no distance from the experience—a procedure which he works to superb effect in his essays but which is partially responsible for the dismal failure of much of his fiction. As I have tried to show, "Third Degree" is deliberately stark and understated. The poet permits himself (and his protagonist) no tears, no self-pity, no raving and ranting, no eloquent denunciations of America's moral fibre or of "the system." His dispassionate coolness is the coolness of the blues. His psychic distancing is the same process whereby the bluesman of "Out of Work," denied relief by the WPA, is able to sidestep rhetoric and instead sing with a measure of ironic triumph:

A year and a day in this
Great big lonesome town!
I might starve for a year but
That extra day would get me down.

In "Third Degree," as so often, Hughes employs the distancing technique of the folk tradition, which ought to be to his credit, especially since the technique works. The poem *conveys* the experience of police brutality, and the victim's thoughts and emotions, *as a dramatic action.* One would have to be unusually insensitive not to think the victim's thoughts or feel the blows as they land. Successful drama or dramatic presentation, as in this poem, forces its audience to become actors as well as spectators, participants from inside and outside the experience at the same time. And that is no simple matter.

In the same review, Baldwin complains that Hughes "has not forced [black speech] into the realm of art where [its] meaning would become clear and overwhelming. 'Hey, pop! / Re-bop! / Mop!' conveys much more on Lenox Avenue than it does in this book, which is not the way it ought to be." In other words, black speech makes more sense to blacks, who inhabit Lenox Avenue, than it does to whites, the only readers of "this book" to whom the meaning of black speech might not be "clear and over-whelming"—especially since Baldwin seems to view black speech as above all a secret code, a system of "hieroglyphics" (his word) decipherable by blacks alone. And he says this ought not to be the case, that black speech ought not to make more sense to blacks than to whites (suddenly we're back to the old dead horse of "universality"!). Which is to say, at least judging from this review, that Baldwin sees the black artist as primarily, if not exclusively, an apostle to the gentiles (whites), a missionary-explainer of "what it means to be a Negro," a perpetual protester, an "orphic messenger" to the West. This conception of the black artist's primary responsibility and audience is, thankfully, passé. Although it was common enough in Hughes's own day, he certainly did not share it, as the closing paragraph of "The Negro Artist and the Racial Mountain" and his work of four decades make quite clear.

It should be pointed out that jazz musicians, from whom the phrase "Hey, pop! / Re-bop!" is borrowed, made and still make no effort to explain their idiom, musical or verbal, to white listeners. Would Baldwin say that they have therefore "not forced" that idiom "into the realm of art"? That if the meaning of their work is not "clear and overwhelming" outside Lenox Avenue, they must therefore be judged to have failed? And it's no use taking refuge in some cliché about music being some sort of "universal language" instantly understandable and enjoyable to alien audiences, which we all know very well it is not. If the demand to come out of the parochial "ethnic province," to decode the "hieroglyphics" of black art-speech so it can be understood by "all" (outside Lenox Avenue, that is), cannot legitimately be made on the black musician, how does anyone justify making that demand on the black writer?

In any case, as Hughes argued in his Spingarn speech, there is nothing especially provincial or parochial about black life or black speech. The communication of private meaning is hardly the most important function of black speech. Black speech is not always in code, not even most of the time; and when it is, it is not always deliberately so, slavery and continued white hostility notwithstanding. On the contrary, by far the greater portion of black speech is understandable to and understood by whites. At the very least, that portion of it which Hughes uses, including the scat singing of "Hey, pop! / Re-bop!," can be understood by anyone who cares to. As Baldwin himself pointed out in his essay "Stranger in the Village," [3] white Americans, by their long centuries of intimate association with blacks, could never, as their European cousins perhaps could, rightly claim innocence or ignorance of the meaning of black life. If they are ignorant, it is because they choose to be so (and to keep their children so). Their claims of innocence will always be spurious, whether in politics ("What do you people want?"), or in art ("Hey, pop! / Re-bop! / Mop! / Y-e-a-h!").

The claim that black speech or music is in need of clarification outside the black community, or that its validity depends upon such clarification, is even less tenable when one considers that for over fifty years black music has penetrated and influenced practically every aspect of America's musical life, the chief exception being the marble symphony halls where European "classical" music is supported with tax dollars and tax-exempt dollars for the enjoyment of the few; that black music earns millions of dollars each year for the white controllers of the industry (rarely for the black artists—blacks make the product, whites own it, much as in slavery days); and that all-American white "standard English" continually augments and vitalizes itself with huge dosages of those same unreconstructed, unmellowed "hieroglyphics" of black speech.

In short, Baldwin asks the wrong questions, poses the wrong problems, makes illegitimate demands upon Hughes's art, and evaluates it with criteria that are untenable and invalid.

Nathan Huggins, writing ten years later, presses somewhat similar charges:

> One would be right in saying that Langston Hughes backed out of the Negro-artist dilemma by choosing not to deal with art as serious "high culture." His casual and almost anti-intellectual attitude about art permitted him a wide freedom of subject and a personal honesty. It allowed him to make the very important point that the people's language, and voice, and rhythms were legitimate stuff of poetry. But this same freedom deprived him of the control and mastery that might make each (or indeed any) of his poems really singular. Langston Hughes avoided the Scylla of formalism only to founder in the Charybdis of folk art.[4]

One could respond to Huggins's assessment in one of three ways. One could, for instance, work up a definition of the "really singular" poem, then proceed to point out and analyse those of Hughes's poems which meet the definition. Or one could argue that a poet does not have to write "really singular" poems, that it is quite possible to be a good or even great poet without writing any "really singular" poems (and perhaps name a few such great poets); that a poet's greatness may reside not in isolated single poems, but in whole books or sequences of poems, such as Hughes's *Montage of a Dream Deferred* or the "Madam" poems, or even in the totality of a poet's work, his *oeuvre*. A third approach is simply to ignore the assessment, somewhat in the same spirit (unfortunately) as one might ignore Selden Rodman when he writes:

> Until recently there hasn't been any Afro-American verse that was more than that—verse. When I was editing anthologies in 1938, and again in 1946, I remember going through the complete works of Countee Cullen, Claude McKay, Langston Hughes, and the others, hoping desperately to find a *poem*, and falling back reluctantly on the spirituals and blues. . . .[5]

(Well! Even Winston Churchill, and during those same years, found a poem by Claude McKay that he could use. But then, Churchill was not an American anthologist!). Rodman, like Huggins, searched through Hughes and did not find a "really singular" poem, not even a half-way decent poem worthy of inclusion in an anthology of American poetry! Another anthologist gave the following reason for excluding black poets: "We couldn't agree on *which black poet* to include." [6] Note that it is not even *poets*, but *poet*. Is the search for the singular poem really very different from the search for the singular (token) poet?

Some will say that I am unfair to Huggins, bracketing him with these dumb white critics. But then, it is Huggins who, in an otherwise brilliant study of the Harlem Renaissance, casually dismisses the whole movement and era in these words: "nothing that was produced then can compare with the fruits of recent years" [7]—a judgment which just happens to coincide with Selden

Rodman's assertion (in 1969) that no poetry worthy of the name was written by Afro-Americans "until recently." This judgment, whether rendered by a white critic or a black one, would in effect exclude from the canon of American literature Langston Hughes's poetry, Jean Toomer's *Cane*, and James Weldon Johnson's *God's Trombones*. True, the Harlem Renaissance fell short of its promise; but to dismiss it so completely is, to say the least, foolhardy.

It might be useful, just as an exercise in perspective, to compare ever so briefly, say, Hughes's "Madam" poems with T. S. Eliot's "The Love Song of J. Alfred Prufrock" [8] and Ezra Pound's "Hugh Selwyn Mauberley." [9] Each of these poems is far more complex, obviously, than whatever aspects of them one might choose to isolate for a brief comparison. At least two approaches would seem to be in order: one could treat all three poems as though their visions and esthetics were the same, and on that basis decide how far each poem succeeds or fails; or one could point out their differences of vision and esthetic which would preclude identical expectations on the part of the reader. Using the first approach, one could take, for instance, the matter of incapacity for love in "Madam" ("Madam and Her Might-Have-Been") and "Prufrock," and perhaps properly conclude that "Madam" affords the reader a more profound insight into human realities than "Prufrock" does. Alberta's incapacity for love issues from her disillusion from hard experiences. Her disappointments have driven her to the conclusion that love is selfish and exploitative; and when therefore she encounters something that does not conform to what she has come to believe is love's reality, she is intimidated by it, rejects it and takes refuge behind a dehumanizing shield of paranoia.

Prufrock, on the other hand, appears to be the victim of a chronic psychological disease. Despite its sonorous phrases, the poem is devoid of ultimate insight—insight, that is, into the social, environmental, or genetic foundations of the disease. The disease itself—Prufrock's neurotic inability to make advances to a woman—is fully described; we feel its quality and see its (non-) results. But whereas "Madam" not only exhibits something of the hard-bitten numbness of the protagonist but also the kind of teeth and slant of bite, "Prufrock" forces the reader to look outside the poem for some explanation of essential causes—to look to the author's (non-existent) notes, to the popular Freudianism of the day, or to some inadequate post-Victorian notion of *l'homme moderne*.

The second (broader) approach would seem, on the whole, more fruitful. All three poems deal with the life experiences (struggles) of the protagonist, but the experiential grid of each, as embodied in the incidents, is different. "Madam" is a journey of the sensibility through the harsh urban ghetto of black America, "Mauberley" a journey through the harsh literary world of Edwardian London, and "Prufrock" a journey through one man's tortured psyche. The essential trait of each protagonist is successfully presented: Madam's unassailable resilience, Mauberley's mocking brashness and confident superiority, and Prufrock's Hamletian indecisiveness. These are qualities of the poems as much as of their protagonists. Each poem is consistent in language, tone, and attitude with the socio-psychological milieu which it explores: the nitty-gritty ghetto dialect and sassy humor, the cynical polished talk of literary London, and the bookish ruminations of Prufrock's active mind in inactive body. In short, to fault one poem for not being more like the other, for not dealing with the matter and in the manner of the other, is to err in judgment.

Hughes's social and philosophical universe is no more circumscribed or parochial than the universes of Aeschylus, Aristophanes, Dante, Shakespeare, Milton, Wordsworth, Keats, Whitman, Dostoevsky, Hopkins, Joyce, Pound, Eliot, Gide, or Sartre. His philosophical system, the hidden infrastructure of ideas and procedures over and around and onto which his art is molded, is as firm, complete, autonomous, and valid as theirs. Entry into the particular world of any of these writers, Hughes included, is accomplished only by an effort of the imagination. The black life experiences which Hughes soul-mirrors may indeed be foreign and distant to white readers; but how close or familiar to black readers is the spiritual dessication and emotional emptiness of the white middle and upper classes which Eliot repeatedly mourns in his poetry, or the details of European history, mythology, literature, and art which Pound so copiously copies into his? It is only by an effort of the imagination—by projection of the self into an alien environment, by deliberate assumption of alien perspectives, by sympathetic identification—that a 20th-century reader in any part of the black world could comfortably enter into the world of the *Divina Commedia, Hamlet, Paradise Lost, Ulysses, The Waste Land,* or *L'Immoraliste.* Hughes's *Montage of a Dream Deferred,* or his *Ask Your Mama,* or any other black work of magnitude, exacts an equivalent white effort.

A well-worded rebuke to the excessive devotion to formal complexity, which characterizes the modernist sensibility and which is largely responsible for the low esteem of Hughes's poetry among the critics, is now and always in order. Regardless what the elitist, antidemocratic, modernist schoolmen think and teach, poetic value is not commensurate with difficulty of comprehension, nor with erudition exhibited in masses of esoterica and obscure allusions, nor with the paucity of the audience to whom a poet chooses to address his work. Hughes did not choose to address his work to little circles of "experts," nor to members of some secret society of "Art." His aim, to borrow the happy phrase of the younger generation, was to unite the academy and the street—to write in such a way that both the minimally educated and the maximally schooled would find themselves maximally rewarded in reading his work. And his poetry is evidence, if evidence were needed, that even in the 20th century lucidity of surface and depth of meaning are not mutually exclusive.

As Margaret Larkin noted in an early review, Hughes's work represents a contribution to the effort in the early part of this century to free poetry "from the stiff conventions which Anglo-Saxon prosody inflicted upon it." [10] What Pound and Eliot, taking their cue from Whitman, did for poetry using standard English, Hughes, taking his cue from Dunbar, Sandburg, and Lindsay, did for it using black English. Hughes participated in the task of exploding the old boundaries of poetry in English by infusing it with a black sensibility independent of the received stereotypes, by expanding it to accommodate the black experience and language and style. This is his particular achievement as a prosodist, that in spite of the nay-sayers, white and black, he succeeded in bringing into the overall poetic arena, away from the locus of side-shows, such forms as the jazz poem, the blues poem, the sermon, the gospel shout, and the exhortatory call-and-response of black theatre. By so doing, Hughes helped pave the way for the Beat movement of the 50s, for the Black Arts revolution of the 60s and 70s whose impact on white American poetry and drama is yet to be measured, and for the burgeoning Ethnopoetics movement of the 70s. The ethnopoets, led by Jerome Rothenberg, [11] are successors to the Beats and fellow-laborers with the black poets in the same vast vineyard, in a universe of poetry whose substance and example is all of the primal word-deeds of the world's vast variety of cultures. Their emphasis, both as translators and as original poets, is on the oral act, on performance, on the poem as noumenal sound rather than as written letter. In these movements which Hughes preceded and influenced, the unification of written with oral poetry is for the first time a realistic possibility.

Hughes's poetry exhibits many of the characteristics of oral poetry the world over. [12] It is marked by an economy of means, by an almost ruthless exclusion of extraneous embellishments, resulting in a lean, spare, uncluttered style, and in efficient structure and logistics that permit no tedious or unnecessary diversions. Its commitment to the auditory, which in oral poetry is primary and definitive, and to a popular mass audience, makes indispensable a lucidity of surface, normal syntax, a contemporary and colloquial rather than archaic or learned idiom, and vivid, concrete, and evocative imagery—in short, felicitous speech and mellifluous motion. Hughes's poetry is to be commended both for its fidelity to traditional forms and themes and for its transposition, manipulation, and adaptation of them.

Hughes's technically efficient poetic machinery, modeled on and assembled with parts borrowed from the oral tradition, is in the service of a sweeping social vision, is a vehicle for moving matters that are of importance to the poet's community. Hughes is very much aware of his historical placement, of the imperatives of his *race, moment, milieu;* and he makes his art respond to those imperatives, which include the raising of consciousness among an oppressed people, the affirmation, conservation, and onward transmission of their culture, and the battling of injustice through exposition and protest. The black artist's mission, as Hughes originally defined it for himself and his contemporaries in "The Negro Artist and the Racial Mountain," calls for depth of vision, breadth of sympathies, passion, and courage. Hughes's passion and courage are obvious from the tenacity of his views and methods, but the intensity of his anger is not, mainly because he usually holds it at a distance, controlled and barricaded behind the sardonic humor of the blues, wrapped in irony, satire, wit and a general playfulness:

> This mornin' for breakfast
> I chawed de mornin' air.
> This mornin' for breakfast
> Chawed de mornin' air.

> But this evenin' for supper
> I got evenin' air to spare. [13]

> Great names for crowns and garlands!
>   Yeah!
> I love Ralph Bunche—
> But I can't eat him for lunch. [14]

Hughes wears a genial mask that fits so well it is possible to mistake it for his face. But a careful second glance, even without a visit to the backstage dressing room, is enough to reveal a man burning with a rage as absolute as the fiery furnaces of LeRoi Jones or Sonia Sanchez. Indeed, we miss Hughes's rage only if we wilfully elect to concentrate on his humor. Usually he manages to mold his anger into the porcelain of his poetry—but without blunting its sharp and bitter edges; on the contrary, the jagged edges stand out even more fiercely against the smoothness:

> I could tell you,
> If I wanted to,
> What makes me
> What I am.

> But I don't
> Really want to—
> And you don't
> Give a damn. [15]

I said before that Hughes's work is swept by the two positive compulsions or radical energies which may be said to dominate Afro-American literature—in its impulse toward the oral tradition and toward a literature of social struggle. Much of Afro-American literature of any consequence utilizes and projects black folk culture to a greater or lesser degree, and handles its matter in a way that would enhance the black struggle. In a sense the two propositions are one or can become one: some works hold the two impulses in equilibrium, give them more or less equal play, or fuse and compel them to function as an undifferentiated whole. This is the case with Hughes. In his work these dual energies are not only greatly visible, prolonged, and relentless in their operation, but they are held in balance and quite often fused, so that the form becomes the function, the instrument the purpose, the medium the message. In Hughes, black folk culture is the weapon, black social and economic sufficiency the prize fought for. By utilizing the black heritage so fully in his work, Hughes preserves and transmits that heritage and thereby aids the survival of Afro-Americans as a distinct people. One of the far-reaching effects of his esthetic, and of its elaborations and extensions by others, is to compel us, in evaluating a black writer, to take into account his attitude to himself and his people and heritage, and what use he makes or fails to make of that heritage. In other words, we must consider the presence, balance, and power of the positive compulsions in his work. Perhaps more than any other writer of his generation, Hughes permits these positive energies the most uninhibited, prolonged and unified play.

Notes

PREFACE

1. J. Saunders Redding, *To Make a Poet Black* (Chapel Hill, University of North Carolina Press, 1939), p. 3.

2. See Addison Gayle, Jr., ed., *The Black Aesthetic* (New York, Doubleday, 1971); LeRoi Jones, *Home: Social Essays* (New York, William Morrow, 1966).

CHAPTER 1: HUGHES'S BLACK ESTHETIC

1. Cullen, "The Shroud of Color," *Color* (New York, Harper, 1925), pp. 26–35.

2. Hughes, "Color," *Jim Crow's Last Stand* (Atlanta, Negro Publication Society, 1943), p. 7.

3. See Hughes, "The Negro Artist and the Racial Mountain," *The Nation*, June 23, 1926, pp. 692–94. For an account of the influence of Langston Hughes and other writers of the Harlem Renaissance on Leopold Senghor, Aimé Césaire, and Leon Damas, the founders of the *negritude* movement, see Lilyan Kesteloot, *Black Writers in French: A Literary History of Negritude*, tr. Ellen Conroy Kennedy (Philadelphia, Temple University Press, 1974), pp. 55–74.

4. W. E. B. DuBois, *The Souls of Black Folk* [1903] (New York, New American Library, 1969), p. 45.

5. George S. Schuyler, "The Negro-Art Hokum," *The Nation*, June 16, 1926, pp. 662–63.

6. Ibid.

7. See Melville J. Herskovits, *The Myth of the Negro Past* [1941] (Boston, Beacon, 1958).

8. Herskovits, "The Negro's Americanism," in Alain Locke, ed., *The New Negro* [1925] (New York, Atheneum, 1968), pp. 353–60.

9. Countee Cullen, interview with Lester Walton, *The World*, May 15, 1927, p. 16M. See also Nathan Huggins, *Harlem Renaissance* (New York, Oxford Univ. Press, 1971), p. 209.

10. "Countee Cullen," *Chicago Bee*, December 24, 1927.

11. Claude McKay, *A Long Way From Home* [1937] (New York, Harcourt, Brace, 1970), p. 27.

12. Ibid., p. 28.

13. See Hippolyte-Adolphe Taine, Introduction to his *History of English Literature* (1863).

14. *The Nation*, June 23, 1926, pp. 692–94. Reprinted in Addison Gayle, *The Black Aesthetic*, pp. 167–72.

15. "Langston Hughes Speaks," *Negro Digest*, May 1953, p. 279. A selection of Hughes's proletarian pieces was recently published under the title *Good Morning Revolution: Uncollected Writings of Social Protest*, ed. Faith Berry (New York, Lawrence Hill, 1973). "Langston Hughes Speaks" is reprinted on pp. 143–45.

16. Hughes, "To Negro Writers," in Henry Hart, ed., *American Writers' Congress* (New York, International Publishers, 1935), pp. 139–41. Reprinted in *Good Morning Revolution*, pp. 125–26.

17. Hughes, "Letter to the Academy," *International Literature*, July 1933, p. 112. Reprinted in *Good Morning Revolution*, p. 3.

18. Hughes, "The Negro," in Jacob Burck, *Hunger and Revolt: Cartoons by Burck* (New York, The Daily Worker, 1935), pp. 141–42.

19. "To Negro Writers."

20. "Langston Hughes Speaks."

21. See *Good Morning Revolution*.

22. Hughes, "My Adventures as a Social Poet," *Phylon*, 8, No. 3 (1947), pp. 205–12. Reprinted in *Good Morning Revolution*, pp. 135–43.

23. "Some Practical Observations: A Colloquy," *Phylon*, 11, No. 4 (Winter 1950), p. 307.

24. The terms "social poetry" and "lyric poetry" are misleading in that "social poetry" may be lyrical and "lyric poetry" may deal with matters of social and political weight. Certainly such is the case in Hughes's poetry, as, for instance, in his "Dream Variation" and "Our Land" (*The Weary Blues* [New York, Knopf, 1926], pp. 43, 99), or in "Sweet Words on Race," "Dream Dust," and "Slum Dreams" (*The Panther and the Lash* [New York, Knopf, 1967], pp. 75, 93, 95). But these are Hughes's own terms, and I find them useful in distinguishing two broad categories of his poetry: "social poetry" for those poems which are preeminently social and / or "racial," i.e., those with immediate socio-political import as well as those modeled on black folk song forms such as jazz, blues, ballads, and gospel; and "lyric poetry" for poems that are not modeled on black folk forms and that are more private and personal than public and political. Thus, blues poems, though lyrical and private, would be classifiable as "social poetry" because of their black folk song form, whereas poems like "Sport" (*Fine Clothes to the Jew* [New York, Knopf, 1927], p.

40) and "Drum" (*Dear Lovely Death* [Amenia, New York, Troutbeck Press, 1931], n.p.), though drawing their images from black music, are primarily private and therefore "lyric." By the same token, "When Sue Wears Red" (*Weary Blues*, p. 66), whose form and spirit derive from gospel, is primarily a love poem and therefore "lyric."

25. Charles S. Johnson, "The Negro Enters Literature," *The Carolina Magazine*, May 1927, pp. 3–9, 44–48.

26. Hughes, *The Big Sea* [1940] (New York, Hill and Wang, 1963), p. 263.

27. "My Adventures as a Social Poet."

28. "Is Hollywood Fair to Negroes?," *Negro Digest*, April 1943, pp. 19–21.

29. "The Task of the Negro Writer as an Artist," *Negro Digest*, April 1965, pp. 65, 75. Italics in original.

30. Ibid.

31. Hughes, "Jazz as Communication," *The Langston Hughes Reader* (New York, George Braziller, 1958), pp. 492–94.

32. See Alain Locke, *The Negro and His Music* [1936] (New York, Arno, 1969); Marshall Stearns, *The Story of Jazz* (Oxford Univ. Press, 1956); Andre Hodeir, *Jazz: Its Evolution and Essence* (New York, Grove, 1956); Gunther Schuller, *Early Jazz* (Oxford Univ. Press, 1967); Maude Cuney-Hare, *Negro Musicians and Their Music* (New York, Associated Publishers, 1936).

33. *Big Sea*, p. 62.

34. Ibid., p. 85.

35. "Lenox Avenue: Midnight," *Weary Blues*, p. 39.

36. Ibid.

37. "Jazz as Communication."

38. Ibid. This rebuke, sometimes attributed to Fats Waller, is part of jazz lore.

39. Ibid.

40. "Lady's Boogie," *Montage of a Dream Deferred* (New York, Henry Holt, 1951), p. 44.

41. J. A. Rogers, "Jazz at Home," in Locke, *The New Negro*, pp. 216–24.

42. "Jazz as Communication."

43. Ibid.

44. Epigraph, *Big Sea*.

45. Ibid., p. 335.

46. Quoted in Nat Hentoff, "Langston Hughes: He Found Poetry in the Blues," *Mayfair*, August 1958, pp. 27 ff.

47. Hughes's phrase, used as a section title in his *Selected Poems* (New York, Knopf, 1959), p. 31.

48. Hughes, "White Folks Do the Funniest Things," *Negro Digest*, February 1944, p. 34.

49. Hughes, "Humor and the Negro Press," address at the Windy City Press Club Banquet, Chicago, Illinois, January 10, 1957. Hughes Archive, Schomburg Collection, New York Public Library.

50. Ibid.
51. Hughes, "Laughing at White Folks," *Chicago Defender*, National Edition, September 8, 1945, p. 12.
52. Hughes's Spingarn Medal Acceptance Speech, NAACP Convention, St. Paul, Minnesota, June 26, 1960. Hughes Archive, Schomburg Collection.
53. "The Negro Artist and the Racial Mountain."
54. "Laughers," *Fine Clothes*, pp. 77–78.
55. Charles S. Johnson, "Jazz Poetry and Blues," *The Carolina Magazine*, May 1928, pp. 16–20.
56. Allison Davis, "Our Negro 'Intellectuals,' " *The Crisis*, 35, No. 8 (August 1928), pp. 268–69 ff.
57. Benjamin Brawley, *The Negro Genius* (New York, Dodd, Mead, 1937), p. 248; Hughes, *Big Sea*, p. 266.
58. Hughes, Letter to the Editor, *The Crisis*, 35, No. 9 (September 1928), p. 302.
59. See n. 52.
60. Ibid.
61. Charles S. Johnson, "Jazz Poetry and Blues."

CHAPTER 2: SHADOW OF THE BLUES

1. Unless otherwise indicated, the poems cited below are in the opening section of *The Weary Blues*, pp. 23–39.
2. "Harlem Dance Hall," *Fields of Wonder* (New York, Knopf, 1947), p. 94.
3. "Jazz Band in a Parisian Cabaret," *Fine Clothes*, p. 74.
4. "Saturday Night," ibid., p. 41.
5. "Sport," ibid., p. 40.
6. "Jazz Band in a Parisian Cabaret."
7. "Dream Boogie," *Montage*, p. 3.
8. *Narrative of the Life of Frederick Douglass* [1845] (New York, New American Library, 1968), p. 32.
9. L. S. Senghor, "À New York," *Ethiopiques*, in *Poèmes* (Paris, Editions du Seuil, 1974), p. 117.
10. "Songs Called the Blues," *Langston Hughes Reader*, pp. 159–61.
11. "Jazz as Communication."
12. "Songs Called the Blues."
13. "The Negro Artist and the Racial Mountain."
14. "A Note on the Blues," *Fine Clothes*, p. xiii.
15. "Jazz Band in a Parisian Cabaret."
16. "Out of Work," *Shakespeare in Harlem* (New York, Knopf, 1942), p. 40.
17. "Hard Luck," *Fine Clothes*, p. 18.
18. Lonnie Johnson, "When You Fall For Someone That's Not Your Own," in Samuel Charters, *The Poetry of the Blues* (New York, Oak, 1963), pp. 63–64.
19. "Songs Called the Blues."

20. Reported in John S. Wilson, *Jazz: The Transition Years: 1940–60* (New York, Appleton-Century-Crofts, 1966), p. 55.

21. Sterling Brown, "The Blues as Folk Poetry," in Langston Hughes and Arna Bontemps, eds., *Book of Negro Folklore* (New York, Dodd, Mead, 1958), p. 373. See also Paul Oliver, *The Meaning of the Blues* (New York, Macmillan, 1969).

22. Paul Oliver, *The Meaning of the Blues*, p. 325.

23. Sterling Brown, "Blues as Folk Poetry."

24. *The Leadbelly Songbook* (New York, Oak, 1969), pp. 68, 73.

25. Sterling Brown, "Blues as Folk Poetry," p. 378.

26. "Still Here," *Jim Crow*, p. 19.

27. "Census," *Simple's Uncle Sam* (New York, Hill and Wang, 1965), pp. 1–3.

28. "Feet Live Their Own Life," *Simple Speaks His Mind* (New York, Simon and Schuster, 1950), pp. 3–7.

29. "Empty Houses," *Simple's Uncle Sam*, pp. 12–16.

30. Alain Locke, "Common Clay and Poetry," *Saturday Review*, April 9, 1927, p. 712.

31. However, Hughes did publish topical blues, especially during World War II. See James Emanuel, *Langston Hughes* (New York, Twayne, 1967), pp. 40–41.

32. "Letter," *Shakespeare*, p. 10.

33. "Little Old Letter," *One-Way Ticket* (New York, Knopf, 1949), p. 96.

34. "Life is Fine," ibid., pp. 38–39.

35. "The Backlash Blues," *Panther*, pp. 8–9.

36. Johnny Temple, "My Pony," Oliver, p. 144.

37. The Yas Yas Girl, "Easy Towing Mama," Oliver, pp. 145–46.

38. Bessie Smith, "Empty Bed Blues," Oliver, pp. 148–49. Oliver devotes his fourth chapter to popular love blues. See also Charters, ch. 7.

39. "Ma Man," *Fine Clothes*, p. 88.

40. "Minnie Sings Her Blues," ibid., p. 64.

41. "Hey-Hey Blues," *Shakespeare*, pp. 52–53.

42. "Song for a Banjo Dance," *Weary Blues*, p. 36.

43. "The Cat and the Saxophone," ibid., p. 27.

44. "Negro Dancers," ibid., p. 26.

45. "Morning After," *Shakespeare*, pp. 44–45.

46. "Hard Daddy," *Fine Clothes*, p. 86.

47. "Beale Street Love," ibid., p. 57.

48. "Bad Man," ibid, p. 21.

49. "Early Evening Quarrel," *Shakespeare*, pp. 113–14.

50. "Gal's Cry for a Dying Lover," *Fine Clothes*, p. 82.

51. "Widow Woman," *Shakespeare*, pp. 107–8.

52. "Lover's Return," ibid., pp. 119–20.

53. "Monroe's Blues," *One-Way Ticket*, p. 108.

54. "Only Woman Blues," *Shakespeare*, pp. 50–51.

55. "In a Troubled Key," ibid., p. 49.

56. "Love Again Blues," ibid., pp. 103–4.
57. "Midwinter Blues," *Fine Clothes*, p. 84.
58. "Workin' Man," ibid., p. 59.
59. "Black Gal," ibid., p. 66.
60. "Evil Woman," ibid., p. 62.
61. "Bad Luck Card," ibid., p. 60.
62. "Lament Over Love," ibid., p. 81.
63. "Suicide," ibid, p. 20.
64. "Too Blue," *One-Way Ticket*, p. 102.
65. "Life is Fine," ibid., p. 39.
66. "Gypsy Man," *Fine Clothes*, p. 22.
67. "Blues Fantasy," *Weary Blues*, pp. 37–38.
68. "Twilight Reverie," *Shakespeare*, p. 3.
69. "Supper Time," ibid., p. 4.
70. "Bed Time," ibid., p. 5.
71. "Po' Boy Blues," *Fine Clothes*, p. 23.
72. "Misery," ibid., p. 19.
73. "Listen Here Blues," ibid., p. 85.
74. "Cora," ibid., p. 58.
75. "Lonesome Corner," *One-Way Ticket*, p. 99.
76. "A Ruined Gal," *Fine Clothes*, p. 63.
77. "Midnight Chippie's Lament," *Shakespeare*, pp. 105–6.
78. "Mississippi Levee," ibid., pp. 46–47.
79. "Down and Out," ibid., pp. 101–2.
80. "Bad Morning," *One-Way Ticket*, p. 98.
81. "Homesick Blues," *Fine Clothes*, p. 24.
82. "Bound No'th Blues," ibid., p. 87.
83. "Blues Fantasy," *Weary Blues*, p. 37.
84. "Hey-Hey Blues," *Shakespeare*, p. 53.
85. "Pay Day," ibid., pp. 8–9.
86. "Daybreak," ibid., p. 6.
87. Hughes, "Jazz as Communication."
88. Ralph Ellison, "Richard Wright's Blues," *Shadow and Act* (New York, New American Library, 1966), p. 104.
89. Charles S. Johnson, "Jazz Poetry and Blues."
90. See Alain Locke, *The Negro and His Music*, pp. 4–6, and "The Negro Spirituals," *The New Negro*, pp. 199–210. Also James Weldon Johnson, introduction to his *Book of American Negro Spirituals*, I, II [1925, 1926] (New York, Viking, 1969); prefaces to his *Book of American Negro Poetry* [1922, 1931], (New York, Harcourt, Brace, 1959).
91. Hughes, "My Adventures as a Social Poet."
92. Unless otherwise indicated, the poems that follow are cited from *Fine Clothes*, pp. 45–53.

93. "Sunday Morning Prophecy," *One-Way Ticket*, pp. 35–37.
94. "Communion," *Fields of Wonder*, p. 98.

CHAPTER 3: JAZZ, JIVE, AND JAM

1. "Railroad Avenue," *Fine Clothes*, p. 27.
2. Vachel Lindsay, "The Congo," *Selected Poems* (New York, Collier-Macmillan, 1967), pp. 47–50.
3. Hughes, *Big Sea*, pp. 28–29.
4. "Song for a Banjo Dance," *Weary Blues*, p. 36.
5. "Harlem Night Club," ibid., p. 32.
6. Johnson, "Dialect Poems," *St. Peter Relates an Incident of the Ressurrection Day* (New York, Viking, 1935), p. 70.
7. "Jitney," *One-Way Ticket*, pp. 131–33.
8. "Man into Men," ibid., p. 85.
9. "Brass Spittoons," *Fine Clothes*, pp. 28–29.
10. "Laughers," ibid., pp. 77–78.
11. "Mulatto," ibid., pp. 71–72.
12. "Closing Time," ibid., p. 32.
13. "The Cat and the Saxophone," *Weary Blues*, p. 27.
14. "Death in Harlem," *Shakespeare*, pp. 57–64.
15. Prefatory Note, *Montage*. Subsequent references to this volume will be cited in parentheses in the text.
16. "Cross," *Weary Blues*, p. 52.
17. "Third Degree," *One-Way Ticket*, p. 130.
18. See Jonathan Kozol, *Death at an Early Age* (New York, Bantam, 1967), pp. 194–96.
19. Quoted on back cover of *Saturday Review of Literature*, March 31, 1951.
20. Nat Hentoff, "He Found Poetry in the Blues."
21. *Ask Your Mama* (New York, Knopf, 1961), p. 3. Subsequent references to this volume will be cited in parentheses in the text. Indented quotations will be rendered in block capitals as in the original, all other quotations in conventional lettering.
22. For examples and/or discussion of the dozens, see: the closing lines of Hughes's "Feet Live Their Own Lives," *Simple Speaks His Mind*, pp. 3–7; H. Rap Brown, *Die Nigger Die!* (New York, Dial, 1969), pp. 26–31; Roger D. Abrahams, *Deep Down in the Jungle*, First Revised Edition (Chicago, Aldine, 1970), pp. 39–60; William H. Grier and Price M. Cobbs, *The Jesus Bag* (New York, McGraw-Hill, 1971), pp. 3–9; the closing lines of LeRoi Jones's "Experimental Death Unit #1," *Four Black Revolutionary Plays* (New York, Bobbs-Merrill, 1969), p. 15; the monkey's address to the lion in any version of "The Signifying Monkey"; the title of Julius Lester's *Look Out, Whitey! Black Power's Gon' Get Your Mama* (New York,

Dial, 1968); Alan Dundes, ed., *Mother-Wit From the Laughing Barrel* (Englewood-Cliffs, N.J., Prentice-Hall, 1973).

23. H. Rap Brown, *Die Nigger Die!*, p. 27.

24. "Birmingham Sunday," *Panther*, p. 47.

25. "The Backlash Blues," ibid., p. 9.

26. "Christ in Alabama," *Scottsboro Limited* (New York, Golden Stair Press, 1932), n.p.

27. Blacks suddenly turn white, or take over the South, or disappear temporarily or permanently. See, for instance, George Schuyler, *Black No More* (New York, Macaulay, 1931); William Melvin Kelley, *A Different Drummer* (New York, Doubleday, 1962); Douglas Turner Ward, *Day of Absence*, in *New Black Playwrights*, ed. William Couch, Jr. (Baton Rouge, Louisiana State University), 1968, pp. 25–59.

28. "Rude Awakening," *Simple's Uncle Sam*, pp. 127–32.

CHAPTER 4: OR DOES IT EXPLODE?

1. LeRoi Jones (Amiri Baraka), "State / Meant," *Home: Social Essays* (New York, Apollo, 1966), p. 251.

2. "Afro-American Fragment," *Dear Lovely Death*, n.p.

3. See "Dream Variation" and "Our Land," *Weary Blues*, pp. 43, 99.

4. "The Negro Artist and the Racial Mountain."

5. "Afraid," "Poem: For the Portrait of an African Boy," *Weary Blues*, pp. 101,102.

6. "Lament for Dark Peoples," ibid., p. 100.

7. "The Jester," ibid., p. 53; "The Black Clown," *The Negro Mother* (New York, Golden Stair Press, 1931), pp. 8–11.

8. Paul Laurence Dunbar, "We Wear the Mask," *Complete Poems* (New York, Dodd, Mead, 1913), p.71.

9. "Summer Night," *Weary Blues*, p. 103.

10. "Disillusion," ibid., p. 104.

11. "Danse Africaine," ibid., p. 105.

12. "Mother to Son," ibid., p. 107.

13. "The Negro Mother," *Negro Mother*, pp. 16–18.

14. "Final Call," *Panther*, p. 21.

15. "I, Too" ("Epilogue"), *Weary Blues*, p. 109.

16. Walt Whitman, "Song of Myself" [1855], *Leaves of Grass and Selected Prose* (New York, Holt, Rinehart, 1964), p. 23.

17. "The Negro Speaks of Rivers," *Weary Blues*, p. 51.

18. Zora Neale Hurston, "High John de Conquer," *Book of Negro Folklore*, p. 95. Italics hers.

19. "Madam to You," *One-Way Ticket*, pp. 3–27.

20. "Magnolia Flowers," *Fine Clothes*, p.70.

21. "The South," *Weary Blues*, p. 54.
22. "Mulatto," *Fine Clothes*, p. 71.
23. "Flight," *Dear Lovely Death*, n.p.
24. "Blue Bayou," *Jim Crow*, p. 10.
25. "Southern Mammy Sings," *Shakespeare*, pp. 75–76.
26. "Ku Klux," ibid., pp. 81–82.
27. "Song For a Dark Girl," *Fine Clothes*, p. 75.
28. Claude McKay, "The Lynching," *Selected Poems* (New York, Bookman Associates, 1953), p. 37.
29. "Lynching Song," *A New Song* (New York, International Workers Order, 1938), p. 30.
30. "Silhouette" *One-Way Ticket*, p. 56. For a discussion of America's sexual mythology, see Calvin C. Hernton, *Sex and Racism in America* (New York, Doubleday, 1965); LeRoi Jones, "American Sexual Reference: Black Male," *Home*, pp. 216–33; Eldridge Cleaver, *Soul on Ice* (New York, McGraw-Hill, 1968), pp. 155–210; Nathan Huggins, *Harlem Renaissance*, ch. 6.
31. "The Bitter River," *Jim Crow*, pp. 11–13.
32. "Justice," *Scottsboro Limited*, n.p.
33. "Scottsboro," ibid.
34. "Christ in Alabama," ibid.
35. "Bible Belt," *Panther*, p. 38.
36. "My Adventures as a Social Poet." Also, *I Wonder As I Wander* [1956] (New York, Hill and Wang, 1968), p. 46.
37. "The Town of Scottsboro," *Scottsboro Limited*, n.p.
38. "Sharecroppers," *Shakespeare*, p. 77.
39. "West Texas," ibid., p. 79. Cf. Malcolm X contrasting house slaves and field slaves: "If someone came to the field Negro and said, 'Let's separate, let's run,' he didn't say, 'Where we going?' He'd say, 'Any place is better than here.' " "Message to the Grassroots" [1963], *Malcolm X Speaks* (New York, Grove Press, 1966), p. 11.
40. "One-Way Ticket," *One-Way Ticket*, pp. 61–62.
41. "Ku Klux," *Shakespeare*, pp. 81–82.
42. "Third Degree," *One-Way Ticket*, p. 130.
43. "Who But the Lord?," ibid., p. 73.
44. *Panther*, p. 17.
45. "Open Letter to the South," *New Song*, p, 27.
46. "Scottsboro Limited," *Scottsboro Limited*, n.p.
47. "Let America Be America Again," *New Song*, p. 9. Subsequent references to this volume will be cited in parentheses in the text.
48. "God to Hungry Child," *The Workers Monthly*, March 1925, p. 234, reprinted in *Good Morning Revolution*, p. 36.
49. "Johannesburg Mines," *The Crisis*, February 1928, p. 52, reprinted in *Good Morning Revolution*, p. 10.
50. "Advertisement for the Waldorf-Astoria," *New Masses*, December 1931,

pp. 16–17. This and the poems and essays cited below are reprinted in *Good Morning Revolution.*

51. "The Black Man Speaks," *Jim Crow,* p.5.
52. "How About It, Dixie," ibid., p.9.
53. "Freedom," ibid., p. 7.
54. *Freedom's Plow,* in *Selected Poems,* p. 296.
55. "Oppression," *Panther,* p. 63. Subsequent citations from this volume will be given in parentheses in the text.
56. "Hold Fast to Dreams," *Lincoln University Bulletin,* No. 67, 1964, pp. 1–8.
57. *Ask Your Mama,* pp. 4–5.

CHAPTER 5: THE DREAM KEEPER

1. See chapter 1, n. 24 for my definition of social and lyric poetry.
2. Unless otherwise indicated, the poems immediately following are cited from these three sections of *The Weary Blues.*
3. Dunbar, *Complete Poems,* pp. 82, 178.
4. "Poème D'Automne," *Weary Blues,* p. 45.
5. "March Moon," ibid., p. 47.
6. "Heaven," *Fields of Wonder,* p. 3. The poems immediately following are cited from this volume unless otherwise indicated.
7. *Earth-Being: The Autobiography of Jean Toomer* (unpublished), excerpted in *The Black Scholar,* 2, No. 5, January 1971, pp. 2–13.
8. "Dear Lovely Death," *Dear Lovely Death,* n.p.
9. "Drum," ibid.
10. "Mammy," *Fine Clothes,* p. 76.
11. "Exits," *Fields of Wonder,* p. 65.
12. "Tower," *Dear Lovely Death,* n.p.
13. "Sport," *Fine Clothes,* p. 40.
14. "Boarding House," *One-Way Ticket,* p. 119.
15. "Grave Yard," *Fields of Wonder,* p. 21.
16. "There," ibid., p. 88.
17. "Request for Requiems," *One-Way Ticket,* p. 115.
18. "Fantasy in Purple," *Weary Blues,* p. 46.
19. "Cabaret Girl Dies on Welfare Island," *Shakespeare,* p. 66.
20. "Sailing Date," *Fields of Wonder,* p. 86.
21. "Death of an Old Seaman," *Weary Blues,* p. 81.
22. "Sylvester's Dying Bed," *Shakespeare,* p. 67.
23. "Berry," *The Ways of White Folks* (New York, Knopf, 1934), p. 175.
24. See *I Wonder as I Wander,* p. 291.

CHAPTER 6: HUGHES AND THE EVOLUTION
OF CONSCIOUSNESS IN BLACK POETRY

1. W. E. B. DuBois, "Of Our Spiritual Strivings," *Souls of Black Folk*, pp. 46–47.

2. Don L. Lee, "Black Poetics," *Don't Cry, Scream* (Detroit, Broadside Press, 1969), p. 15.

3. Phillis Wheatley, "On Being Brought From Africa to America," *Poems on Various Subjects, Religious and Moral* (London, A. Bell, Cox and Berry, 1773), p. 18.

4. "To the University of Cambridge, in New England," ibid., p. 15.

5. Ibid., p. 74.

6. Jupiter Hammon, "A Dialogue Intitled the Kind Master and the Dutiful Servant," in Benjamin Brawley, ed., *Early Negro American Writers* (New York, Dover, 1970), p. 26.

7. George Moses Horton, "On Liberty and Slavery," ibid., pp. 114–15.

8. James Whitfield, "America," ibid., p. 228.

9. Frances E. W. Harper, *Moses, A Story of the Nile, in Idylls of the Bible* (Philadelphia, 1906), pp. 3–4.

10. Dunbar, "The Poet," *Complete Poems*, p. 191.

11. James Weldon Johnson, Preface to *The Book of American Negro Poetry*.

12. See Helen M. Chesnutt, *Charles Waddell Chesnutt: Pioneer of the Color Line* (Chapel Hill, University of North Carolina, 1952), p. 21.

13. See Johnson, *Book of American Negro Poetry*, p. 17; Johnson, *The Autobiography of an Ex-Colored Man* [1912] (New York, Hill and Wang, 1968), pp. 87–88.

14. Quoted in Arna Bontemps' introduction to *Cane* (New York, Harper, 1969), pp. viii–ix.

15. W. S. Braithwaite, "In a Sunken Pool," *Selected Poems* (New York, Coward-McCann, 1948), p. 27.

16. "Sic Vita," ibid., p. 49.

17. Johnson, *Book of American Negro Poetry*, p. 99.

18. Ibid., p. 233.

19. Cullen, "Yet Do I Marvel," *Color*, p. 3.

20. "The Shroud of Color," ibid., pp. 26–35.

21. "To Certain Critics," *The Black Christ* (New York, Harper, 1929), p. 63.

22. "Uncle Jim," *Copper Sun* (New York, Harper, 1927), p. 9.

23. "After a Visit," *The Medea and Some Poems* (New York, Harper, 1935), pp. 67–68.

24. Tolson (1898–1966) was actually a member of Hughes's generation but did not publish his first book until 1944.

25. "Rendezvous with America," *Rendezvous with America* (New York, Dodd, Mead, 1944), pp. 5, 9.

26. Tolson, *Harlem Gallery* (New York, Twayne, 1965), p. 19.

27. Ibid., p. 83.

28. Ibid., pp. 81, 82.

29. Ibid., p. 70.

30. Ibid., p. 124.

31. Ibid., p. 173.

32. Robert Hayden, "Middle Passage," *A Ballad of Remembrance* (London, Paul Breman, 1962), pp. 60–66.

33. "Runagate Runagate," *Selected Poems* (New York, October House, 1966), pp. 75–77; *Angle of Ascent: New and Selected Poems* (New York, Liveright, 1975), pp. 128–30.

34. "Idol," *Selected Poems*, p. 31; *Angle of Ascent*, p. 93.

35. "A Ballad of Remembrance," *A Ballad of Rembrance*, pp. 6–7; *Selected Poems*, pp. 39–40; *Angle of Ascent*, pp. 99–100.

36. Don L. Lee, "Black Poetics."

37. Gwendolyn Brooks, *Report From Part One* (Detroit, Broadside Press, 1972), p. 45.

38. "The Sundays of Satin-Legs Smith," *A Street in Bronzeville* (1945), reprinted in *The World of Gwendolyn Brooks* (New York, Harper and Row, 1971), p. 29.

39. Ibid., pp. 5, 122, 123.

40. "The Ballad of the Light-eyed Little Girl," *Annie Allen* (1949), ibid., p. 106.

41. "Life for my child is simple, and is good," ibid., p. 104.

42. Ibid., p. 31.

43. Ibid.

44. *In the Mecca*, ibid., pp. 400–1.

45. "The Third Sermon on the Warpland," *Riot* (Detroit, Broadside Press, 1969), p. 11.

46. "Speech to the Young. Speech to the Progress-Toward," *Family Pictures* (Detroit, Broadside Press, 1970), p. 23.

47. Allen Ginsberg, "Howl," *Howl* (San Francisco, City Lights, 1956), p. 17.

48. LeRoi Jones, "Hymn for Lanie Poo," *Preface to a Twenty Volume Suicide Note.* . . . (New York, Totem Press, 1961), p. 8.

49. "The Insidious Dr. Fu Man Chu," ibid., p. 41.

50. "Notes for a Speech," ibid., p. 47.

51. Hughes, "Afro-American Fragment," *Dear Lovely Death*, n.p.

52. Jones, "The New Sheriff," *Suicide Note*, p. 42.

53. Jones, "Black Dada Nihilismus," *The Dead Lecturer* (New York, Grove Press, 1964), p. 63.

54. Ibid., p. 64.

55. Jones, *A Black Mass*, in *Four Black Revolutionary Plays* (New York, Bobbs-Merrill, 1969), p. 31.

56. Ibid., p. 39.

57. "Look for You Yesterday, Here You Come Today," *Suicide Note,* p. 15.
58. Jones, "An Explanation of the Work," *Black Magic: Collected Poetry, 1961–1967* (New York, Bobbs-Merrill, 1969).
59. "A School of Prayer," ibid., p. 121.
60. "W.W.," ibid., p. 137.
61. "The Legacy of Malcolm X," *Home,* p. 248.
62. "The Revolutionary Theatre," ibid., p. 210.
63. "Ka 'Ba," *Black Magic,* p. 146.
64. "The Revolutionary Theatre," *Home,* p.211.
65. Ibid., p. 212.
66. "Black Art," *Black Magic,* p. 116.
67. "Black People!," ibid., p. 225.
68. Jones, "It's Nation Time," *It's Nation Time* (Chicago, Third World Press, 1970), pp. 21, 23–24.
69. For a discussion of contemporary varieties of "black nationalism" and "black power," see Solomon P. Gethers, "Black Power: Three Years Later," *Black World,* December 1969, pp. 4–10, 69–81.
70. "For Tom Postell, Dead Black Poet," *Black Magic,* p. 153.
71. "The Liar," *Dead Lecturer,* p. 79.
72. "Leroy," *Black Magic,* p. 217.
73. Marvin X, *The Black Bird,* in Ed Bullins, ed., *New Plays From the Black Theatre* (New York, Bantam, 1969), pp. 109–18.
74. Don L. Lee, *We Walk the Way of the New World* (Detroit, Broadside Press, 1970), p. 71.
75. Ron Karenga, "Black Cultural Nationalism," in Addison Gayle, *The Black Aesthetic,* p. 36.
76. Sonia Sanchez, "Liberation Poem," *We a BaddDDD People* (Detroit, Broadside Press, 1970), p. 54.
77. David Nelson, "No Time For Blues Now," *Black Impulse* (New York, Drum Publications, n.d.), n.p.
78. Don L. Lee, "Don't Cry, Scream," *Don't Cry, Scream,* p. 28.
79. Ibid.
80. LeRoi Jones, "State / Meant," *Home,* p. 252.
81. David Nelson, "Die Nigga," *Black Impulse,* n.p.
82. Omar Ben Hassen, "Niggers are Scared of Revolution," *The Last Poets* (phonodisc), New York, Douglas Music Corp., #3, 1970.
83. Gil Scott-Heron, "The Revolution Will Not Be Televised," *Small Talk at 125th and Lenox* (phonodisc), New York, Flying Dutchman, 1970.
84. Nikki Giovanni, "Ego Tripping," *Truth is On Its Way* (phonodisc), Right On Records, #RR05001, 1971.

CHAPTER 7: CONCLUSION

1. James Baldwin, review of the *Selected Poems of Langston Hughes, New York Times Book Review,* March 29, 1959, p. 6. The quotations that follow are taken from the same review.

2. See pp. 117–18.

3. Baldwin, "Stranger in the Village," *Notes of a Native Son* (Boston, Beacon Press, 1957), pp. 159–75.

4. Huggins, *Harlem Renaissance,* p. 227.

5. Quoted by Walter Lowenfels in "The White Literary Syndicate," *Liberator,* 10, No. 3, March 1970, p. 8. Emphasis in original.

6. Quoted by Lowenfels, ibid., p. 9. Emphasis added.

7. Huggins, *Harlem Renaissance,* p. 307.

8. T. S. Eliot, "The Love Song of J. Alfred Prufrock," *The Complete Poems and Plays, 1909–1950* (New York, Harcourt, Brace, 1958), pp. 3–7.

9. Ezra Pound, "Hugh Selwyn Mauberley," *Selected Poems* (New York, New Directions, 1957), pp. 61–77.

10. Margaret Larkin, "A Poet of the People," *Opportunity,* March 1927, p. 84.

11. See Jerome Rothenberg, *Technicians of the Sacred* (New York, Doubleday, 1968), and *Shaking the Pumpkin* (New York, Doubleday, 1972); Jerome Rothenberg and George Quasha, *America A Prophecy* (New York, Random House, 1973). See also *Alcheringa: Ethnopoetics,* "A First Magazine of the World's Tribal Poetries," founded in 1970 by Jerome Rothenberg and Dennis Tedlock.

12. The passage that follows is adapted from Onwuchekwa Jemie, Chinweizu, and Ihechukwu Madubuike, "Towards the Decolonization of African Literature," *Okike,* No. 7, April 1975, pp. 80–81; *Transition,* No. 48, April 1975, p. 56.

13. Hughes, "Evenin' Air Blues," *Shakespeare,* p. 38.

14. Hughes, "Crowns and Garlands," *Panther,* p. 6.

15. Hughes, "Impasse," ibid., p. 85.

Bibliography

I. BIBLIOGRAPHIES

There is one nearly complete bibliography: Donald C. Dickinson's *A Bio-Bibliography of Langston Hughes, 1902–1967* (Hamden, Conn., Shoe String Press, 1967). (In actuality, it goes only up to 1965).

Also, three good selected bibliographies, by: James Emanuel in his *Langston Hughes* (New York, Twayne, 1967); Ernest Kaiser in *Freedomways*, 8, No. 2, Spring 1968, pp. 185–91; and Therman B. O'Daniel in *CLA Journal*, 11, No. 4, June 1968, pp. 349–66. See also Darwin T. Turner, *Afro-American Writers*, Goldentree Bibliographies (New York, Appleton-Century-Crofts, 1970), pp. 58–61; and Theresa G. Rush et al., *Black American Writers Past and Present: Biographical and Bibliographical Dictionary*, 2 vols. (Metuchen, N.J., Scarecrow Press, 1975).

II. WORKS BY HUGHES

Poetry

The Weary Blues. New York, Knopf, 1926.
Fine Clothes to the Jew. New York, Knopf, 1927.
Dear Lovely Death. Amenia, New York, Troutbeck Press, 1931.
The Negro Mother. New York, Golden Stair Press, 1931.
The Dream Keeper and Other Poems. New York, Knopf, 1932.
Scottsboro Limited. New York, Golden Stair Press, 1932.
A New Song. New York, International Workers Order, 1938.

Shakespeare in Harlem. New York, Knopf, 1942.
Freedom's Plow. New York, Musette Publishing Co., 1943.
Jim Crow's Last Stand. Atlanta, Negro Publication Society, 1943.
Fields of Wonder. New York, Knopf, 1947.
One-Way Ticket. New York, Knopf, 1949.
Montage of a Dream Deferred. New York, Henry Holt, 1951.
Selected Poems. New York, Knopf, 1959.
Ask Your Mama: 12 Moods for Jazz. New York, Knopf, 1961.
The Panther and the Lash. New York, Knopf, 1967.

Novels

Not Without Laughter. New York, Knopf, 1930.
Tambourines to Glory. New York, John Day, 1958.

Short Stories

The Ways of White Folks. New York, Knopf, 1934.
Laughing To Keep From Crying. New York, Henry Holt, 1952.
Something in Common and Other Stories. New York, Hill and Wang, 1963.

"Documentary" or "Editorial" Fiction

Simple Speaks His Mind. New York, Simon and Schuster, 1950.
Simple Takes a Wife. New York, Simon and Schuster, 1953.
Simple Stakes a Claim. New York, Rinehart, 1957.
The Best of Simple. New York, Hill and Wang, 1961.
Simple's Uncle Sam. New York, Hill and Wang, 1965.

Plays

Five Plays. Bloomington, Indiana University Press, 1963.

Autobiographies

The Big Sea. New York, Knopf, 1940.
I Wonder as I Wander. New York, Rinehart, 1956.

General Anthologies of His Work

The Langston Hughes Reader. New York, George Braziller, 1958.
Good Morning Revolution: Uncollected Writings of Social Protest. Ed. Faith Berry. New York, Lawrence Hill, 1973.

Histories

A Pictorial History of the Negro in America. With Milton Meltzer. New York, Crown Publishers, 1956.
Fight for Freedom: The Story of the NAACP. New York, Norton, 1962.
Black Magic: A Pictorial History of the Negro in American Entertainment. With Milton Meltzer. Englewood Cliffs, New Jersey, Prentice-Hall, 1967.

Histories and Biographies for Younger Readers

The First Book of Negroes. New York, Franklin Watts, 1952.
The First Book of Rhythms. New York, Franklin Watts, 1954.
Famous American Negroes. New York, Dodd, Mead, 1954.
The First Book of Jazz. New York, Franklin Watts, 1955.
Famous Negro Music Makers. New York, Dodd, Mead, 1955.
The First Book of the West Indies. New York, Franklin Watts, 1956.
Famous Negro Heroes of America. New York, Dodd, Mead, 1958.
The First Book of Africa. New York, Franklin Watts, 1960.

Uncollected Essays and Speeches

"The Negro Artist and the Racial Mountain." *The Nation*, June 23, 1926, pp. 692–94.
Letter to the Editor, *The Crisis*, 35, No. 9, September 1928, p. 302.
"When I Worked for Dr. Woodson." *Negro History Bulletin*, May 1950, p. 188.
"Ten Ways to Use Poetry in Teaching." *CLA Bulletin*, Spring, 1951, pp. 6–7; *CLA Journal*, June 1968, pp. 273–79.
"Writers: Black and White." *The American Negro Writer and His Roots.* New York, American Society of African Culture, 1960, pp. 41–45.
"Problems of the Negro Writer." *Saturday Review*, April 20, 1963, pp. 19–20, 40.
"Langston Hughes' Acceptance of the Spingarn Medal, NAACP Convention, St. Paul, Minnesota, June 26, 1960." New York, Schomburg Collection, Hughes Archive.
"Tribute to W. E. B. DuBois." *Freedomways*, Winter 1965, p. 11.
"The Twenties: Harlem and its Negritude." *African Forum*, Spring 1966, pp. 11–20.

Phonograph Recordings of His Own Work

Simple Speaks His Mind. Folkways Records FP 90, 1952.
The Story of Jazz. Folkways Records FP 712, 1954.
The Dream Keeper and Other Poems. Folkways Records FP 104, 1955.
Rhythms of the World. Folkways Records FP 740, 1955.
The Weary Blues and Other Poems. MGM Record LPs E3697, 1958.

III. WORKS ON HUGHES

Biography

Meltzer, Milton. *Langston Hughes: A Biography.* New York, Crowell,
1968.

Essays, Reviews and Books

Alexander, Lewis. Review of *Fine Clothes to the Jew,* in *The Carolina
Magazine,* May 1927, pp. 41–44.
Baldwin, James. Review of *Selected Poems* in *New York Times,* March 29,
1959, p. 6.
Bontemps, Arna. Review of Countee Cullen's *On These I Stand* and
Hughes's *Fields of Wonder,* in *Saturday Review,* March 22, 1947, pp.
12, 13, 44.
CLA Journal, special Langston Hughes issue, 11, No. 4, June 1968.
Clarke, John Henrik. "Langston Hughes and Jesse B. Semple." *Freedom-
ways,* Spring 1968, pp. 167–69.
Cullen, Countee. Review of *The Weary Blues,* in *Opportunity,* February
1926, pp. 73–74.
Davis, Arthur P. "The Harlem of Langston Hughes' Poetry." *Phylon,* 13,
Winter 1952, pp. 276–83.
——— "Langston Hughes: Cool Poet." *CLA Journal,* 11, No. 4, June 1968,
pp. 280–96.
Deutsch, Babette. "Waste Land of Harlem." Review of *Montage of a
Dream Deferred,* in *New York Times,* May 6, 1951, p. 23.
Emanuel, James A. *The Short Stories of Langston Hughes.* Ph.D. disser-
tation, Columbia University, 1962.
——— *Langston Hughes.* New York, Twayne, 1967.
——— "The Literary Experiments of Langston Hughes," *CLA Journal,* 11,
No. 4, June 1968, pp. 335–44.
Fauset, Jessie. Review of *The Weary Blues,* in *The Crisis,* March 1926,
p. 239.

Gibson, Donald (ed.). *Five Black Writers*. New York, New York University Press, 1970.

Hentoff, Nat. "Langston Hughes: He Found Poetry in the Blues." *Mayfair*, August 1958, p. 27ff.

Jackson, Blyden. "A Word About Simple." *CLA Journal*, 11, No. 4, June 1968, pp. 310–18.

O'Daniel, Therman B. (ed.). *Langston Hughes: Black Genius*. New York, William Morrow, 1971. (An expanded version of the special Hughes number of *CLA Journal*, June 1968).

Wagner, Jean. *Black Poets of the United States*. Tr. Kenneth Douglas. Urbana, Univ. of Illinois Press, 1973.

Waldron, Edward E. "The Blues Poetry of Langston Hughes." *Negro American Literature Forum*, 5, No. 4, Winter 1971, pp. 140–49.

IV. GENERAL

Abrahams, Roger D. *Deep Down in the Jungle*. First Revised Edition. Chicago, Aldine, 1970.

Baraka, Amiri (see Jones, LeRoi).

Bone, Robert. *The Negro Novel in America*. Revised edition. New Haven, Yale, 1968.

Braithwaite, William Stanley. *Lyrics of Life and Love*. Boston, Turner, 1904.

—— *The House of Falling Leaves*. Boston, Luce, 1908.

—— *Selected Poems*. New York, Coward-McCann, 1948.

Brawley, Benjamin. *The Negro Genius*. New York, Dodd, Mead, 1937.

Brooks, Gwendolyn. *A Street in Bronzeville*. New York, Harper, 1945.

—— *Annie Allen*. New York, Harper, 1949.

—— *The Bean Eaters*. New York, Harper, 1960.

—— *Selected Poems*. New York, Harper, 1963.

—— *In the Mecca*. New York, Harper, 1968.

—— *The World of Gwendolyn Brooks*. New York, Harper, 1971.

—— *Riot*. Detroit, Broadside Press, 1969.

—— *Family Pictures*. Detroit, Broadside Press, 1970.

—— *Report From Part One*. Detroit, Broadside Press, 1972.

Brown, H. Rap. *Die Nigger Die!* New York, Dial, 1969.

Brown, Sterling A. *Southern Road*. New York, Harcort, Brace, 1932.

—— *Negro Poetry and Drama* (1937) and *The Negro in American Fiction* (1937). Issued together in one volume. New York, Atheneum, 1969.

—— "The Blues as Folk Poetry." *Book of Negro Folklore.* Ed. Langston Hughes and Arna Bontemps. New York, Dodd, Mead, 1958, pp. 371–86.

Bullins, Ed. *Five Plays.* New York, Bobbs-Merrill, 1968.

—— (ed.). *New Plays From the Black Theatre.* New York, Bantam, 1969.

Burck, Jacob. *Hunger and Revolt: Cartoons by Burck.* New York, The Daily Worker, 1935.

Charters, Samuel. *The Poetry of the Blues.* New York, Oak, 1963.

Chesnutt, Helen M. *Charles Waddell Chesnutt: Pioneer of the Color Line.* Chapel Hill, N.C., University of North Carolina, 1952.

Cleaver, Eldridge. *Soul on Ice.* New York, McGraw-Hill, 1968.

Cook, Mercer, and Henderson, Stephen. *The Militant Black Writer.* Madison, University of Wisconsin, 1969.

Cullen, Countee. *Color.* New York, Harper, 1925.

—— *The Ballad of the Brown Girl.* New York, Harper, 1927.

—— *Copper Sun.* New York, Harper, 1927.

—— (ed.). *Caroling Dusk: An Anthology of Verse By Negro Poets.* New York, Harper, 1927.

—— *The Black Christ and Other Poems.* New York, Harper, 1929.

—— *The Medea and Some Poems.* New York, Harper, 1935.

—— *On These I Stand.* New York, Harper, 1947.

Cuney-Hare, Maude. *Negro Musicians and Their Music.* New York, Associated Publishers, 1936.

Davis, Allison. "Our Negro 'Intellectuals.' " *The Crisis,* 35, No. 8, August 1928, pp. 268–69ff.

Douglass, Frederick. *Narrative of the Life of Frederick Douglas* (1845). New York, New American Library, 1968.

DuBois, W.E.B. *The Souls of Black Folk* (1903). New York, Fawcett, 1968.

Dunbar, Paul Laurence. *Complete Poems.* New York, Dodd, Mead, 1913.

Dundes, Alan (ed.). *Mother Wit From the Laughing Barrel.* Englewood Cliffs, N.J., Prentice-Hall, 1973.

Eliot, T. S. The *Complete Poems and Plays, 1909–1950.* New York, Harcourt, Brace, 1952.

Ellison, Ralph. *Invisible Man.* New York, Random House, 1952.

—— *Shadow and Act.* New York, Random House, 1964.

Essien-Udom, E. U. *Black Nationalism* (1962). New York, Dell, 1964.

Ferlinghetti, Lawrence. *A Coney Island of the Mind.* New York, New Directions, 1958.

—— *Starting From San Francisco.* New York, New Directions, 1967.

—— *The Secret Meaning of Things.* New York, New Directions, 1968.

Frazier, E. Franklin. *Black Bourgeoisie.* New York, Free Press, 1957.

Gayle, Addison (ed.). *The Black Aesthetic.* New York, Doubleday, 1971.

Giovanni, Nikki. *Black Judgment.* Detroit, Broadside Press, 1968.

—— *Re:Creation.* Detroit, Broadside Press, 1970.

Grier, William H., and Cobbs, Price M. *Black Rage.* New York, Bantam, 1968.

—— *The Jesus Bag.* New York, McGraw-Hill, 1971.

Hare, Nathan. *The Black Anglo-Saxons.* New York, Macmillan, 1970.

Harper, Frances Ellen Watkins. *Idylls of the Bible.* Philadelphia, The Author, 1906.

—— *Sketches of Southern Life.* Philadelphia, Ferguson, 1888.

Hart, Henry (ed.). *American Writers' Congress.* New York, International Publishers, 1935.

Hayden, Robert. *A Ballad of Remembrance.* London, Paul Breman, 1962.

—— *Selected Poems.* New York, October House, 1966.

—— *Words in the Mourning Time.* New York, October House, 1970.

—— *Angle of Ascent.* New York, Liveright, 1975.

Hernton, Calvin C. *Sex and Racism in America.* New York, Doubleday, 1965.

Herskovits, Melville J. *The Myth of the Negro Past* (1941). Boston, Beacon, 1958.

Hodeir, Andre. *Jazz: Its Evolution and Essence.* New York, Grove, 1956.

Huggins, Nathan Irvin. *Harlem Renaissance.* New York, Oxford, 1971.

Hughes, Langston, and Bontemps, Arna (eds.). *Book of Negro Folklore.* New York, Dodd, Mead, 1958.

Joans, Ted. *Black Pow-Wow: Jazz Poems.* New York, Hill and Wang, 1969.

Johnson, Charles S. "The Negro Enters Literature." *The Carolina Magazine,* May 1927, pp. 3–9, 44–48.

—— "Jazz Poetry and Blues." *The Carolina Magazine,* May 1928, pp. 16–20.

Johnson, James Weldon. *The Autobiography of an Ex-Colored Man* (1912). New York, Hill and Wang, 1968.

——*Fifty Years and Other Poems.* Boston, Cornhill, 1917.

—— (ed.). *The Book of American Negro Poetry.* New York, Harcourt, Brace, 1922, 1931.

—— and Johnson, J. Rosamond. *The Book of American Negro Spirituals.* New York, Viking, 1925 (Vol. I), 1926 (Vol. II), 1969 (combined).

—— *God's Trombones*. New York, Viking, 1927.

—— *St. Peter Relates an Incident of the Resurrection Day*. New York, Viking, 1935.

Jones, LeRoi (Amiri Baraka). *Preface to a Twenty Volume Suicide Note*. New York, Totem Press, 1961.

—— *The Dead Lecturer*. New York, Grove Press, 1964.

—— *Home: Social Essays*. New York, William Morrow, 1966.

—— *Four Black Revolutionary Plays*. New York, Bobbs-Merrill, 1969.

—— *Black Magic: Poetry 1961–1967*. New York, Bobbs-Merrill, 1969.

—— *It's Nation Time*. Chicago, Third World Press, 1970.

Kaufman, Bob. *Solitudes Crowded With Loneliness*. New York, New Directions, 1965.

—— *Golden Sardine*. San Francisco, City Lights, 1967.

Kesteloot, Lilyan. *Black Writers in French: A Literary History of Negritude*. Tr. Ellen Conroy Kennedy. Philadelphia, Temple University Press, 1974.

Kozol, Jonathan. *Death at an Early Age*. New York, Bantam, 1967.

Leadbelly (Huddie Ledbetter). *The Leadbelly Songbook*. New York, Oak, 1969.

Lee, Don L. *Don't Cry, Scream*. Detroit, Broadside Press, 1969.

—— *We Walk the Way of the New World*. Detroit, Broadside Press, 1970.

Lindsay, Vachel. *Selected Poems*. New York, Macmillan, 1967.

Locke, Alain (ed.). *The New Negro* (1925). New York, Atheneum, 1968.

—— "Common Clay and Poetry." *Saturday Review*, April 9, 1927, p. 712.

—— "The Message of the Negro Poets." *The Carolina Magazine*, May 1928, pp. 5–15.

—— *The Negro and His Music* (1936). New York, Arno, 1969.

Lowenfels, Walter, "The White Literary Syndicate." *Liberator*, 10, No. 3, March 1970, pp. 8–9.

Malcolm X. *Autobiography*. New York, Grove, 1966.

—— *Malcolm X Speaks*, New York, Grove, 1966.

Marvin X. *The Son of Man*. Fresno, Calif., Al Kitab Sudan, 1969.

—— *Fly to Allah*. Fresno, Calif., Al Kitab Sudan, 1969.

—— *The Black Bird*, in Ed Bullins, *New Plays From the Black Theatre*. New York, Bantam, 1969.

McKay, Claude. *Songs of Jamaica*. Kingston, Jamaica, Aston Gardner, 1912.

—— *Constab' Ballads*. London, Watts, 1912.

—— *Spring in New Hampshire and Other Poems*. London, G. Richards, 1920.

—— *Harlem Shadows*. New York, Harcourt, Brace, 1922.

—— *A Long Way From Home* (1937). New York, Harcourt, Brace, 1970.

—— *Selected Poems*. New York, Bookman, 1953.

—— "On Becoming a Catholic." *The Epistle: A Quarterly Bulletin Published by the St. Paul Guild*, New York, No. 2, Spring 1945, pp. 43–45.

—— *Right Turn to Catholicism* (typescript). New York, Schomburg Collection, 1946.

Muhammad, Elijah. *Message to the Blackman in America*. Chicago, Muhammad Mosque No. 2, 1965.

Nelson, David. *Black Impulse*. New York, Drum Publications, n.d.

Oliver, Paul. *The Meaning of the Blues*. New York, Macmillan, 1969.

Pound, Ezra. *Selected Poems*. New York, New Directions, 1957.

Redding, J. Saunders. *To Make a Poet Black*. Chapel Hill, University of North Carolina, 1939.

Rowan, Carl T. "How Racists Use 'Science' to Degrade Black People." *Ebony*, May 1970, pp. 31–34ff.

Sanchez, Sonia. *Homecoming*. Detroit, Broadside Press, 1969.

—— *We a BaddDDD People*. Detroit, Broadside Press, 1970.

Schuller, Gunther. *Early Jazz*. Oxford Univ. Press, 1967.

Schuyler, George S. "The Negro-Art Hokum." *The Nation*, June 16, 1926, pp. 662–63.

—— *Black No More*. New York, Macaulay, 1931.

Stearns, Marshall. *The Story of Jazz*. Oxford Univ. Press, 1956.

Tolson, Melvin B. *Rendezvous With America*. New York, Dodd, Mead, 1944.

—— *Libretto for the Republic of Liberia*. New York, Twayne, 1953.

—— *Harlem Gallery*. New York, Twayne, 1965.

Toomer, Jean. *Cane*. New York, Boni and Liveright, 1923.

Wheatley, Phillis. *Poems on Various Subjects, Religious and Moral*. London, A. Bell, Cox and Berry, 1773.

—— *The Poems of Phillis Wheatley*. Ed. Julian D. Mason, Jr. Chapel Hill, Univ. of North Carolina, 1966.

Wilson, John S. *Jazz: The Transition Years: 1940–60*. Oxford Univ. Press, 1970.

V. PHONODISCS

Bontemps, Arna (ed.). *Anthology of Negro Poets*. New York, Folkways #FL 9791, 1954, 1966.

Giovanni, Nikki. *Truth is On Its Way*. New York, Right On Records, 1971.

Jones, LeRoi (Amiri Baraka). *It's Nation Time*. Detroit, Motown, 1972.
The Last Poets. *The Last Poets*. New York, Douglas Music Corp #3, 1970.
Malcolm X. *Message to the Grassroots*. Detroit, Afro-American Broadcasting and Recording Co., n.d.
Scott-Heron, Gil. *Small Talk at 125th and Lenox*. New York, Flying Dutchman, 1970.

VI. FILM

Black History: Lost, Stolen, or Strayed. CBS-TV, "Of Black America" Series, 1968.

Index